Archive Books
Igor Zabel Association for Culture and Theory

Beti Žerovc

When Attitudes Become the Norm

The Contemporary Curator and Institutional Art

Table of Contents

Introduction

 Beti Žerovc

The present book offers a selection of articles on contemporary art curators and curatorship, which were written between 2002 and 2012. My attention was drawn more or less naturally to the phenomenon of the curator of contemporary art. In the early 1990s, when I started working professionally in the art field and wished to understand my new environment and learn its basic principles, curating was the big topic in the art world. Contemporary art curatorship seemed to be irreversibly expanding, with curators popping up like mushrooms in every corner of the globe; at the same time, there was a proliferation of very vocal debates as to whether this was a good thing, what the consequences of the trend might be, and what effect it would have on art and the role of the artist. As a researcher, I wanted not only to ponder the most obvious facts – that the profile of the curator of contemporary art was quite different from that of the traditional art curator; that this new sort of curator had an enormous influence on the artist; and that, with this curator, the exhibition of contemporary art was also changing as a medium – but also to develop my reflections into a more comprehensive and analytical understanding of why this form of curatorship was, in fact, occurring and, indeed, who the curator actually was and what sort of activities, responsibilities, and powers belonged specifically to him.

When I began my research on contemporary curatorship, I soon realised that to understand the phenomenon it had to be examined in its broader social, political and economic contexts, and, especially, in relation to the radical changes that had taken place in the art field in the previous century. The 20th century had given rise to an extraordinary faith in art, and in the positive dimensions of art, all around the globe – that was something historically new. This general, socially established positive attitude toward art provided the foundation, both philosophically and materially, for the development of curatorship. Society's positive attitude toward art generated a remarkable influx of money and other resources into the art field, which allowed for the creation of a gigantic and still-growing highly diverse institutional platform for contemporary art and, with it, a permanent need for a large workforce to manage, explain, and organise this platform.

In the book, I analyse the curator as a figure who appears, evolves, and tirelessly participates in the institutionalisation of contemporary art. Arm in arm with the development of the institutional platform for contemporary art, and its requirements, the figure of the curator is structured simultaneously as a bureaucratic, managerial, and producing figure, as someone who is actively involved in the conception, development, and interpretation of art, and as someone who is able to create an attractive discourse and set of events that give meaning to this kind of art production and that support its exceptional importance in contemporary society. With the curator, institutional art achieves its fullest expression; he takes it to a new level: art is created not merely with the idea and hope that it might one day end up in an art institution, as part of an exhibition or even in its permanent collection, but it is actually made in close collaboration with the art institution and is designed to fit the institution's space and needs.

The present book brings together a variety of texts – analytical essays, case studies, and interviews – in the desire to illuminate the topic as fully as possible and from different perspectives, while at the same time telling a story that is vivid and engaging. Because I have written extensively on curatorship, and from various angles, in the book I limit myself to the four topics I find most interesting: the history and evolution of the figure of the contemporary art curator; the leftist politicisation of contemporary art as it occurred, and is still occurring, in connection with the curator; the phenomenon of the contemporary art exhibition and the curator's role in it; and the exhibition of contemporary art as a set of institutional rituals and the potential effect of such rituals.

The first section of the book provides a historical and contextual framework for understanding the phenomenon of curatorship. Using, in particular, comparisons with older professional profiles in the visual art field, this section outlines the basic range of the contemporary art curator's powers and activities, which are, in fact, still being constantly developed. The period after the Second World War appears as an important time of preparation for the development of curatorship, as secularised Western countries in particular devoted more and more attention and resources to contemporary art and made it an active part of both their domestic and foreign politics. The work of their increasingly powerful cultural ministries and other similar public institutions, the creation of effective alliances between private capital and public funds, and the notably rapid pace of institutionalisation are only a few of the factors that gradually brought about a

　　　　　　　　Beti Žerovc

state of remarkable prosperity in the field of contemporary art. Under such favourable conditions, the rise of the contemporary curator began in the late 1960s, when, working in art galleries and museums, he was able to establish himself as a direct producer of contemporary art – among other things, art started being made literally as a consequence of his invitations to artists to participate in projects – and, with respect to exhibitions, as a creative figure. Eventually, the "curatorial" exhibition of contemporary art achieved wide acceptance; such exhibitions are noticeably different from their historical predecessors in that the curator can mark them with his own personal imprint and, quite plainly, define their ideas, philosophy, politics, etc. This kind of subjectivised exhibition seeks to become more and more an exhibit in itself, a distinctive event, and as such hopes to attract ever greater attention from the media and the public. A significant part of the narrative in the first section of the book is told through interviews with people who played important roles in the pioneering period of contemporary curatorship: Pierre Restany, Zoran Kržišnik, Harald Szeemann, and Daniel Buren. Through their stories, important differences between old and new principles, and different work practices, are revealed, as well as specific antagonisms, such as the tensions that occurred between artists and curators.

I move from the first to the second section of the book with the article "Networking, Curatorship and Social Capital", which portrays as the curator's existential environment the highly ramified global network of the art system with its characteristic rules of operation as it developed at the end of the 20th century. The article summarises the state of affairs at the end of the "Heroic Age of Curating", when in the last quarter of the century contemporary curatorship established itself intensively, taking root in existing art institutions, creating, with extraordinary ingenuity and true missionary zeal, many new structures and institutions, and spreading rapidly around the world. The spread of curatorship, which often coincided with the spread of capitalism and neoliberalism into new territories, was accompanied by a highly politicised discourse about how contemporary art and its institutions could help to construct a better, more democratic, more equal, and freer world. Fifteen years later, from today's perspective, more visible changes can be seen only within the art system itself: for instance, it seems that in terms of power relations the traditional dominance of the West is easing, that people in the art field are today less passionate about taking sides and making explicitly political statements, and that a fondness for individual mythologies is again on the rise. But in structural terms, there has been no serious change or deviation. The contemporary art system and curatorship are today more successful and more widespread than ever, while the established models of practice are perpetuated in ever greater numbers.

The tendency toward a highly politicised left-leaning contemporary art, which I alluded to above, might be described as the first artistic genre that developed in explicit connection with curators – under their aegis, we could say, or at least with the curator as co-creator. Here we are talking about ideas that seem to have become less attractive and less prevalent in recent years but that were only recently extraordinarily vital, especially in the 1990s, when certain curators fervently presented the ethical dimension as nothing less than a structural feature of curatorship, and exhibitions as an effective tool for the emancipation of society. In the second section of the book, therefore, I analyse this curatorial stance and ask whether the exhibition can be a socially emancipatory practice with extra-artistic effects and whether the curator can be an effective socio-political activist. The essay "The Curator and the Leftist Politicisation of Contemporary Art" offers a critical reflection on such possibilities through an analysis of curatorial training. In my interview with Charles Esche, a curator who has very explicitly declared his leftist views in the field of contemporary art, we open up the aporias of such a position, one after the other, on the basis of his own personal practice. The essay "Beautiful Freedom" presents certain key thoughts about why such institutionalised political activity does not deliver the socio-political results it proclaims, or at least desires, but instead produces, literally, the very opposite effect, in that, primarily, it provides ideological cover for promoting the interests of those who maintain and finance the art system.

In the third and fourth sections of the book, I devote my attention largely to the phenomenon of the contemporary art exhibition: I attempt to define its essence and nature and to elucidate what and how it actually communicates to us. The curated exhibition of contemporary art has in recent decades become both a privileged form in the contemporary art field and a practically unavoidable element in the creation and existence of a large segment of contemporary art. It is the format in which con-

     Beti Žerovc

temporary art occurs, lives, and breathes. Today contemporary art is so vitally connected to the exhibition medium and the art institution that much of this art is incapable of any worthwhile existence outside this environment.

Such a state of affairs sparks reflections in several different directions. Among other things, I examine whether the curated exhibition can itself be an independent work of art and what is actually artistic about it. I also look for answers and analogies – at times, I admit, somewhat strained – from outside the visual arts, especially in other creative fields. In the essay "The Exhibition as Artwork, the Curator as Artist: A Comparison with Theatre", I consider the artistic potential of curatorship in dialogue with theatrical directors who have found the medium of the contemporary art exhibition so intriguing that they have employed it as a form of their own production. I also look in more detail at how the exhibition's authorship is structured. Can this be defined as individual authorship or does it make more sense to speak of collective authorship? What is the curator with respect to the exhibition: expert, artist, a mix of the two and then some, or some entirely third thing? Indeed, in this connection I consider whether, with the contemporary art exhibition, it (still) makes any sense at all to think about authorship in such terms and I ask if the curator is merely one who executes the characteristic forms of institutionalised rituals, in which he is unavoidably bound to established models and prescribed formats.

One thing that should become clear in this part of the book is that the physical exhibition is often, and increasingly, merely one element, a kind of background, in the broader complex of the exhibition, in which the curator, armed with an arsenal of the most diverse means and mechanisms, produces a focused set of events and a discourse by which he guides us in our thinking about the chosen topic. The events and the curator's discourse are part of a flow of events and discourse in which the institution deftly interweaves and homogenises all that it produces – and this "flow" seems today to be the chief product of the individual contemporary art institution. Here we can see plainly the institution's tendency to reduce everything to a common denominator; capable of the most extraordinary harmonisation of multiplicities, the institution is like some truly marvellous milling machine: whatever drops into it, no matter how indigestible it seems, is ground into a pleasing porridge. The flavour differs, of course, depending on the institution's focus, locality, and so on; questions about flavour and the correct way to make the porridge are the subject of constant debate and sometimes even very heated dispute. But this is precisely how the system lubricates itself – how the institutionalised rituals of contemporary art consumption are perpetuated with considerable uniformity all over the world.

Toward the end of the book I reflect on the fact that so many of us, ordinary viewers and art professionals alike, gain a sense of ourselves and feel fulfilled as cognitive, emotional, ritualistic and political beings specifically in the institutional setting and in the context of curated events, and I ask if these are still areas that can be perceived and defined with any success. What I mean is that, for the most part, we in the art world would rather not think or speak about these issues. We want to experience the institutional setting, as much as possible, as a neutral, even benevolent place. We want our discussions to be focused primarily on theorising over exhibitions and artworks – the kind of theorising, of course, that omits, or takes but little account of, the fact that in recent decades art institutions have not only been housing and exhibiting artworks but also commissioning and producing them, organising their use, and overseeing their meaning. I am convinced there is urgent need for a more thorough consideration of the implications of the processes I describe. All the more because art institutions have become commissioners and producers of contemporary art of a type and on a scale similar only to what the aristocracy and the Church were in the past.

There was once great discussion about how removing artworks from their original context and installing them in the museum meant their certain death. Today, it seems, we need to be thinking about different questions. Does the institution of visual art bring something to life if within it we create enough materials, structures, and rituals that are in many aspects similar to religious ones? And what, in fact, are we summoning to life?

With two exceptions – "The Exhibition as Artwork, the Curator as Artist: A Comparison with Theatre" and "Why Is It Important in the Art Field to Think About Art Events?" – the essays in this book were written, at least in the main details, before the spring of 2007 as chapters for my doctoral dissertation. The chapters were later developed into articles, and what appears in the present book are more or less reprints of their first publication in English. Although the essays are not necessarily one hundred per cent congruent with my thinking today, I did not wish to change them, as this would mean sacrificing their relevance to their own time, when, in their responsiveness to current issues, they contributed to the animated conversation around the figure of the curator. I felt it was important, too, to preserve the texts' "vital juices": their directness, their feelings of grievance, their impassioned speech – aspects, in other words, that are usually first to go when we are tidying things up in retrospect. All the texts, however, have been newly edited, and a few have been slightly shortened: at times I wanted to avoid repetition, while in some of the interviews I left out passages that strayed from curatorial topics.

In the original Slovene texts, I used masculine grammatical forms when speaking in the abstract about the curator, the artist, etc. – gender-neutral reference is not as prevalent in Slovene writing as in English – and this is also reflected in the translations. My use of masculine pronouns, however, is entirely generic and should not be taken as implying anything about gender. But given that when it comes to the most influential positions in curatorship this otherwise very feminised profession quickly turns into a predominantly white male world, the selection of exclusively male interview subjects seemed entirely appropriate.

I fear that certain terminological difficulties may confuse or mislead the reader. The terminology for contemporary art curatorship is not (yet) fully established in individual languages, let alone internationally harmonised. As a result, writers on the subject resort to arduous descriptive definitions or use general labels even when a fuller understanding might require more specific terms. I hope my readers will understand what kind of exhibition I mean when I say "exhibition" (usually I am thinking of the thematic group exhibition of contemporary art that allows the curator to develop his own potential), and, most importantly, that they will understand when "curator" means the kind of contemporary art curator we have seen in recent decades and when it means the more traditional museum curator, for which I sometimes also use the term "art custodian" (perhaps creating further confusion). In Slovene, we have different words for these two forms of curatorship, a fact that caused quite a few difficulties when it came to the English translation. (Incidentally, it might be wise to ask what, in fact, motivates the persistence in English of one term for two such very different work ethics and practices.)

I would like to offer my sincere thanks to all those who participated in my research and assisted me during the writing and publication of the texts. The support I received from the Slovenian Research Agency was indispensable to my work, as it paid for nearly all of the research that forms the basis of what I write in this book.

For her dedication, her professional support and friendship, and the great patience she showed during the making of this book, I give warm thanks to my editor Urška Jurman.

I also sincerely thank my dear collaborator Rawley Grau, who translated most of the texts in this book, and who, indeed, usually translates my texts. For this book he meticulously reviewed his earlier translations and made improvements. Rawley plays an essential part in my communication with the wider world, and our translation "marriage" goes back so many years that sometimes I think he knows what I want to say better than I do myself.

I am also very grateful to Mary Anne Staniszewski for contributing her thoughts on my writing and on the topics I discuss. Her agreeing to write the Afterword to my book means so much to me because her book *The Power of Display: A History of Exhibition Installations at the Museum of Modern Art* was from the beginning an important inspiration for my own research on curatorship.

Finally, I thank my husband and friend, Andrej Savski, for all our conversations, for his advice, and for lovingly dispelling the clouds from all sorts of difficulties, doubts, and dilemmas.

The Role of the Contemporary Art Curator: A Historical and Critical Analysis

First published (in a slightly different version) as "The Role of the Contemporary Art Curator: A Historical and Critical Analysis, *MJ – Manifesta Journal* (Ljubljana and Amsterdam), no. 5, spring/summer 2005, pp. 138–153.

There can be little doubt that today the curator of contemporary art is a figure of extraordinary influence in the art system. Given that this influence derives in part from his assumption of certain attributes, tasks, and powers once enjoyed mainly by other art-world figures, it makes sense, in any detailed discussion of the curator's function, to examine the similarities and differences between his activities and other support roles in the art field that were typical of the period before his arrival. At the same time, I should stress that these powers and tasks are to various degrees still in the hands of these traditional figures, although they are increasingly being covered by curators as well, at least partially and in certain contexts.[1]

———————

Although the contemporary curator appears to be logically related to the traditional museum custodian, this is less true than we might think. Despite the fact that the curator today is usually

[1] If "combining" activities in this way is rarely problematised, this may be due to the fact that it is hardly new and that other figures, too, in the field of contemporary art often wear several hats at once and, to achieve greater results, simultaneously perform activities that are supposed to be strictly separated, at least according to general ideas about the correct way to do things and the complete difference between vocations that lead to different artistic professions and work principles.

Today this can easily be seen, for instance, with certain famous mega-collectors, who are, at the same time, buyers and sellers of art, occasionally curators, often leading figures in museums, publishers of art books, overviews, catalogues, etc., and, as needed, philanthropic art-loving patrons. Some of them, if perhaps not the most important, are also artists (Alain Quemin, *L'art contemporain international: Entre les institutions et le marché (Le rapport disparu)*, Artprice, Nîmes, 2002, pp. 123–131). Indeed, it was artists who – if they had a talent for selling and brokering sales, or could offer good advice on the most diverse aspects of these matters – were adept in the past at such combining of activities; in fact, before the establishment of the museum custodian as impartial expert, artists were often the custodians of art collections (Wolfgang Hardtwig, "Privatvergnügen oder Staatsaufgabe? Monarchisches Sammeln und Museum 1800–1914", in *Sammler, Stifter und Museen: Kunstförderung in Deutschland im 19. und 20. Jahrhundert*, Ekkehard Mai and Peter Paret (eds.), Böhlau, Cologne, Weimar, and Vienna, 1993, p. 89).

The art world is filled with all kinds of "public secrets", which are known to many in this world, who rely on them in their work but are reluctant to speak of them publicly – this, after all, would undermine the entire mythology of art, compromising the whole thing and them with it. For more on this topic, and on the peculiar relationship people in the art world have to the truth, see Raymonde Moulin, *The French Art Market: A Sociological View*, Rutgers University Press, New Brunswick, NJ, and London, 1987, pp. 3–6.

employed by a particular (normally public or non-profit) institution or operates on a freelance basis for various institutions, and that some of his tasks overlap with those of the museum custodian, his role unites and intertwines all sorts of features that can even seem, at least outwardly, incompatible with the tasks and powers of the institutional employee.

For example, the curator has assumed many features of the private gallerist and is deeply involved in the way money is distributed in the art system. Not only has the curator absorbed the sexy pioneering stance of the post-war gallerist who has a nose for the new and is ready to risk exhibiting and supporting the most contemporary trends, but the artist has also become largely dependent on the curator for his survival and therefore less so on the gallerist. That is to say, in a situation where the most important buyers of contemporary art – museums and private collections – usually act on the advice of a curator when purchasing art, both artists and gallerists find themselves to a certain extent dependent on curators.[2]

Especially in recent decades, when "academic" funding has become increasingly important to an artist's work and survival – in the form of stipends, all manner of public and private awards and commissions, paid residencies and travel grants, per diems, exhibition honoraria, material funds for executing works and other sums connected with exhibiting, etc. – it is again the curator who plays a significant role in the distribution of this income. Indeed, one reason why he is today able, like the private gallerist, to have a certain group of "his own" artists is precisely his vast arsenal of ways to support them.

2 Curators are also very often directly involved in all sorts of art/financial speculation. One of the most typical and simple schemes, which can be used in different settings and at various levels, is known as *la peau de l'ours* or *la peau de lion* (*the bear skin* or *the lion skin*). It supposedly goes something like this: the curator meets with, say, nine financial investors. The investors put up funds, which the curator uses to buy artworks, usually covertly, while at the same time, through his work both inside and outside the museum, he tries as much as he can to increase their value. After a few years, or decades, of course, when the prices are rising, everything that was thus purchased and "ennobled" is now sold, and the profit divided into ten shares, of which one share is the curator's payment. My sources for this subject have wished to remain anonymous. Reports about this type of art speculation, or similar schemes, can be found in the literature, especially for the first decades of the 20th century (*Understanding International Art Markets*, Iain Robertson (ed.), Routledge, London and New York, 2005, p. 52).

As I said, the curator has supplanted the gallerist even in his pioneering relationship to art. Because of these different sources of funding and because of the changes in our understanding of what belongs in a museum and what constitutes quality, the curator today has vast opportunities and even the obligation to lend his support to the most original and most innovative projects – unlike in earlier times, when such work was denied access to "serious" institutions. Then, it was most often the private gallerists who, at their own expense and sometimes even at the risk of their livelihood, oversaw such projects and gave them the space they needed. As a result, even up into the 1980s, many of these "avant-garde" gallerists had a certain hip reputation, some even star status.[3]

Still, it would be surprising if gallerists complained very much about a loss of privilege to the curator, since the new state of affairs is greatly to their advantage. When all kinds of public and non-profit institutions for contemporary art started to appear and the traditional museums and galleries opened their doors first to contemporary art and, later, to even very young artists, they became giant display windows for the art dealer's wares, supplying catalogues and scholarly expertise at virtually no cost to the dealer and all the while whetting the appetites of collectors. The smart gallerist knows how to benefit from this situation, since those institutions and the curator have freed him from having to make large initial investments in artists all on his own, and they do not even share in his later profits.[4] Dealers, therefore, have a clear interest in maintaining good relations with curators: their activities support each other and are not mutually exclusive.[5]

3   Sandy Nairne, "The Institutionalization of Dissent", in *Thinking about Exhibitions*, Bruce W. Ferguson, Reesa Greenberg, and Sandy Nairne (eds.), Routledge, London and New York, 1996, pp. 401, 404.

4   An example of a gallerist who built his strategy not on opposing the art institution but rather on using its wind to "fill his sails" was the now-famous Leo Castelli (Raymonde Moulin, *Le marché de l'art: Mondialisation et nouvelles technologies*, Flammarion, Paris, 2000, p. 31). Castelli is also an example of a dealer who becomes a big star with his own mythology.

5   Through their enthusiastic collaboration with the art market, curators at the same time contribute to its "ennobling". For instance, through their intensive participation in art fairs, curators help make these fairs seem more like "disinterested" cultural events, almost a kind of biennial and not a marketplace at all. See my interview with Charles Esche, pp. 161–164.

That the curator's involvement in the sale of art is an awkward topic we can see from the fact that it is rarely discussed. Also, in most of the current attempts to compile a history of curating – a task being undertaken by a number of curators – the role of the private gallerist is usually left out, although curators could well see him as their predecessor on a number of levels.[6] Given that the curator simultaneously exhibits and popularises art, and is even indirectly involved in selling art, it makes sense to examine his position by comparing it with the gallerist's work. As early as the second half of the 19th century, an "ideological dealer" (Robert Jensen's term), such as Paul Durand-Ruel, for example, exhibited and popularised art in ways that are largely recognisable today. For instance, he successfully cultivated ties with a group of new, up-and-coming artists and played an active role in their breakthrough; he also quite successfully employed various exhibition techniques, such as group shows and (at the time not so common) solo shows, thematic shows, and exhibitions in his own home, where, of course, he anticipated the positive effect of the intimate setting. We might also consider him a predecessor of contemporary exhibition-making in that he supported his activities with the kind of promotional techniques used by museums and galleries today, not only by, for example, instrumentalising any sort of scandal but also by founding his own art magazines so he would not have to rely solely on reviews in the independent press.[7] What is more, he also designed his role as someone who separated economic concerns from his "true" higher interests; he presented himself as engaged in a self-sacrificing battle for a truly special, new kind of art that was superior to the rest and, therefore, in the public interest.

Clearly more interesting for the history of exhibitions and curatorship are certain private gallerists for whom selling art was, or at least seems to have been, more of a secondary pursuit and who are known primarily as genuine art enthusiasts and producers of what in their day was alternative art. Such, for instance,

6   I addressed such issues systematically in my interviews with curators and found that, as a rule, they would try and avoid questions about buying and selling art. The rare statements they made on the topic were often entirely deleted from the final versions of the interviews, since they refused to authorise them.

7   Robert Jensen, *Marketing Modernism in Fin-de-Siècle Europe*, Princeton University Press, Princeton, NJ, 1994, pp. 18–69.

 Beti Žerovc

was Herwarth Walden, who at the beginning of the last century succeeded in less than 10 years – through the art association he founded, his own gallery, a newspaper, strong international ties, etc. – in creating an entire platform for launching contemporary art.[8] We should note that we are again dealing with a case where a range of functions is united in a single individual. In this respect, Walden could rely on the older example of the famous Berlin art merchant Paul Cassirer.

In such histories, just before the first more prominent appearances of the curator, we might expect to find mentioned more often such unusual gallerists as George Maciunas. We could say that, while Maciunas was perhaps a rather unsuccessful gallerist and art dealer, he was very successful as a kind of producer of all things imaginable, including some highly unusual events and projects. Maciunas is unique, and for ambitious curators, I expect, a very inspirational example in which the aura of being the "spiritual leader" of a movement goes hand in hand with the work of the curator.[9]

If, in the past, the bond between artist and gallerist included yet a third figure – the art critic – who provided art with a theoretical grounding and ideological "cover", then, in today's configuration, the curator has taken over this job as well, at least on certain levels. There are a number of reasons for this substitution, and they are linked not only to the curator's financial and production capabilities but also, among other things, to the strong public relations apparatus that art institutions have today. This makes it possible

8   Describing the differences between the old methods of selling art and Walden's company, Robin Lenman underscores in particular certain properties of the latter that correspond completely to the desired attitude of the contemporary curator. Apart from selling their art, Walden offered artists "not only genuine sympathy and understanding, but also indestructible energy, journalistic talent, and a willingness to shoulder the increasingly important managerial duties" (Robin Lenman, "Der deutsche Kunstmarkt 1840-1923: Integration, Veränderung, Wachstum", in *Sammler, Stifter und Museen: Kunstförderung in Deutschland im 19. und 20. Jahrhundert*, p. 139. See n. 1).

9   Ina Conzen, "From Manager of the Avant-Garde to Fluxus Conductor", in *Fluxus. Eine lange Geschichte mit vielen Knoten: Fluxus in Deutschland 1962-1994*, Institut für Auslandsbeziehungen, Stuttgart, 1995, exh. cat., pp. 18-29.

for the institution itself to publicise its own productions and even to suggest – and disseminate through all possible channels – a particular, and of course very favourable, view of its activities. Given such resources, the independent critical review, which as a rule is published only once, becomes increasingly dispensable. The materials sent to journalists and media outlets by an institution's PR department, which are normally brimming with factual information, have become the usual basis for public announcements and writing about art events, while the journalistic report increasingly replaces and overshadows works of original art criticism.

Critical writing is also less influential in positioning a given artist or artwork, since, with today's methods of presenting and consuming art, it is often the exhibition itself that provides the context for positioning a particular work of art. Complicating these relationships further is the tendency to expand the exhibition context. Alongside the show itself, there is, in particular, the catalogue, as well as accompanying lectures, symposia, and other events, all of which very often focus on, and direct us toward, various interdisciplinary activities, discussions on the most diverse topics, and so on, but which are concerned less and less with a critical analysis of the exhibited works, let alone their formal qualities. The works themselves are often selected for the exhibition mainly because they fit a certain curatorial concept, illustrate a certain curatorial idea, etc.; with such a gravitational shift in the criteria for selecting artworks, it seems increasingly pointless to try and seek out and reveal the artistic qualities of the works themselves, nor are there any uniform criteria for such a task. Practically the only reasonable way to deal with an exhibition, it seems, is to critique or analyse the exhibition as a whole along with its curatorial concept.

The position of the art critic is, then, becoming more and more precarious and, in terms of the actual relationships in the art field, we can say that, in contrast to the situation a few decades ago, today the support of an important curator is far more helpful for an artist's career than that of an important art critic. This turnabout has occurred with remarkable speed. Studies of the art system published in the 1980s, which may otherwise be excellent, today seem out of date precisely because, in comparison to today's situation, they place too much emphasis on the critic's role, and many aspects related to the positioning of

          Beti Žerovc

artworks, then in the domain of the critic, are now part of the curator's domain.[10]

Given the abundance of areas in which a curator can work and have influence, we might well expect him to at least stay clear of the work of the art historian and art theoretician. And to a certain degree he does. Rarely do we find the curator as the author of in-depth and solidly grounded art-theoretical studies. Nevertheless, it appears he is deeply involved in interpreting, as well as historicising and (in connection with this) canonising, artworks. In this capacity, he works through his exhibitions and catalogues, as well as, more and more frequently, by authoring a wide variety of books and surveys on contemporary art that are often equipped with lush visual materials.[11] Although he may not contribute any thorough discussions of the artwork in these books, he is the one who chooses the artists and the art, which is something that in the field of art history can be of crucial importance. Since we usually merely skim through such books, reading them almost like we would picture books, their main message is conveyed to us through the visual materials far more than through the accompanying texts.

But undoubtedly, the curator's strongest trump card in this area is the exhibition catalogue. As early as the 1980s, Ekkehard Mai found that the exhibition catalogue was not only handsomer and more appealing than the dry book of scholarship was, it was also less expensive, since it had larger print runs (and a wider

10   Here I am thinking especially of Carol Duncan's essay "Who Rules the Art World?", written in 1983 and republished in her book *The Aesthetics of Power: Essays in Critical Art History*, Cambridge University Press, Cambridge and New York, 1993, pp. 169–188. There has been much discussion on the topic of criticism's recent decline, and many reasons and causes have been found to explain this phenomenon. One such view, which is directly connected to our subject, looks at things from a completely different perspective: it presents the curator as the ultimate legitimisation and affirmation of the critic in that he has moved from written instructions to the manipulation of living material. See Raymonde Moulin, *Le Marché de l'art: Mondialisation et nouvelles technologies*, pp. 38–39 (see n. 4); and the interview with Pierre Restany included in the present volume, pp. 54–64.

11   Here we should include the catalogues of the big exhibitions, especially the recurring ones, and the kinds of books that have appeared in recent years, such as the *Cream* series and *Vitamin P* (both Phaidon).

audience), and was often better subsidised; moreover, it had the additional advantage of being widely advertised in conjunction with the exhibition.[12] Also, because it is linked to the experience of a certain event, the catalogue serves as a souvenir, which means that its effect is quite different from that of a scholarly work, which has no such associations.[13] Furthermore, because it helps keep an exhibition alive, so to speak, even long after it has closed, the catalogue can be an important factor in maintaining a link between the art and the exhibition. It is, indeed, one of the curator's "miracle tools", making it possible for his subjective selections to take up lasting residence on our bookshelves and, especially, in our memories. The catalogue encourages our propensity to draw connections among works and artists that are, increasingly, more in line with the curator's groupings – and outside their "natural" contexts – and to box them away in our memory with such labels as *Zeitgeist*, *Magiciens de la terre*, documenta x, etc., rather than in the sort of stylistic categories we once used. When it comes to the art of recent decades, it seems that, alongside certain formal features, basic concepts and images, and the names of key artists – things that spring to mind when we think of earlier art periods – our memory more and more presents us also with images of curators and entities such as Szeemann's documenta, Hoet's *Chambre d'amis*, Fuchs's documenta, Obrist's *Do It*, etc.

Given such conditions, non-curatorial art scholarship appears rather superfluous and quite impotent, especially when we consider that, on the theoretical side, the art field currently seems almost more interested in thoughts and findings from other scholarly fields, such as sociology, political theory, philosophy, anthropology, and the like. And it is the curator who, in a very broad way, incorporates these ideas in the performance and pronouncements of his work, making room for such texts in his catalogues and inviting specialists from these other fields to

12 Ekkehard Mai, *Expositionen: Geschichte und Kritik des Ausstellungswesens*, Deutscher Kunstverlag, Munich and Berlin, 1986, pp. 98–102.

13 In his analysis of documenta as a collective ritual, a kind of modern pilgrimage, Harald Kimpel makes special mention of the catalogue, which, he says, is more a magic object than a study object, more a symbol than an aid, more a collector's item than reading material. It serves in a way as proof of its owner's art competence: as visits to documenta and purchased catalogues multiply, it attests to the owner's *non-parvenu* status, which in turn obliges him to keep coming back to Kassel (Harald Kimpel, *documenta: Mythos und Wirklichkeit*, DuMont, Cologne, 1997, pp. 228–229).

  Beti Žerovc

participate in his symposia. By the same token, even in the traditional vehicles for art writing, such as art catalogues and art magazines, writing about art has been losing its pre-eminence. For some time now, the space allotted to it has been shrinking[14] in favour of things like critical analyses of society and societal problems, ruminations on (predominantly leftist) solutions to global inequities, attempts to solve the problems of the Third World, and so on – in other words, texts that don't merely explain art or, for example, help unravel complex iconographies, but which are also meant to perform a more general function of enlightenment in accordance with ideas about art's social role and its power to exert a positive influence on contemporary society. In short, traditional writing about art has been further jeopardised by what is currently one of the strangest concepts in the visual arts field, namely, the understanding of the art magazine and art catalogue as appropriate and effective vehicles for progressive, egalitarian, and even radical thought.

It is this configuration, so favourable to the curator – and for the time being insufficiently elaborated upon in terms of a critical analysis of his financial and canonising powers, his involvement in maintaining the social structure, and our simultaneous faith in the professional and socially responsible work of institutions – which today allows him to exert direct and constant influence on art and its public without being seriously accused of excessive speculation or involvement in spheres of interest that are usually seen as undesirable in art and criticised. This situation is reinforced by the fact that we are talking about a relatively new profession, and that therefore most conclusions can only be speculative. At the same time, the great variety of practices in contemporary curatorship makes it difficult to summarise all the curator's activities and attributes. Nevertheless, it seems possible to designate the curator as a latter-day mutation of all those mediating figures who, over the past 150 years or more, performed similar tasks in the field of art.

14   Shrinking, that is, in relation to the whole, which not very long ago was devoted entirely to such writing. It is, however, difficult to speak about an actual shrinkage of space, since there is an ever-growing number of art publications of the greatest variety and they are getting thicker and thicker.

We can assume, hypothetically, that these mutations in the figure who stands beside the artist have been vital in keeping the machinery of the art system running smoothly. When it needs to adapt, the highly ramified art system, which tends toward self-preservation, expansion, and naturalisation, is understandably less focused on changing entrenched institutionalised mechanisms of production and distribution; rather, it adapts by changing its smallest and most easily replaceable elements or modifying the relations between them. Through these mediating figures, the system can also, at least superficially, integrate (theoretical) criticism in a way that disperses or covers up the system's "negative" and, at the moment, socially undesirable aspects, especially those that could damage our faith in the institution of art and the legitimacy of the art system. In addition, it uses these mediating figures to present and mediate its own new image with aspects that are socially more desirable.

Such an understanding of the curator's role gains further support when we look at the era in which the curator first emerged as a vital element in the production of contemporary art. Although we can trace his latent presence as far back as the 19th century, and although since the start of the 20th century contemporary art has been drawn closer and closer to official institutions, the curator as we know him today first appears most clearly at the end of the 1960s. This was a time of general social crisis when, along with far-reaching demands for change and criticism of consumerism in all fields, art and art institutions were also being questioned. The seriousness and intensity of the social turbulence of the time clearly demanded more visible changes; still, these changes could occur within the framework of traditional institutions provided that both the institutional and art-critical sides were accommodated. By the major museums and galleries opening their doors directly to radical and institutionally critical contemporary art and introducing other changes that, from today's perspective, seem more cosmetic, both sides clearly got what they wanted: young artists acquired much better access to the official establishment and the market, while traditional institutions regained an appearance of relevance. By successfully integrating something that at first seemed to threaten them with destruction, traditional institutions were able to prove themselves to be spaces that were neither conservative nor on their way to extinction, since they were, after all, also suitable for contemporary production and could assume an active role even in this segment of the art field.

In implementing this process, then, alongside the gallerist, museum custodian, and art critic – "tarnished" figures who were universally criticised – a space opened up for a new figure, who had to be acceptable to both sides as a mediator and the overseer of the process. This new kind of curator was able, at least to some extent, to satisfy the critically minded public and the artist, inasmuch as he, too, usually came from the critically minded community, was an enthusiastic advocate for contemporary art, did his utmost to find funding for the artist, had a special awareness and sensitivity for contemporary production, and so on. At the same time, he could satisfy the traditional system, since he made sure that art would "unfold" within the traditional framework and be distributed in the usual way with no real change in the system's hierarchy and values, although all these things would now have a somewhat modified and modernised "image". At this point, then, the contemporary curator was acting not only as an agent of change but, even more, as an agent of neutralisation, of reconciliation between the traditional system and contemporary art and its demands. At a time when reconciliation seemed impossible, the curator exerted a calming influence through his unusual appearance and stance, which, from the perspective of both sides, allowed him to act as part of the solution and not part of the problem. He offered pledges to both the art community and the traditional institution: a pledge to recognise what is new, excellent, and interesting and to present it in real time, at the very moment of its creation and emergence, and a pledge to bring this art safely into the arms of the institution and watch over it there.

Today it is no longer so unusual to encounter the observation (no longer expressed with such great astonishment) that it was precisely when critical and conceptual art began to be exhibited in the institutional "establishment" that large corporate sponsorships entered art in a major way. Given the content and declared intentions of the art of the time, this is something that should seem at the very least strange, if not a total contradiction in terms. But when we consider the arrival of the curator and the musealisation of such art in the way I have described, then this situation, too, becomes much easier to grasp. Indeed, it is the curator we often find orchestrating such compromises and serving as mediator between such (seemingly) incompatible sides.[15]

In this conflict, then, it was traditional institutions, with the backing of capital, which proved to be acting with the greatest long-term foresight, since when "alternative" art began to happen right in the museum itself, it came under the museum's direct control. In one fell swoop, traditional institutions set in motion a means for preventing the damage a critical and subversive art might cause in real space – stirring second thoughts, igniting criticism, holding public demonstrations, etc. – and at the same time, the institutions found a way to ensure wise and "correct" acquisitions for their collections: the curator, after all, with his unique provenance, work methods, and position, would not fail to choose art that might one day enter History. He would not, so to speak, install *pompiers* or *juste-milieu* artists in the museum, but only "the real deal" – the Monets, Gauguins, and Cézannes of today – and he would do it right away.[16]

The system of producing and discovering artists and art, partly because it had learned from the repeated lessons of history, thus acquired a new safety valve, its own personal agent, someone directly involved in the most progressive alternative

15 A now-famous example of such a connection between corporate sponsorship and the institutionalisation of young art that happened through the curator is Szeemann's exhibition *When Attitudes Become Form* (Kunsthalle Bern, 1969), which was sponsored by Philip Morris Europe. See my interview, included in this volume, with Harald Szeemann, pp. 83–88; and John A. Murphy, "Sponsor's Statement for 'When Attitudes Become Form'", in *Art in Theory: 1900–1990. An Anthology of Changing Ideas*, Charles Harrison and Paul Wood (eds.), Blackwell, Oxford, UK, and Cambridge, Mass., 1995, pp. 885–886. For other early situations and examples of this sort, especially in America, see Mary Anne Staniszewski, *The Power of Display: A History of Exhibition Installations at the Museum of Modern Art*, MIT Press, Cambridge, Mass., and London, 1998, pp. 281–287, 341; and Alexander Alberro, *Conceptual Art and the Politics of Publicity*, MIT Press, Cambridge, Mass., 2003, pp. 1–16.

16 Supporting this rough sketch of the transition period and entry into the "age of the curator" are recent writings by people who participated in the events of that time. From their retrospective viewpoints, they describe a decline in the more radical possibilities and ideas, in the number of people who refused to compromise, and so on. See, for instance, Carel Blotkamp, "1969", in *Conceptual Art in the Netherlands and Belgium 1969–1975: Artists, Collectors, Galleries, Documents, Exhibitions, Events*, Suzanna Heman, Jurrie Poot, and Hripsime Visser (eds.), Stedelijk Museum and NAI Publishers, Amsterdam and Rotterdam, 2002, pp. 16–27.

          Beti Žerovc

scenes. At the same time, all of this gave the curator a basis for assembling a gradually expanding portfolio of authorities and mechanisms by which he could, in a very real way, conduct the musealisation and canonisation of his chosen artists.[17]

The history of important exhibitions, as we understand it today, confirms this temporal placement of the contemporary curator. This history extends from the independent shows of Courbet and Manet, through the Secessions, the exhibitions of the avant-garde groups of the early 20th century, the *Armory Show* and similar presentations, special forms like Duchamp's *Boîte en valise,* Malraux's "imaginary museum" and Seth Sieglaub's journal-based exhibition, the shows of Yves Klein, Arman, Kounelis, and others in private galleries, all the way to its culmination in institutional, often museum, exhibitions, when the curator joins this group in the late 1960s. This now fairly established "official" history of exhibition making consists of shows that, considered along the line of their exhibition spaces, originated for the most part in private and commercial venues. Meanwhile, if we follow the line of authorship of these events, we find that in the majority of cases they were created by artists, though often with the help of others in the art field. But in the late 1960s, following the lines of both venue and authorship, we see the public or large non-profit institution and the curator entering this history in a major way and in direct correlation. And accordingly, we find that, from this point on, all the historically interesting shows are, by and large, group exhibitions.[18]

---

17   For example, simply by exhibiting certain artworks in a museum, he can, as a rule, regularly ensure that their market value increases. If he combines this, as is quite usual, with purchasing the works for the museum and other collections, publicising them, sparking media interest, and so forth, then his ability to consecrate an artwork is, indeed, unequalled, and his "magic touch" can have a truly remarkable effect.

18   The historicisation of exhibitions, of course, existed before the arrival of the curator, but, logically enough, in the era of the curator it has become very popular. At the same time, curators have to some extent adapted this history in their own fashion as a way of ennobling their practice. For an example of such a history, see "A Short Chronology of Curatorial Incidents in the 20th Century", compiled by Alison Green, in *Curating in the 21st Century*, Gavin Wade (ed.), University of Wolverhampton and The New Art Gallery, Walsall, 2000, pp. 156–165.

That the field was truly ready for the arrival of a new figure can be seen in the way curatorship flourished in the 1980s and, especially, the 1990s. The curator became, indeed, one of the key players in contemporary art, and whenever he moved from one institution to another, this would generate sensational coverage in art magazines as if he were a famous football coach who was changing teams. Also in the 1990s, the practice of contemporary art curating underwent a process of intense professionalisation – through the establishment of local and international professional associations, the setting of guidelines for curatorial work (for example, at various curating symposia and in public debates), the search for materials that would confirm and ennoble the curator's position (especially through the development of a curatorial literature and the aforementioned historical legitimisation of curatorship),[19] and the founding of curating schools in every corner of the globe.

If we now return to our initial search for differences and again compare the curator with his predecessors, we find that this new configuration around new and current art production is precisely where the contemporary curator has developed the essential difference that separates him from his immediate predecessor, the museum custodian. Although the work of both figures involves presenting art in a medium common to them both – the institutional exhibition – the curator is no longer simply a self-effacing, studious, and meticulous figure who documents, with as little imagination as possible, an already established situation;[20] rather, because of the new situation and, especially, the central-

19 Even events and publications that have an entirely different "official" purpose can fulfil such functions. A good example would be the various symposia where the art profession takes a critical look at itself and the art system (*Changing the System? Artists Talk about Their Practice*, Åsa Nacking (ed.), NIFCA, Helsinki, 1999; *Stopping the Process? Contemporary Views on Art and Exhibitions*, Mika Hannula (ed.), NIFCA, Helsinki, 1998).

20 In fact, even at the most local level, museum custodians are exposed to similar trends and pressures from the environment, which lead them away from a concentration on the material to the organisation of events that will be as attractive as possible. Nathalie Heinich and Michael Pollak have discussed the role of the traditional museum custodian in relation to the new *auteur* role of the contemporary designer of exhibitions (and not only art exhibitions) and indicated several differences between these two roles in terms of their work and status (Nathalie Heinich and Michael Pollak, "From Museum Curator to Exhibition Auteur: Inventing a Singular Position", in *Thinking about Exhibitions*, pp. 231–250. See n. 3).

  Beti Žerovc

isation of previously dispersed powers and responsibilities in the person of the curator, he can play a much more active role in the presentation of artworks. He can even act as a creator, or at least co-creator, of new art trends, calling forth out of "nothing" the latest thing in art, the art world's new stars, etc. At the same time, his exhibition becomes less and less a transparent institutional medium or scholarly presentation; on the contrary, it is increasingly his own individual creation and original event, which in many cases has both the aspiration and the possibility of itself becoming a historical point of reference. The modern-day curator of contemporary art uses his exhibitions to present his own ideas and, through the artwork of others, to illustrate and narrate his own stories.[21] Consequently, we might say that the museum custodian and the new curator are committed to different truths. Whereas the former attempts (at least officially) to treat the material with the greatest possible objectivity and impartiality, as he has, supposedly, received it from history, the latter "selects" with greater flexibility that to which he commits himself – for example, certain artistic criteria, political correctness, other political convictions, private obsessions, etc. – he devises his own concepts and messages and in accordance with these can even commission new works from artists to suit the needs of his exhibitions.

Another thing that sets the curator entirely apart from the museum custodian is the very clear eroticisation of his work, and his own personal image, which comes with his status as an independent creator and his handling of living artists and their careers. In this regard, the boring museum worker has nothing on the curator, who, if he is famous enough, will be pursued wherever he goes by droves of artists eager for success. After all, his "magic touch" can transform unknown and little-appreciated objects into major works of art (with a commensurate market value) and can validate the people who made these objects as genuine artists – a validation that carries a multitude of benefits. It is not unusual, therefore, that whenever a well-known curator comes to a city in preparation for an exhibition or biennial,

---

21 Lucy Lippard writes: "As a writer, I equate curating with choosing the illustrations for a book. This won't please artists, but most exhibitions do in fact illustrate some curator's ideas" (*Words of Wisdom: A Curator's Vade Mecum on Contemporary Art,* Carin Kuoni (ed.), Independent Curators International, New York, 2001, p. 102).

artists politely and patiently line up to present themselves and their work to him personally – if they've been invited to do so by whoever is organising these meetings, usually a local institution compatible with the curator.

If we now turn to the dealings between the curator and the artist, we see that rituals of this sort are evidence enough that this relationship is hardly an equal one. We will understand it more easily if in our analysis we always keep in mind that today the curator is present at every point of the artist's inclusion in the professional art world, and is thereby practically indispensable for the artist. The curator is involved in the market, in exhibition-making, in the historicisation of art, in contacts with the media, etc., and so collaborating with him and seeking his mediation appear as the artist's most effective way to enter and actively participate in the professional structures of the art world.

If we keep all of this in mind, it will also be easier to understand why, despite the ever-increasing visibility of exhibitions, the artist seems to be losing the possibility of speaking for himself, his independence, and a wide range of skills, all to the advantage of the curator, without the artist ever really complaining or trying to halt or change the situation.[22] What is peculiar about this new mediating figure who stands next to the artist is that he is taking over tasks and roles not only from the support personnel and middlemen of the art world, but also, and quite intensively, from the artist himself. Since the shift in boundaries and transfer of roles between the artist and the curator is most easily measured in the exhibition itself, I will try to explain what has oc-

22   There has, of course, been criticism of the curator's role, especially in the early period of curatorship, but no war cries or calls for boycotts, which is what we might expect given the seriousness of the situation. What usually happens is that artists criticise an institution on a very abstract level without implicating curators at all. More rarely, artists might criticise a curator for intruding into their realm and trying to be an artist who uses their artwork to create his own work – although this tendency has been quite obvious from the very beginning. Today, the now-classic texts on the topic are the critiques by Daniel Buren and Robert Smithson. See *The Museum as Arena: Artists on Institutional Change*, Christian Kravagna (ed.), Verlag Walther König, Cologne, 2001, pp. 12–17, 40–42; and Eric Banks, "October 1972", *Artforum*, vol. XLI, no. 2, 2002, p. 56.

          Beti Žerovc

curred by examining the changes and new position and structure of this medium.

While certain things about the exhibition of contemporary art have stayed in place – it still usually happens in an exhibition space, there are still artworks on display, a catalogue is still published, its market effect remains undiminished, etc. – an additional new level has opened: it has become extremely important today who is making the exhibition. On this level, the conceptualisation of the exhibition/event, as well as the selection and placement of the artworks in it, are viewed, increasingly, as distinctly original and creative activities, even as artistic activities – though still with a theoretical underpinning. We tend, then, to read such an exhibition as a new entity in itself with a specific message of its own that is separate from the messages of the individual artworks on display, even as it serves as the foundation, context, and "guide" for deciphering, reading, and understanding these other messages. Today these two levels – the exhibition as a whole and the artworks it presents – exist side by side; but since the curator and his concept/message are explicitly foregrounded, they are what mostly reach the public and form the main topic of conversations, despite the fact that the artworks remain right where they have always been in exhibitions. To understand the relationship between these two levels, and the range of information they convey, we need to go beyond the traditional "intellectual" approach of seeking the exhibition's message solely in the exhibition itself and the artworks on view. Instead, we must accept the fact that the exhibition, especially because of its intense media support, is able to communicate its message and extend its effect far beyond the exhibition space; indeed, most of the people it reaches come into contact with it and become aware of its presence, orientation, and impulse primarily through various media. At the same time, however, the people who actually go to a contemporary art exhibition do not usually consume it in its "ideal" state – they do not normally read the catalogue, they don't necessarily understand all the works or look at them long enough or closely enough, etc. But these same consumers are repeatedly exposed to the curator's clearly stated message. In other words, while the artist's message lurks encoded in the artwork on display, the curator, through a brief but pointed explanation repeated over and over and an exhibition title that is as resonant as possible, conveys his own message to us and, at the same time, explains, or at least suggests, the message that is being sung by the "chorus" of artworks. What is often overlooked in discussions about the curator's role is the fact that, in addition to the exhibition itself and the catalogue, he has at his disposal an entire apparatus of the most diverse promotional and pedagogical channels for distributing his message: the press release that gets published by a huge number of media outlets, interviews and media statements, exhibition wall labels, guided tours, etc.

But even here the curator manages to escape criticism. It is, after all, literally written in his job description that he must do all he can, and be as vocal as possible, to get the greatest possible response from the media for a given exhibition – in contrast to the artist, for whom it is still quite unbecoming to seek out media attention or opportunities for press statements. At the same time, the curator's job description justifies and even encourages his popularised explications and crude simplifications, all of which are of course supposed to entice the public, sponsors, etc., and bring only benefit to art and the artist. And from the public's perspective, this again makes the curator more attractive – and more memorable – than the exhibited artworks, which are probably not so populistically eloquent.[23]

To put it simply, not only is the curator today able to directly influence artworks in the most diverse ways, but when they are part of his exhibition he can also define them in the context of his own narrative and, what is more, overshadow them. His mediation, therefore, is hardly innocent; it radically shapes our ideas about art, all the more so as it leaves us with the firm belief that we have been exposed directly and exclusively to art, and so surrender ourselves to his mediation usually without a second thought. When we come into contact with the curator's

23   Today it is very unusual for an artist who takes part in a certain exhibition to comment on, or even correct, the curator and his narrative in public. If an artist is not happy with the curator's concept or message, he can either stay in the show and be quiet or leave, since the exhibition is entirely the curator's domain. We all know that the exhibition is the curator's "property", just as it is also generally well known how troublesome those few artists are, like Daniel Buren, who want to be in exhibitions – since they think they have a certain right to this – but at the same time, if they disagree with something, will express their own views in opposition to the curator (Daniel Buren, "Ausstellung einer Ausstellung", in *documenta 5. Befragung der Realität: Bildwelten heute*, Harald Szeemann, Marlis Grüterich, Katia von den Velden, and Jennifer Gough-Cooper (eds.), Kassel, 1972, exh. cat., pp. 17–29; see the interview with Daniel Buren on pp. 94–109).

 Beti Žerovc

production, which is "inhabited" entirely by art, we do not give any special consideration[24] to the fact that we are being addressed by someone who has, on the one hand, an enormous array of opportunities and channels for delivering his message and, on the other hand, a responsibility to the people who have actually commissioned his messages and pay him for them. In order to preserve the integrity of the entire enterprise, the curator's immediate relations with his employers and funders, as well as any clear causal connection between their biases and the curatorial content, must be pushed aside.[25] I suspect that the desire to keep such associations and implications as discreet and distant as possible is one of the reasons why the curator and curatorial activity – parallel with the increasing public visibility of him and his exhibition – has been shifting (and been allowed to shift) more deeply into art itself, which is something he, too, has been intensively pushing for.[26] At this level, after all, the curator is no longer just an art scholar; his exhibitions are created from his own artistic impulses and inner tendencies, even profound personal crises, his commitment to certain political ideals, etc. People today speak about exhibitions as they do about artworks, referring to the curator's talent, his "special something" and similar mystical gifts; they bestow on him such key artistic values

24 For instance, the exhibition is usually presented as if the art itself were speaking to us directly, but in fact, the real source of the speech, who exactly is addressing us, where exactly this message is coming from – is all rather blurred and hazy. Are we being addressed by the curator, the artist, the art, or indeed the exhibition itself? Is the curator with us now as an artist or as an art scholar? And so on.

25 This relationship is usually alluded to only by small logos in special places and on certain pages in the catalogue – kept separate from the artwork and texts – and the curator is never compelled to say, "Because I am being paid by Such-and-Such Bank, I am sincerely committed, in particular, to reducing global inequities," or "Although I am being paid by Such-and-Such Bank, I am sincerely committed to finding a way out of the unjust capitalist system," or anything like this. But such logo use entirely determines our reading, in the sense that the logo is a kind of frame that tells us how to react toward whatever carries the logo. See Henry A. Giroux, "Benetton's 'World without Borders': Buying Social Change", in *The Subversive Imagination: Artists, Society and Social Responsibility*, Carol Becker (ed.), Routledge, London and New York, 1994, pp. 187–207.

26 Though not entirely. These are complex relations, where the specific situation of the art field both supports and hinders such a shift by the curator and forces him into an ambivalent position regarding his creative and artistic role. For more on this, see pp. 176–196.

and attributes as imagination, authenticity, personal sincerity, autonomy, commitment to an ideal, play, improvisation, "that magic touch", and so on. [27]

Let me conclude by returning to the question of why the artist lets all this happen, since, by definition, he should not put up with being trapped in the system and having his personal freedom and power so curtailed. Maybe it really is true that, as I said earlier, he sees no other alternative and, more importantly, does not consider this way of working to be especially problematic. But it is also true that the system and its operations are extremely convenient for the artist, precisely because, among other things, it gives the curator some extraordinary ways to take care of the artist, almost maternally, and make his life very comfortable. Not only does the system offer many artists numerous social and material benefits but, what is more, it does this in a way that allows the artist to think of himself and his work in a rather romantic light, since with the curator's help he does not have to be involved in marketing or organisational matters. In fact, the curator has been very successful in providing the artist with a mode of discourse and an enthusiastic environment that are free of such unwelcome concerns; instead, he fills the artist's world with

27   If we are speaking about "curatorial art", then the advice offered to the younger generation by 60 top curators in the collection *Words of Wisdom* confirms clearly just how much the curator today is involved in art production itself and how much he determines what art will be on all levels, even where we have been accustomed to think of such decisions as being made by the artist. But the opinions of these advice-givers are obviously very divided about where the curator's proper place is in regard to art and the artist – from those who are bold enough to compare their work methods to the artistic process and even to refer to themselves as artists and curating as a form of art, to the, perhaps, most frequently offered piece of advice in the book, namely, the warning to at all costs not forget that curating is not art, that the curator is not an artist, and that the artist should be left in peace to do his work. See comments by Dan Cameron (p. 39), Maria Lind (p. 100), Fumio Nanjo (p. 125), Jana Ševčíková and Jiři Ševčík (p. 153), Mari Carmen Ramírez (p. 138), and Marcia Tucker (p. 172), Jean-Christophe Ammann (p. 22), Robert Fleck (pp. 63–64), Maaretta Jaukkuri (p. 88), Paul Schimmel (p. 150), and Igor Zabel (p. 175) in *Words of Wisdom: A Curator's Vade Mecum on Contemporary Art* (see n. 21). While these two understandings of the curator's position are mutually opposed, they both point to the indisputable fact that the curator is today deeply involved in art production itself – for if his roles and activities were clearly separate from those of the artist, there would be no need to remind us that, for instance, the curator is not an artist.

    Beti Žerovc

other, more appealing issues, so that everyone involved, from the artist to the public, feel themselves part of an enlightened, intellectual, and critical international elite.[28]

To put it another way, for the artist to remain in a secure and enthusiastic environment as he goes about saving the world with the finest of intentions, it is also in the *artist's* interest – and not only that of capital, corporations, bourgeois forces, and similar bogeymen – that the curator be recognised as an artist and author, an inspired thinker with great personal integrity who is far more committed to such ideals than he is to the forces of capital and politics, which directly hire him. This, it seems, is the main reason why – instead of the conflicts and complications we might expect from our naive assumptions about the artist's freedom-loving, rebellious nature and his critical stance toward such unjust systems as the art world – the bond between artist and curator usually develops in an atmosphere of friendship.

28 In this way, the curator today assumes the role of a "screen" between the world and his chosen artist – a role that once most often fell to the gallerist. In modernism, as a rule, the artist and art dealer are not the same person; rather, the dealer is precisely that screen which allows the artist to block out all economic concerns and enables him to appear entirely oblivious to worldly affairs. On the dealer–artist relationship and the "denied economy", and especially on the fact that to prosper in this "denied economy" a person must have a good mastery of it, see Pierre Bourdieu, *The Rules of Art: Genesis and Structure of the Literary Field*, Polity Press, Cambridge, UK, 1996, pp. 149, 168.

Joséphin Péladan: A Proto-Curator?

First published (in a slightly different version) as "Joséphin Péladan – protokurator?" ["Joséphin Péladan: A Proto-Curator?"], *Dialogi* (Maribor), vol. 43, no. 5–6, 2007, pp. 26–34.

A quintessential aspect of aesthetic modernism in the 19th century is that it produced not only a body of artworks and a profusion of *-isms*, but also a body of institutions and a template of practices that, unlike the art itself, were accepted almost without protest by the European and American art public.[1] As early as the late 19th century, the field of exhibition making also had isolated examples of figures similar to that of the independent curator of contemporary art – though, of course, without the institutional support that is usual today. One such "proto-curatorial" figure[2] was Joséphin Péladan, who, among other things, was the founder and director of the Catholic Rosicrucian Order of the Temple and the Grail (L'Ordre de la Rose-Croix Catholique du Temple et du Graal) in Paris. In the 1890s, Péladan organised large group exhibitions as the order's main public events, ones in which he presented artists who had been selected in accordance with his very particular conceptions of art. Viewed from today's perspective, he was a typical independent curator who, at every level and wherever present, defended his "particular position" in art, communicating it through his public image and lifestyle as well.[3]

1   Robert Jensen, *Marketing Modernism in Fin-de-Siècle Europe*, Princeton University Press, Princeton, NJ, 1994, p. 3.

2   "Proto-curator" is, of course, a provisional term for these individuals; though of all the possible professions in the art field, that of the modern-day curator most closely fits their work. Certainly, they had little in common with either the traditional museum custodian or the private gallerist.

    In France, we find a few interesting examples of "proto-curators" even before Péladan. A very early one is Mammès-Claude Pahin de La Blancherie, who in the second half of the 18th century was especially appalled by the cruelty of the American slave trade and devoted himself to liberating art and science from the bonds of tradition. Among other activities connected with his ideological views, he also organised a few exhibitions. These were temporary art shows, produced and conceived by Pahin himself and presented in the rooms of his own salon, which operated with the help of important sponsors. One appealing characteristic of his exhibition practice was that his catalogues also listed works he wanted to exhibit but was unable to borrow for the show. These were marked by an asterisk. See Francis Haskell, *The Ephemeral Museum: Old Master Paintings and the Rise of the Art Exhibition*, Yale University Press, New Haven and London, 2000, pp. 14–22.

3   Today, the best-known curators normally have certain well-developed philosophical positions, on which their work is based and which they feel committed to – or at least very passionately defend. They present these views as part of both their personal and professional identities, use them to set themselves apart from other curators, actually "compete" with them against each other, and so forth. See, for instance, my interview with Charles Esche, pp. 149–155.

Today, Péladan is not well known for his curatorial work, not because he was so far ahead of his time that, say, his contemporaries did not understand him, but rather because, when it came to positioning himself successfully in art with an enduring place in history, he made several "mistakes". Among other things, Péladan, despite his hard work and the genuinely large influence he enjoyed in his day, did not do enough and, above all, was not convincing enough to ensure that he would be "right" in art history. He did not persevere long enough in this work, did not assemble a coherent enough group of artists, and was too little connected with the market. Furthermore, he was so extremely pompous and so obviously contradictory that it was difficult for anyone later to take up his cause openly and in all seriousness. Mario Praz described him as heroic in intention and comic in result.[4] Péladan experienced a small revival in the late 1960s, when symbolism as a movement again acquired a certain general importance.[5] Hippies, too, found him interesting because of his strange attire, his fascination with magic and the Near East, his rejection of weapons, and the like.

Péladan

A brief look at the life of this bizarre, complex individual is needed if we want to understand his proto-curatorship and compare it with contemporary curatorial practices. Joseph Péladan (1858–1918), as he was originally called (he later changed his first name to Joséphin), was born in Lyons to the family of the fervent Catholic journalist and mystic Louis-Adrien Péladan. He thus acquired his zeal for mysticism and Catholicism from his family, while his delight in costumes, mysteries, and unusual rituals and names (Sâr Mérodack, among many others) was not his alone but was common among occultists of the time and could also very often be found in artistic circles (we need only recall, for example, the group Les Nabis).[6] Péladan carefully crafted his external

4　Mario Praz, *The Romantic Agony*, Oxford University Press, London, 1954, p. 316.
5　Philippe Jullian, *The Symbolists*, Phaidon, London, 1973, p. 26.
6　Edward Lucie-Smith, *Symbolist Art*, Thames & Hudson, London, 1972, pp. 98–102.

appearance: he wore long tunics, silk and lace, had long hair and a long beard, and sported eye-catching, provocative accessories.

He travelled in Italy as a young man, after which he arrived in Paris filled with fervour and loudly announced his mission in the press. Among other things, in a review of the 1883 Salon, he wrote: "I believe in the Ideal, in Tradition, in Hierarchy."[7] In short, he declared war on every kind of realism. In 1884, he published his first major literary work, the novel *Le Vice suprême*, which was followed not only by other novels but also many plays, articles, reviews, and scholarly works on art. He even published two travelogues of sorts – *La Terre du sphinx* (on Egypt) and *La Terre du Christ* (on the Holy Land) – and some esoteric "self-improvement" books, including one on becoming a magus and one on becoming a fairy. Among his many other extraordinary accomplishments, he claimed to have discovered a new location of the tomb of Christ. He called his vast cycle of novels *La Décadence latine*: his belief that the corrupt and irreligious Latin race must fall appears as a common thread and motto in most of the works. The novels reflect his fear of democracy and the coming of the barbarians. They deal with mysticism and strange events, usually plotted around Péladan himself in the guise of a literary character. His hero is always in pursuit of the Ideal, for which he makes the greatest sacrifices and renounces everything worldly, as deeply infatuated noblewomen try to seduce and distract him. Only rarely is this formula abandoned. Art is normally involved as well – its redeeming potential, the struggle for true art, and so forth. For example, in the novel *L'Androgyn*, Péladan promises to crusade against all that is ugly, all that is vulgar, both in his novels and in real life.[8] To this end, he advocates an indivisible art as the thing that can take us back to the Catholicism of the Renaissance, which, he argues, was when the greatest number of masterpieces were made. And for him, the masterpiece is the highest proof of the existence of God.

Despite his enduring fascination with the occult, Péladan was an idiosyncratic and fanatical Roman Catholic who zealously promoted the Catholic faith. He believed that while the church opposed sorcery, it was not against magic and even supported it.

7   Ibid., p. 109.
8   Joséphin Péladan, *Der Androgyn*, Georg Müller, Munich, 1924; originally published in French in 1891. The foreword to the German edition of Péladan's novel series was written by August Strindberg.

The bombastic fanfare around the publication of his novel *Le Vice suprême* brought the occultist Stanislas de Guaïta to him, and together in 1888 they revived the Rosicrucian order (L'Ordre de la Rose-Croix) in Paris. Philosophical differences soon led to internal disputes, and at the start of the 1890s Péladan founded his own Catholic Rosicrucian order, the Order of the Temple and the Grail. The members of the order performed works of mercy to prepare for the coming age of the Holy Spirit and, most importantly, sought an inner perfection that would allow them to live a contented life on a perverted earth. The main focal points of the order's work were aesthetic, and its most visible public events were, in fact, exhibitions – art salons held regularly from 1892 to 1897. These were typical oppositional exhibitions, which essentially announced that, unlike the once-official Salon and similar contemporary art shows, they were presenting "true" art. This, of course, meant art as it was understood by the enthusiastic curator Péladan, who with great fervour and pomposity invited his chosen artists to exhibit.[9]

Péladan, the Proto-Curator

What aspects, then, of Péladan's manner of exhibiting the art of his day make him seem so close to the modern-day curator?

The first is, certainly, the simple fact that, quite unusually for his time, he decided to convey his philosophical and critical views and ideas about art not only in writing but also through large group exhibitions. He evidently decided on the exhibition form

9   Robert Pincus-Witten, *Occult Symbolism in France: Joséphin Péladan and the Salons de la Rose-Croix*, Garland Publishing, New York, 1976, p. 90. Despite the fact that the exhibitions were official events of the Rosicrucian order, I propose viewing them as primarily Péladan's affair in both their organisation and content, which is how they have been treated by previous writers who have discussed them. I do not compare them with similar exhibitions put on by different artists' associations of the time, since, in the latter, the group's dynamics, work, interests, and goals were, as a rule, explicitly in the foreground. Many original materials connected with Péladan's Rosicrucian order and its exhibitions are available on the Internet (e.g. through the electronic library Gallica), while in the work cited above, Pincus-Witten provides a precise description of the order and the exhibitions in English.

because it allowed him to use other people's works to illustrate and communicate his worldview, and the beliefs he was advocating. This understanding of the exhibition makes his approach identical to the modern-day view, where it is not only a medium for showing art but also a vehicle that can work toward a variety of goals, for instance, to encourage social renewal. Apart from his love for art, what justified and confirmed Péladan in his commitment to such work was his dedication to a higher goal, the Catholic renewal of society. This, to be sure, makes him ideologically distant from contemporary curators' commitment to fight global capitalism or support politically correct views, but the principle is basically the same.

Because of this "utilitarian" attitude toward exhibition-making, Péladan is, in fact, already a typical curator with a particular position, one that defines all his projects in a characteristic way and stamps them with a distinctive mark. Turning things around a bit, we can say that by enforcing his own ideas, dictating the messages, using a characteristic "form" for his exhibitions, and choosing very specific artists, Péladan developed a distinct authorial style of curating where his name alone at once told viewers what kind of exhibition they could expect.

Like modern-day curators, Péladan also established his own circle of artists, for whom he was a fervent supporter and advocate. He made it easier for these artists to do their work – he brought them into a network (an international one), found spaces and funding for public presentations of their work, etc.; at the same time, however, he dressed them in a kind of shared external image, one that perhaps did not suit all his exhibited artists and obscured their differences. As is true today, the curator's proximity meant, for the artist, considerable help in becoming established, but also that the curator's worldview, narrative, and speech would considerably define his art, shaping an interpretation and staking out an understanding of him and his work that he himself might not necessarily embrace.

Furthermore, with Péladan's work, we can already witness the merging into a single job of the two positions that are usually kept separate in the art world, namely, those of producer and artistic director; indeed, it is this specific combination that gives the curator such extraordinary power. The ability to organise and direct numerous large productions thus also provides the producer with a direct means for establishing his ideas, views, and artistic aspirations, since in the process the producer is not divorced from the creative function but rather defines even the exhibiting artists and their work, and conceptualises the event as a whole. It is understandable, then, that such a curator-as-producer also takes the lion's share of the prestige and fame, as the greatest part of such bonuses attaches specifically to his name.[10]

Péladan, the Producer

If, of the two positions just mentioned, we first look a little closer at the producer's side, we find that Péladan performed this role very well and used work methods that are completely modern. He knew how to acquire devoted collaborators, the necessary funding, and a prestigious venue, and how to promote the event in a way that would attract media attention and the widest possible public. Let us take his first salon as an example.

Labelled a *geste esthétique* and *acta Rosae crucis* (acts of the Rose Cross), the exhibition was held at the Galerie Durand-Ruel from 10 March to 10 April 1892. Describing the show in today's

10 Péladan's obvious knack for promotion, including of course self-promotion, has been noted by earlier art historians, who compare him to the more famous Marinetti. Like the celebrated futurist after him, Péladan worked tirelessly on proclaiming his positions and organising events, while at the same time he was largely also drawing attention to himself. "Like Marinetti, Péladan seems to have been a compulsive exhibitionist, whose greatest artistic creation was his own personality" (Edward Lucie-Smith, *Symbolist Art*, p. 109. See n. 6). In the history of contemporary art, Péladan may well be more important than we now imagine, among other reasons because of his potential influence on art-world figures such as Diaghilev, Marinetti, and others, who started appearing not long after him. Péladan, who was also very active in the areas of conceiving and organising musical and theatrical events, is further connected with such figures by his desire to produce the most auratic events possible, where what was essential was not so much the chosen medium or art form but rather the ultimate effect of the whole, which had to be as magnificent as possible. Thus, a musical event or art exhibition would be "directed" very much like a theatre production. Compare my text "The Exhibition as Artwork, the Curator as Artist: A Comparison with Theatre," pp. 198–215. On the synaesthetic effects of the different artistic media at the Rosicrucian salons, and on Péladan's extraordinary enthusiasm for Wagner, see Laurinda S. Dixon, "Art and Music at the Salons de la Rose-Croix," in *The Documented Image: Visions in Art History*, Gabriel P. Weisberg and Laurinda S. Dixon (eds.), Syracuse University Press, Syracuse and New York, 1987, pp. 165–186.

terms, we would say it took an interdisciplinary and intermedia approach, was conceived as an integrated spatial installation, a kind of "environment", and included many accompanying activities. On opening night, the exhibition rooms were festooned with flowers and fragrant with heavy oriental perfumes, and the guests as they entered were greeted with the prelude from Wagner's *Parsifal*. Among other things, the opening also featured specially composed music by Erik Satie. This whole "circus" (excessive even for those days), which Péladan took in dead earnest, was just what the viewers wanted; they flocked to the show in droves, perhaps looking not so much for aesthetic delights but to satisfy their curiosity and lust for sensation. Those present on the day of the opening included Paul Verlaine, Gustave Moreau, Pierre Puvis de Chavannes, and even Émile Zola,[11] who was hated by the symbolists – names, in other words, that guaranteed the event's reputation as a prestigious occasion. We can conclude that the salon was very successful, despite receiving a mixed response from the critics.[12]

Péladan solved the problem of funding, and made the social connections needed for success, by involving powerful and influential sponsors in his shows. For his first salon, he found such a backer in Count Antoine de la Rochefoucauld, who initially was one of his most important collaborators and also took part in the salon as a painter. De la Rochefoucauld generously supported the first salon financially and put his reputation behind it; he was thus crucially important in creating the initial momentum for

11   Gisèle Ollinger-Zinque, "The Belgian Artists and the Rose-Croix," in *Simbolismo en Europa: Nestor en las Hesperides*, Centro Atlantico de Arte Moderno, Las Palmas de Gran Canaria, 1990, p. 371.

12   Robert Pincus-Witten, *Occult Symbolism in France*, pp. 104-106, 131 (see n. 9). The strong connection between contemporary art exhibitions and the media, even in the 19th century, is evident in the fact that for this first salon, as many as 2,000 invitations were sent to the press! In fact, of all the Rosicrucian salons, the first received the best response from the media; this was, I expect, due in part not only to the initial shock at such an extraordinary project, but also to the show itself, which in fact impressed many as a special kind of *Gesamtkunstwerk*. The salons that followed did not elicit such a response, and the last editions saw a decline in both the size of the shows and the quality of the artwork, as well as in the enthusiasm of sympathisers and financial backers and even in Péladan's own determination and drive. All of this led to an increase in negative responses from the press. See Christophe Beaufils, *Joséphin Péladan (1858–1918): Essai sur une maladie du lyrisme*, J. Millon, Grenoble, 1993, pp. 272-273, 300-301, 313-314, and elsewhere.

Péladan's salons. Nevertheless, even with the first salon, he and Péladan quarrelled a great deal over all sorts of things, and in the end, de la Rochefoucauld evidently had no choice but to leave the group. The salon's main financial backer, who held with Péladan the highest position in the Rosicrucian order, apparently fell into Péladan's disfavour because, among other things, he tried to win acceptance for some of his ideas about the selection and installation of the artworks at the salon.[13]

Péladan designed his art project to be explicitly international; clearly, by then it was already established knowledge that, to win the greatest possible recognition for such an undertaking, international connections and expansion were essential. Thus he exhibited many Dutch artists, including Toorop, as well as such Swiss artists as Schwabe and Hodler – the latter shone at the first salon with his work *Disappointed Souls*. Another well-represented group were the Belgians, who also seem to have been the most enthusiastic about Péladan, especially Jean Delville, who for a time served as a kind of ambassador for him and his order in Brussels, and Fernand Knopff, who provided illustrations for his novels.[14] Although successful in attracting foreign painters to his salon,[15] Péladan was not particularly successful in his attempts

13 Ibid., pp. 225–235, and Robert Pincus-Witten, *Occult Symbolism in France*, pp. 140–144 (see n. 9).

14 The French symbolists who are best known today had no desire to participate in Péladan's salons, although he did all he could to assemble as star-studded a group as possible (partly, I assume, because he was well aware of its promotional and social potential). Thus, he invited both Gustave Moreau and Pierre Puvis de Chavannes to show their work, but he did not receive their permission. He simply idolised Moreau, who, however, evidently had serious doubts about the Rosicrucian hocus-pocus. Even so, the painter sent his students to Péladan to be exhibited. Of the numerous French artists who showed work in his salons, not many are particularly famous today. The ones who do stand out somewhat are Charles Filiger, Alphonse Osbert, Alexandre Séon, Edmond Aman-Jean, Antoine Bourdelle, Georges Rouault, and Armand Point.

    Nor can we say that the group of artists that formed around Péladan's salons was fully coherent in style. Especially in the first salon, several artists had distinctly post-impressionist tendencies; here we could put Count de la Rochefoucauld. As the years passed, the salons became more unified stylistically, though unfortunately with a drop-off in the better-quality artists, while the work of those such as Point, Osbert, and Séon came to be seen, in a way, as the most typically Rosicrucian style of art.

15 But even here he was not always successful, as we learn from an amusing anecdote. One of Péladan's favourite painters was the Englishman Edward Burne-Jones, who was more than a little astonished by Péladan's invita-

to expand the order's network beyond Paris, and its foreign affiliates never really developed. Among other reasons, the order's involvement with visual art was probably too short-lived for such an expansion; Péladan announced that the Paris Rosicrucian salon of 1897 would be the last, and when it closed, he apparently stopped curating contemporary art.

Péladan, the Artistic Director

Presumably, it was Péladan's ability and success as a producer and organiser that secured him the interest and participation of a wide range of artists. Left to fend for themselves on the free market, artists in the 19th century increasingly saw regular exhibiting and press coverage as matters of survival; hence, they were more and more dependent on – and in an unequal relation to – potential exhibitors. Given the comparison with today's curatorial practice, it is particularly important to underscore that Péladan considered exhibition making as a subjective creative challenge where he could have his ideas and views recognised and where he could realise his ambitions, while the artist was left to adapt to all this – or else was invited to participate only if the curator deemed him suitable. With the exhibition so devised, Péladan then saw it and defended it as, essentially, his own intellectual property, explaining and justifying it from his own personal perspective.

As mentioned, Péladan had very clear ideas about which artists he wished to present at the Salon de la Rose-Croix, and which works of art. At the same time, he always made it very clear what he wanted and expected from art; in this way, he tried as much as possible to shape the content of future artworks as well. Although the expression "curatorial concept" was not in use at the time, his writings and public statements define in precise

tion to participate. He wrote about it to his colleague, the painter George Frederic Watts: "I don't know about the Salon of the Rose-Cross – a funny high falutin sort of pamphlet has reached me – a letter asking me to exhibit there, but I feel suspicious of it ... the pamphlet was disgracefully silly" (Quentin Bell, *A New and Noble School: The Pre-Raphaelites*, Macdonald, London, 1982, p. 175).

Joséphin Péladan   47

terms the kind of art he supported and considered "worthy" of being shown in the salon. Péladan did, however, conceptualise his exhibition practice in the form of the order's art programme, which was published as a set of rules. Although the ideas and subject matter of his desired art do not in themselves interest us here (at least not primarily), let me summarise these rules so we can get a sense of the considerable clarity of Péladan's concept, as well as the freedom (or lack thereof) he allowed art and the artist.[16] He writes in Section II of his rules that the Rosicrucian salons strive "to ruin realism, reform Latin taste and create a school of idealistic art." In Section III, he says that the order accepts works by invitation only and "imposes no other programme than that of beauty, nobility, lyricism." Nevertheless, in Section IV, he lists "for greater clarity" the kind of subjects that will be rejected "no matter how well executed, even if perfectly": history painting, patriotic and military painting, "all representations of contemporary, private or public life", portraits (with rare exceptions), "all rustic scenes", landscapes, all still lifes, all seascapes, anything humorous, flowers, etc. "The Order favours first the Catholic ideal and Mysticism," he wrote, followed by legend, myth, allegory, dream, etc., and it wished to see content related to these topics "even if the execution is imperfect." These rules also extended to sculpture, and busts were not accepted except by special permission. Because the art of architecture "was killed in 1789", the only acceptable works in this field were "restorations or projects for fairy-tale palaces."[17] The technique preferred before all else was the fresco. Drawing was also highly favoured, less as a physical than as a psychological technique that more easily crossed the boundary between the earthly and the spiritual. Women were entirely excluded as exhibiting artists.[18]

16 Robert Pincus-Witten, *Occult Symbolism in France*, pp. 211–216 (see n. 9). Longer summaries of the rules can be found in Edward Lucie-Smith, *Symbolist Art*, pp. 111–112 (see n. 6); and Philippe Jullian, *The Symbolists*, p. 227 (see n. 5).

17 Edward Lucie-Smith, *Symbolist Art*, pp. 111–112 (see n. 6).

18 Péladan's similarity to certain modern-day curators can be seen as well in the incoherence of his ideas – he was incredibly enthusiastic about all sorts of things, including, unsurprisingly, things that were completely incompatible. For example, although he banned the portrait genre (with only rare exceptions), he exhibited grandiose portraits of himself, and although he was a devout Catholic and a defender of virtue and purity, he was also a devoted admirer of the Belgian painter and illustrator Félicien Rops, whose drawings and illustrations are often a very perverse kind of pornography. This was an

To such truly "conceptualised" exhibitions, where the selection of artists was combined with rules about the content, Péladan then added a third level, where through focused writings and statements before, during, and after the event he further imprinted his story on the whole entity thus designed. As eloquently and as loudly as possible, he tried to justify his exhibitions and selections as universal, the most sensible, and the best selections of art at the present moment, and to achieve the greatest effect in this effort, he skilfully employed all sorts of operations that are still being used by curators today. For instance, he was very adept at justifying and legitimising new artistic positions by juxtaposing them to established antecedents and emphasising the similarities. Because exhibitions also by this time had an intensive presence in the media realm, his message, in relation to the artist's, was already clearly in the foreground, especially because Péladan, like the successful curator today, was extremely careful about the media coverage of his events and knew how to make himself a very attractive personality for the press.

Accordingly, like modern-day curators, Péladan was criticised for trespassing too far into the artist's domain – but the criticisms did no real damage. In response, and in a way quite characteristic of today's debates on the topic, Péladan would entangle himself in contradictory and contrived-sounding explanations about how he was the one who truly exalted the artist and the artist's freedom, even to the very highest level. When it came to displaying his positive, devoted attitude toward the artist, Péladan could be extremely vocal. For example, in the catalogue of the first salon, he extolled the artist in the following terms:

artist and an art that sprang from completely different views, the very opposite of his own, but still Péladan desperately wanted him for his salons and so always found a way to explain his enthusiasm for the Belgian. For example: "I have seen some of his masterful etchings, of such an intense perversity that I, who am preparing the Treatise on Perversity, was enchanted by his extraordinary talent" (Gisèle Ollinger-Zinque, "The Belgian Artists and the Rose-Croix," in *Simbolismo en Europa*, p. 370. See n. 11). The two men also engaged in a vast correspondence; Péladan wrote to Rops: "May the devil, your supposed master, keep for you the admiration of Catholic artists, to the greater confusion of Protestant pigs and bourgeois swine, Amen!" (ibid.). Rops, in fact, never did exhibit in Péladan's salons, although he provided illustrations for a number of his novels.

Artist, you are the priest: art is the great mystery and when your efforts result in a work of art, a holy beam descends on the altar ... Artist, you are the king: art is the true empire; when your hand writes a perfect line, the cherubims themselves descend to take pleasure in it as if in a mirror ... Artist, you are the magician: art is the great miracle and proves our immortality.[19]

Conclusion

In short, Joséphin Péladan tried to define the art of his day in a manner that was quite rare for the time but is today exceedingly common, since much of what we consume at contemporary art exhibitions is prepared along the same lines. But because the curatorship of contemporary art did not come into its own until much later, we should assume there to be certain clear differences between today's curator and such isolated "proto-examples". So as not to get lost listing every possible specific difference, let us look at a difference that does seem to be at the very heart of the phenomenon. Until at least the first decades of the 20th century, roughly speaking, the situation in the art field as a whole was essentially different; certain segments were already prepared and suitably developed to be compatible with curatorial practice, but others were still far from the situation we have today, which is well in tune with such practices. If in that period a person had the idea of organising large group exhibitions of contemporary art in accord with his own concept, and if he managed to acquire the agreement and participation of artists and a circle of supporters and backers, and if these exhibitions also attracted the clear interest of the public and media, then a distinct difference from today's situation would be the lack of any institutionalisation of such practices that would allow them to happen regularly and widely. In the 19th century, the contemporary art exhibition was still very much in the domain of the market, and many years would pass before it became the preferred form for supporting contemporary art on the part of the big backers and commissioners, politics and capital, as well as the today ubiquitous but then non-existent art institutions. Among other

19   Ibid.

    Beti Žerovc

things, the (large group) exhibition of contemporary art was not yet developed, or understood, as something that, in the ritualised setting of a museum or gallery, could create narratives, generate meanings, shape worldviews, beliefs, and values – and so potentially even influence society in line with the desires of those who commissioned it. For such large structural shifts to occur, it had to become clear that such an exhibition does not only show and sell contemporary art but can also do much more, especially in terms of constructing specific integral messages and communicating them such that the potential ideological implications go unnoticed.

Still, despite the institutional sector not being immediately ready to adopt ambitious proto-curators, it is hard to say that Péladan had no influence at all on the field of contemporary art curatorship. His practices and strategies came into curatorship mainly by indirect routes, mostly through the mediation of artists who in the early 20th century increasingly cultivated a practice similar to Péladan's. Unfortunately, we are only vaguely aware of this current, probably because serious thought about Péladan's influence – even on such central, iconic 20th century artists as Kandinsky, Malevich, Hugo Ball, and Duchamp, and on such groups as the Vienna Secession, Futurists, Dadaists, and Surrealists – is establishing itself in the art-historical discourse slowly, timidly, and in bits and pieces. It seems that we do not wish to see the characteristic practices of the pioneers of contemporary art as linked to similar practices Péladan had employed quite strikingly not long before, to the great attention of both press and public.

Because these iconic artists' influence on the development of the exhibiting of contemporary art – and the development of contemporary curatorship and curatorial practices – is sufficiently well known, I will not discuss it here. Instead, I would like to propose a more active scrutiny of Péladan's influences on these artists in areas where I see a possible connection with contemporary curating. Here I propose three categories of influence, which may have operated separately or, even more often, as a whole, as an effective integrated work model.

First, we should note the importance of Péladan's use of the exhibition medium as a distinctly independent means of expression that is able to tell its own story and so requires a specific kind of "dramaturgy and directing". In this regard, the exhibition is not merely a passive juxtaposition of artworks; rather, it is simultaneously an interdisciplinary and intermedia platform, a "synaesthetic environment", and an intensive media event. We can assume that these aspects were reflected in the pioneering exhibition projects of the key figures of early 20th century art – although, given the scant research into the connections between them and Péladan, it is difficult to determine the exact nature and extent of this reflection.

Second, Péladan's specific logic in constructing his own career in the art field seems to have been very influential: what is important here is the way he established and designed himself as a public persona with a clearly readable identity. Péladan – and we must not forget that he was himself an artist – actively tried to shape his own mythology, to turn anything connected with himself into an event, to develop his profile on different levels and through very different activities, and in a way to transform himself into an institution. While Péladan was certainly not the only one to do this, we need to consider more thoroughly his role in the evolution of the type of artist that came into its own in a real way in the decade before the First World War – the artist who forges his profile not only by creating artworks but through a variety of activities, including writing (among other things, manifestos), public performances, all sorts of organising (of groups, events, etc.), developing networks, a specific way of acting and dressing, unusual gestures, rituals, and the like.

And last of all, however unexpected as it may sound, the influence of Péladan's worldview is also probably greater than it seems at first. I am thinking mainly of his specific view of art in general, its aims and potential. Here the key element is his distinct contribution in raising the status of art, which was based on his understanding of art as a medium for presenting spheres that are supra-rational, and as an effective tool for improving the world. Accordingly, Péladan also raised the status of the artist, who with this sort of responsible, priestly mission was now suddenly in a different position than before, also *vis-à-vis* society. With this understanding of art, a great deal was now expected of the artist, and much more, too, was permitted him. In the 20th century, such views became increasingly established, in the art field as well. Péladan's contribution, however, was overlooked, mainly, I suspect, because his mystical explanations for these views, with their strange combination of Catholicism, elitism,

     Beti Žerovc

conservatism, pomposity, and incoherence, were difficult for a wider audience to accept. But it is worth pointing out that, in the early 20th century, the leading figures of contemporary art themselves very often connected their work to mysticism, even to a mysticism that is sometimes surprisingly close to Péladan's.[20]

20 On connections between Péladan and, for example, Duchamp (the two had many interests in common), see John F. Moffitt, *Alchemist of the Avant-Garde: The Case of Marcel Duchamp*, SUNY Press, New York, 2003, pp. 27, 252; and James Housefield, "The Nineteenth-Century Renaissance and the Modern Facsimile: Leonardo da Vinci's Notebooks, From Ravaisson-Mollien to Péladan and Duchamp," in *The Renaissance in the Nineteenth Century / Le 19e Siècle Renaissant*, Yannick Portebois and Nicholas Terpstra (eds.), Centre for Reformation and Renaissance Studies Publications, Victoria University in the University of Toronto, Toronto, 2003, pp. 73–88, among others. When we consider what traces Péladan left on curatorship, it is essential to stress his potential structural influences. In the present article, therefore, I have largely disregarded his specific ideas, which can be so bombastic that they very quickly drown out everything else and take us in their own direction. Looking at these ideas, we soon find ourselves dealing with instantly obvious comparisons based mainly on content (for example, with Harald Szeemann's body of work).

Interview with Pierre Restany

First published as "Pierre Restany: Intervjuvad av Beti Žerovc" / "Pierre Restany: Interviewed by Beti Žerovc", *Site* (Stockholm), no. 12, 2004, pp. 4–8. The version published here has been abridged.

 Beti Žerovc

The French art critic Pierre Restany (1930–2003) spent his childhood and youth in Morocco, completing his secondary education in Paris. He went on to study aesthetics and art history in France, Italy, and Ireland. His first critical writings were concerned with abstract expressionism, but in the mid 1950s, this was already giving way to an enthusiasm for Yves Klein. From there Restany began moving gradually toward the formation of the New Realism movement and soon became its key theoretician and promoter. By 1963, however, the heyday of the movement was coming to an end. For Restany, this was when his long collaboration and editorship at the Milan art and architecture magazine *Domus* began, as well as a remarkable production of articles, books, and other works, which appeared in every part of the world. In his writings, Restany was interested not only in the strictly artistic aspects and interpretation of contemporary art production but also in the sociological aspects of art, the history of art, the workings of the art system, and so on. The question he would always keep returning to was the meaning of art in the modern world.

At the same time, Restany also travelled tirelessly, participating in the art field on practically every continent; he worked intensively in Argentina, Australia, and Japan, among other countries. Even in the period of the Cold War he took a regular interest in Eastern Europe: he collaborated with the Ljubljana Biennial of Graphic Arts on several occasions, was intensely involved with art periodicals in Prague in the 1960s, and in the second half of the 1980s was very active in the Russian scene. He was also interested in broader social concerns: in 1978, for example, he journeyed with colleagues down the Rio Negro, a tributary of the Amazon, a trip that resulted in the "Rio Negro Manifesto". The manifesto sought to redefine the relationship between nature and culture; it called for a deeper, more creative relationship to nature and for a more constructive co-existence with marginal cultures. In 1999, Restany, who remained active practically to the end of his life, became the honorary president of the Palais de Tokyo exhibition centre in Paris.[1]

---

1   A symposium titled *Pierre Restany's Half Century*, held in Paris in 2006 (organised by the Archives de la Critique d'Art, the International Association of Art Critics (AICA), and the Institut National d'Histoire de l'Art), sought to come to grips with Restany's extraordinary presence in art, not only in Europe but throughout the world. It featured a true cacophony of diverse topics relating to Restany. In 2004, Restany's "home" publishing house,

The main objectives of my meeting with Pierre Restany were to examine how the conditions for contemporary curatorship arose after the Second World War and to discuss the role played by biennials and other recurrent exhibitions in this development. Restany proved an ideal commentator on these phenomena. As early as the 1950s, his role in making New Realism an important art movement went far beyond what had previously been the usual activities and competences of the art critic. As for the second question, I had the impression that after fifty years of working in art around the world there was hardly a biennial in which he had not participated, at least in some capacity.

If our conversation has a slightly unusual emphasis, that is because it took place during the opening of documenta 11 in 2002 in Kassel. Although already ailing, Restany was remarkably robust and in good spirits, so that the entire hotel lobby could eavesdrop half-openly on our chat, which lasted more than two hours. He was, after all, a genuine star, one of the most recognizable figures in the global art scene. Even Andy Warhol, when asked what he thought of the French critic, is said to have replied, "Pierre Restany? A myth."

How do you consider yourself, as a critic or as a curator?
>   Critic, surely.
In one of your interviews from the 1980s, you still talked about people (Harald Szeemann, Achille Bonito Oliva, etc.) – people we would today call curators –, as critics.
>   For me, they can be considered as critics because they changed a lot in the international critical scene. For me, Szeemann is a critic more then a curator, because all the exhibitions that he has conceived have a very strong thematic point and they are built as, let's say, critical proposals. In Kunsthalle Bern, with the exhibition *When Attitudes Become Form*, Szeemann wanted to prove his idea that you can express intellect through installations of objects and this is what he did. Because he gave a verification of something that was in his mind, a kind of a postulate – that we can express

Domus, issued a book about him, edited by Stefano Casciani, with the significant title *Pierre Restany: The Critic That Was an Artist*.

    Beti Žerovc

concept with objects. So I think that when you curate an exhibition of that kind, you do an active critical work. Also, the biennials he curated were interesting precisely because they had this kind of a critical point.

In the interview mentioned above, you were talking about those "critics-curators" in connection with Aperto in Venice in 1980. You criticised things, which in your opinion a critic shouldn't do, especially actions connected with trying to force a new direction in art. Could we say that these are typical aspirations and a way of acting of today's curator and are usually even understood as his qualities?

> Everything is relative. At the beginning of the 1980s, or toward the end of the 1970s, the intellectuals, people like Achille Bonito Oliva or Germano Celant made a revolution in the critical scene of Italy. They changed the structure of critical communication. Before them, at the end of the Second World War, the criticism in Italy was very universitary, very scholastic, and there was a kind of a pyramidal structure, first Lionello Venturi, then Argan and all those kinds of critics that were university teachers. With this new scene, people like Achille Bonito Oliva became in a way managers.

Managers?

> Yes, managers of organisation as well as managers of ideas. They treated ideas the same way managers would treat them, because they wanted them to be the winners. These were the people that were able to act in very different ways and deal with money problems and things like that. The university people never wanted to be like that: active, managerial, etc. I think that now that time is over as well, because in order to curate an exhibition you have to be able to tell if the works that you are showing have a telegenic dimension. If they don't have it, they don't communicate, and today the artists who don't communicate don't exist. Art today is the factor of communication. And this is exactly the problem at the moment. If you curate an exhibition, you have to do that in the spirit of a potentially very good TV programme.

And this guarantees a good exhibition?

> No, no. I'm talking about this moment. This is the sign of time. When you see all the works shown at documenta, you will understand that if they had been able to be provided with a good TV programme of an hour or an hour and a half, you

would have seen the things that are presented there in a much better way – because there are a lot of photographs, especially digital photographs. So when they appear in the totality of the television screen, they have the power of presence that they don't have when you see them on the walls, like drawings or paintings. This means that the new director of documenta had all the time in mind that what he was showing might as well be shown on television. That's the new dimension of visual communication.

You think that that was his aspiration?

> Yes. It's the same today for Szeemann. I've heard that he has this idea in mind. It's this idea that affects the judgement of the curator. The things shown at this documenta have surely been shown with this intention, with this kind of reference.

So, for those curators, one of the criteria of measuring quality of art today would be …

> Yes. Would be a good television programme. I think that those people have the idea that the work of art must communicate and must communicate immediately and for that they take the TV genre. I think TV changed their dimensions a lot.

But let's go back first. I'm interested in this "managerial part" of the curator. After the war, the exhibitions we consider today important, and as such they are presented in histories of curating, were usually held in private galleries and non-institutional spaces. But then, as we approach today, they are moving more and more to big museums and public spaces. So it seems that the curator has taken on a lot of the features of the private gallerist. Especially this idea about the private gallerist, of how he is presenting throughout time the cutting edge art, in a way has become the primary task of the curator, but without taking the real risk that used to be involved before.

> I remember in the 1950s there were a lot of exhibitions that I did, and I always worked with a private dealer. At that time, there were a lot of private galleries that were established out of love and not out of money. That was different.

Who used to work out of love? The private dealer?

> Yes, yes. In Paris, for example, in the 1950s you had people like Larcade, Stadler, Iris Clert and so on. You had a lot of small galleries, which worked only because they loved art. They were not really making money. They were rather

shocking because they acted as laboratories of the new-art-in-progress. The collectors were very rare, but some of them were also very idealistic. They were able to raise the money to sponsor an exhibition. A lot of exhibitions were made that way. Things were absolutely different, that's true; and in that sense, the committed gallerists were capable organisers and very idealistically oriented. I don't know if this kind of patience has been transferred into the curator's mentality. But it's true that you can find in the actual curatorial strategies some part of this kind of strong activity, bearing in mind that you can promote ideas without money, which is quite interesting. Maybe some of the young curators today are still fresh enough to have at least something of that. But otherwise, that post-war period of curatorship and situation is definitely over. Because everything changed when the public got more and more power, through "the ministry of culture", in everyday artistic life. So exhibitions first became very publicly oriented, and then very avid for the financial budget. Also, the art scene became broader and broader, so more and more public manifestations were needed, like the biennials, to control the development of the arts in order to make different statements according to different times, different situations.

To control the arts?

> Yes. By controlling the arts, there is a reason for creativity, for the development of an artist's creativity. Those kinds of controls were very rare and limited to Venice and São Paulo. In fact, they were the shop windows of the artist's creativity. They had this role in a financial way as well. Getting the prize at the biennial augmented the value of your work. A lot. Immediately. That was the way in which the system between the market place and the institutional place was organised.

How did this machinery of biennials start or restart after the war? What was the main reason – in whose interest was it happening?

> The Venice Biennial started in 1895. It aroused broad interest because at that time there were a lot of Italian artists in Paris and some had a lot of power, like Boldini. So Paris was immediately interested in showing in Venice. Italian artists were able to convince Parisian artists, such as Puvis de Chavannes, that the biennial could be a very important thing. Italian "pompier" artists were very important in this convincing

process. And after Paris, of course, all the rest of Europe was interested, too. More and more, very well known artists were coming and they all wanted to get the Venetian prize. This is also the reason why after the Second World War the biennial resisted and survived in spite of the pro-Nazi connotation it got between the war. This is because, after the war, a lot of great artists that had never gotten the prize were still alive, like Matisse, Léger, de Chirico, etc. A lot of big names – and they were interested in showing, getting the prizes. And after reopening, the biennial started to give prizes to these really big names, until the mid 1960s let's say, until 1964, when the prize was given to Rauschenberg and this tradition of giving prizes to big European names was broken. The Venice Biennial became in a way much more globally oriented as well because of that surprise. It was no longer a sort of European matter, but had attained a broader vocation, it became a real worldwide institution. So in that sense, the Venice Biennial is a good example, the first in this development, and at that time it developed in a very smart way.

How and why did this change happen?

> I believe that the jury at that time was more sensitive to the power and importance of the American school. From 1955 on, there was a big explosion of the pre-pop culture; it was the first global moment of culture in the century, and in 1964, when Rauschenberg got the prize, pop culture was totally spread out around the world. Not just pop art, but pop in general, pop songs, the pop way of living, hamburgers, sneakers, jeans and so on. So, the lifestyle of the urban, metropolitan section of New York became the existential model for all the youth of the world. This is important. America won the Second World War, not in 1945, when it dropped the atomic bombs at Nagasaki and Hiroshima, but twenty years later, when pop culture became the global phenomenon. And in that sense, Venice understood this, and the jury understood that it was time to give the prize to America.

If we go back, I asked you about this whole trend of biennials that started in the 1950s, like the São Paulo Biennial, documenta, the Biennial of Graphic Arts in Ljubljana, etc. Why did it happen?

> For very different reasons. The São Paulo Biennial was founded by a very, very rich industrialist – Matarazzo – who was

of Italian origin. He was working in coffee and tin boxes. He was kind of the "Tin Box King". Since he was Italian, he did it as a pure copy of the Venice Biennial. In a way, he copied every Venice Biennial. He was very linked with Venturi, and after that with Argan. Matarazzo understood that after the war there was this new importance to the Venice Biennial and that it could really cover the new artistic activity. He said the biennial in South America would be the dialectical point of dialogue with Venice. It worked like that until very recently, until the 1990s. People who missed the prize in Venice could win the prize in São Paulo, etc.

documenta was totally different. It started in 1955 because a minor professor of drawing at the local academy in Kassel understood the situation. Once the Americans had won the war, they developed a kind of a cultural ostracism towards Germany. They wanted Germany to pay culturally, too. So Germany became totally isolated. The first generations of artists in Germany felt this ostracism since they tried to make contacts with Paris, London – but that was very difficult. So the brilliant idea of professor Bode, the father of documenta, was as follows: if the Western culture doesn't want to come to us, we have to go take the culture and bring it to Germany. But to do that, we have to pay for everything ourselves. And that, exactly, became documenta's system for a long time. Everything was paid by the land of Hessen and by the federal government. That's how people were stimulated to come. So, documenta has a very important role and special dimensions in the post-war German culture. Of course, over the course of time, Germany became rich, closer to Americans, etc., and documenta became a kind of a regular measure of the contemporary artistic activity, like a barometer. Moreover, five years is long enough to do that. Biennials can't have such a role, because two years is just too short a period.

You are very critical of the recent biennials. What, would you say, are the main changes in this almost half-century-long development of these institutions?

> The development of cultural communication and information. In spite of the fact that public television is very often of low quality, there is a communication of art and cultural statements. The communication system of the media changed the structure of the informative system in art. Until

the 1980s, all these kinds of manifestations – like the Venice and São Paulo Biennials, documenta – they all had a role. But with the development of cultural information through the media, their role is getting more and more secondary.

So you think that the manifestations before had a much bigger impact because they were also more "special" than they are now.

> Exactly. I think that the place taken by culture and art in the TV system will increase and will be more of a direct approach to the public.

But how do you explain that more and more people come to such manifestations? What is that? Pure tourism?

> Yes, because more and more people in the entire world also go to the beach and things like that.

So in a way this is just a block-buster effect?

> Yes, exactly.

But how would you set this figure of the curator in this development, since in a way, this is a relatively new figure?

> It is a new figure, but it will disappear soon.

So who will be the one "selecting" the arts?

> People from the field of communication. The curator system is over. If curators continue to exist, they will be anachronistic, because they'll come back to the old idea of the university and scholarly kind of vision. Maybe they will make very specific exhibitions about very specific arguments, like archaeology, or like sociology of the quattrocento, and things like that. I don't think that curators will exist as active protagonists in the field of arts in a few years' time.
>
> You see, at first, art became closer to the art market and after that to large audiences. Now, the audience is getting bigger and bigger, because the art demand today is stimulated by the communication system, by television and things like that. When you see an art broadcast on television it gives you the idea that you might go to the museum. But then the communication system will become stronger and stronger and more efficient and will eliminate this kind of an institutional way of presenting art. The curator might become a master of communication. No longer a manager, no longer an opinion leader ...

But at this moment, the curator still seems to be a very important figure who is at the same time important but

            Beti Žerovc

also not reflected enough. There are very few critical texts about this figure: sitting in several chairs, at the same time promising to everybody – to the artists, the sponsors, the public, etc. – that he or she will do the best for every one of them.

> Of course. Because the curators practice the old strategy of *omertà*. Among themselves. Because they know all those problems, but they don't want to admit them.
>
> One of the reasons why there exists a mafia and things like that is also that art, as a generic kind of category, can easily be used for a lot of things, for different characters, market, protagonists, etc. Curators are easy to manipulate, if you have a lot of money and power. They are easily manipulated by politicians or artists or university professors, just as they are easily manipulated for market purposes. And very soon, curators will become media managers and they will be manipulated by information.

So, would you say that Okwui Enwezor was also manipulated?

> No, hang on, he's a professional. He's a Nigerian, but he was entirely formed by the American educational system, he's a curator of the Chicago Art Institute, so he's a product of a specific dimension of the American educational system, which is very different from the European one. So he can really deal with culture and management. But he is a man of all the frustrations of his time, so he's very much conditioned by the complicated power of the communication system. He's a manager-curator who selects pieces of art because they can easily be inserted into the flux of communication and then attract a big audience.

Curators would like to persuade us that their job is very creative. Do you find this creativity in curating?

> Hardly any. Sometimes a curator can be creative, as in the case of Szeemann like we were talking about, but not always. This is impossible, because a curator has to agree to compromises. He's the master of the compromise. And it's not by reaching compromises that you can really create. Curators have the illusion of being creative people, but that's only their own narcissism or their political strategy as in the case of Enwezor.

For many years, we have been talking about the precarious existence of art, the death of art; you are talking about approaching the end of the curatorial system, etc., but at the same time, the spaces for contemporary art are growing in profoundly shocking figures. How would you comment on that?

> I don't know if this quantitative extension of the art public means that people are more interested in traditional art. I only think that art has developed a new dimension of its social presence in life. A lot of people consider art as a kind of a social or psychological therapy. Or, they consider it as a way for the better adjustment of their own life to the society. There are a lot of motivations for the people who are dealing with this new approach of art, which are absolutely extra-aesthetic. Maybe more ethical than aesthetical. The new public thinks art is going from aesthetics to ethics. You will see that in a very simple, not sophisticated way here in Kassel. You will see works of pro-Palestinian artists who are doing works, installations that are anti-Israeli-oriented. So, these people believe that they are artists because they can express their moral and ideological truth in a visual, modern way, in the form of an installation or multi-media work. Art today has changed it's own function, and a lot of indirectly aesthetical motivations are involved in it today.

   Beti Žerovc

Interview with Zoran Kržišnik

First published as "O kombinacijah: Zoran Kržišnik" ["On Combinations: Zoran Kržišnik"], *Likovne besede / Art Words* (Ljubljana), no. 81–82, winter 2007, pp. 24–31. The version published here has been abridged.

 Beti Žerovc

The Slovene art historian Zoran Kržišnik (1920–2008), who enjoyed a brief singing career right after the Second World War, became the first administrator of the Museum of Modern Art in Ljubljana in 1947 and its director ten years later. He led the institution for nearly forty years, until 1986, when he moved to the MGLC, International Centre of Graphic Arts, which had been established on his initiative. Of all his varied activities and projects, he is best known as the primary founder of the International Biennial of Graphic Arts in Ljubljana, which he launched in 1955 and which received almost immediate international recognition. As for his own personal international recognition, this can be seen in his active involvement in a wide variety of prestigious institutions, committees, and boards all over the world.

Kržišnik belongs to the post-war generation of art figures who at the start of their careers found themselves in a unique situation because of the long conflict that had just ended. State borders seemed firm and unyielding; the different nationalities appeared to have very little in common, while the wrongs that had been committed and different political views made communication literally impossible. Given this serious lack of justifiable reasons for interaction and communication, art with its positive reputation represented one of the few platforms for easing tensions and improving the situation. It offered a way for nations to connect and escape the imposed isolation, while at the same time creating and constructing new and more positive community identities, an opportunity that not only Yugoslavia, in its effort to distance itself from the Eastern bloc, put to good use, but also the former Fascist and Nazi powers of Italy and (West) Germany. The extraordinary scope of this potential could very soon be felt in the exhibiting of contemporary art, including the ability of such exhibitions to very successfully convey the presence in a given society of such abstract values as freedom, modernity, democracy, openness, etc. Institutions of modern and contemporary art thus found themselves becoming a special kind of projector of propaganda and ideology, a role they have maintained ever since.

In this connection, it seems, modern and contemporary art institutions became more important than ever before, while the institutionalisation of contemporary art entered a period of exponential growth that continues to this day. Unsurprisingly, with such new opportunities and obligations, the importance of the directors and chief curators at such art institutions grew as well. No longer were they viewed merely as custodians of art collections, but rather, their socio-political activities began to be understood as, in a way, their central mission.

My conversation with the still very youthful and active 87 year-old Zoran Kržišnik was recorded at his home in the village of Žirovnica in September 2007. His house was filled with important artworks by his friends – painters from Slovenia and other parts of the former Yugoslavia – as well as by such world-famous artists as, for instance, Robert Rauschenberg.

Due to your specific career, you are in an ideal position among Slovene fine art protagonists to comment on the phenomenon of curatorship in contemporary art, particularly as it seems that from the very beginning of your career, you very well understood its rationale. At a time when this could not have been easy, you managed to establish in Slovene art a very strong international exchange and were successful to the extent that you were, among others, also a member of the third documenta committee. You have obviously always been exceptionally good at organising events. The Ljubljana Biennial of Graphic Arts was, for example, from the very beginning structured similarly to other current biennial exhibitions of the time – from its basic aspects, such as strong sponsors from the world of commerce, to details such as a 25 per cent discount on rail tickets for exhibition visitors. The criticisms you received resembled the ones curators receive today, namely that you were too managerial and that you had your pet artists whom you pushed and favoured. So, where exactly do you see yourself in relation to contemporary curatorship?

> I suggest we begin by going as far back as possible. I found myself in the Museum of Modern Art as a representative of the post-war generation that faced the key question of how to wriggle out of the grip of socialist realism. That was our priority, and one of the possibilities was the establishment of a biennial of graphic art in Ljubljana. In Venice, where, in 1952, I assisted commissar Šegedin, I met the Slovene painter Zoran Mušič and we began discussing how we could

relax the existing situation just a little. When Mušič received an award in Cortina d'Ampezzo in the shape of a grant for Paris, he invited me there. And so I went to Paris, somehow bypassing official channels – the Museum of Modern Art – for consultations with artists and it was there that our biennial was actually organised. I collected 144 graphic works, practically the entirety of the École de Paris, and smuggled them to Ljubljana. This was the foundation of the biennial. Various curators and directors of institutions began to appear at viewings in Ljubljana, such as Gustave von Groschwitz, the director of the biennial of graphic arts (colour lithography) in Cincinnati. At that time, there were already a few exhibitions specialising in graphic arts, such as the *Bianco e Nero* [*White and Black*] in Lugano, where Slovene artist Božidar Jakac was among the artists who exhibited, and, after his return, he proposed a similar exhibition in Ljubljana. As you mentioned documenta, let me tell you that Arnold Bode, its organiser, also came to Ljubljana at that time. We talked a great deal. I explained to him my idea of a graphics biennial in Ljubljana, while he talked about his idea of documenta.

That's interesting, which year are we talking about?

> That was in the early 1950s.

Why did Bode come to Ljubljana?

> I think he was simply travelling, collecting data, refining his thoughts on how his event would look in practice. Later, I went to the documenta twice as a commissar from my country. So, if we now consider the difference between us and today's curators, I don't really see any great differences, except in those specific factors that result from a differently shaped society. Just like today's curators, I knew very well then that if I wanted to start the biennial, I had to have, for example, the whole of the École de Paris behind me as a kind of a "visiting card" that would open doors and ensure that others would also want to work with us. And that's exactly how it was. On the strength of the fact that I had persuaded the reputable École de Paris to participate, twelve countries replied that they would also take part. If you compare the organisation of a similar modern event, such as Manifesta, I don't see any great difference.

But what you describe is already very removed from the activities and position of a traditional museum custodian

who is, above all, a guardian of objects, which he or she – closed in a museum – nurtures, studies, and describes.

> Of course. For me, it was the social aspect that was most important in this work. We set up the biennial in order to make our way into the world. It was a way of opening doors. And – thankfully – I managed to attract important graphic arts experts for the jury, such as the well-known critic from Venice Giuseppe Marchiori. They were key personalities in the whole of fine arts. This was a confirmation that our event was the beginning of something that was worthy of mention. This first biennial represented the first step with which we indicated to the Yugoslav authorities that another way existed. Of course, there were always political difficulties, especially during the period when the East reacted strongly to abstraction. At that time, for example, Khrushchev spoke about abstract painting, saying: "Abstract paintings look like daubs done by a donkey's tail." A serious "examination" of the event took place at that time. Thankfully, Krste Crvenkovski came to Ljubljana upon Tito's order, an open-minded, literary man and a Slavic studies specialist, while also the vice-president of the Yugoslav government and minister for culture. After seeing the biennial, he supported us and after that things began to run their course fairly smoothly. In order to convince him even further, I accompanied him to Paris and Venice. It was a funny situation. He never said where he was going and they were looking for him all over Ljubljana. In short, I think that at least the basic origins of what is now termed curatorship were already established then.

If I were to give a very rough assessment of what a younger protagonist in the art world would now think, it would be that, after the Second World War, Slovene fine art was somehow completely divorced from that in the rest of the world, in the West, until the late 1980s, early 1990s, when some kind of exchange between the two blocs was established, which could at least conditionally be called a unification, or at least an incorporation. You probably did not experience this polarisation in the same way?

> The political withdrawal from extreme Russian socialism was also in a way a withdrawal from social realism. Later, the idea of non-alignment arose and at that time I proved to Marshal Tito, via Crvenovski, that the biennial of graphic

     Beti Žerovc

arts was actually a materialisation of what was being referred to as openness, which was then seen as non-alignment. We were already talking about a dialogue between West and East and attracted China and Russia to the first biennial. This was approximately seven or eight years before the Russians returned to the Venice Biennial. But we approached them differently, with a direct invitation to present whatever they wanted. We did not interfere in the selection as we did, for example, with École de Paris, where we wanted to get specific representatives, the best of that school; the Russians and the Chinese did their own selection. Our establishment of a kind of a symbiosis between East and West was achieved. All the subsequent biennials were organised on these foundations, and so we became a unique environment in the graphic arts, i.e. we exhibited everything, practically the whole world. This aspect was then combined with the most competent juries possible. The members were always verified individuals of the highest rank, such as the directors of museums like the Guggenheim, the Tate Gallery, the Moderna Museet in Stockholm, the Museums of Modern Art in Tokyo, Melbourne, Rome, and so on. To me, the jury was at that moment just as important as the artists, as it created the ultimate seal of approval on the global fine arts scene.

So, you didn't experience the transition in the late 1980s so drastically?

> No. I just continued the main plan, both officially and "under the table". If I remember, for example, how things went with the Russians: at subsequent biennials we somehow got an opportunity to get, via Riga, everything that was on the "black list" in Russia. That was one thing, for example.

You have to explain this more clearly. What did you get via Riga?

> Those works of Russian artists which would never be sent by Moscow officially, as they were not recognised, but we simply included them as a special group in addition to the official selection.

Who were these artists? And how and why via Riga of all places?

> Artists there and those in Russia who had channels in Riga contacted us themselves. At the biennial, we then arranged

them among the "pure" representatives of social realism. It was a kind of a diversionary tactic for enriching the biennial.

And the Russian officials had no problem with this?

> No, none. We also had very good relations with the Bulgarians and were given very progressive things from them. The Krakow Print Biennial was started at that time, following the Ljubljana example. There, they even came up with the idea of setting up an event alternating between Ljubljana and Krakow, but to be honest I wasn't keen on that and we didn't agree to it. Later, biennials spread all over the world, but we, having been among the first, had good relations with the newer events. Tokyo, for example, established its biennial following our example, and thus we always had good contacts in the Far East. We were quite frequent guests at the Museum of Modern Art in Tokyo and we somehow managed the whole of the Far East from there. I always took care of these contacts personally and when an opportunity arose, I proposed Masayoshi Honma, the director of the museum in Tokyo, as a member of the Conseil International des Musées d'Art Moderne (CIMAM) and invited him to be a member of the jury for a major exhibition of graphic arts in San Francisco. And thus Honma, Bill Lieberman, the director of MoMA New York, and I were on the jury. This was an exhibition at which eleven thousand graphic works were collected, and we had to examine them as if they were on a conveyor belt. Janez Bernik won, followed by Kosuke Kimura. This is how personal ties were formed and Ljubljana somehow participated in coordinating the world fine arts stage.

Are you among those who believe that the difference that existed during the post-war decades between Yugoslavia and other Eastern countries is now less apparent? As if no one feels like dealing with the special status Yugoslavia once held anymore and therefore it just gets bundled up with other Eastern countries?

> We definitely enjoyed a special status. When we used to arrive at the Venice Biennial, it was always something special. For nearly a decade we had a very specific dialogue with the Spanish pavilion, which represented a kind of a Fascist state on the extreme right, while we were on the other side, open Informbiro people if you like, representatives of a country that was escaping extreme socialism, while still being con-

nected to it. And we always received attention. It is interesting that in spite of everything, we always had good relations with the custodian of the Spanish pavilion, who was a Franco supporter, but at the same time professionally quite progressive. Franco somehow tolerated him because Franco himself was actually a "Sunday painter". The Italian prime minister at the time, Amintore Fanfani, was also a "Sunday painter" and as he was good enough, I personally invited him to our biennial and he did in fact exhibit here. During the exhibition he came to Ljubljana and said to me at dinner: "You know, I haven't come to just look at my exhibition, but to ask if you can help me establish contact with your Tito; the situation is such that we on the right and those on the left who are more open should talk to each other." I established contact via Slovene politician Stane Dolanc, who was sufficiently open to such things. I know I have digressed here, but what I'm trying to say is how curiously these things are unintentionally connected with politics. On the global stage and especially on the axes Ljubljana-Vienna and Ljubljana-Klagenfurt we often talked in this way. Whenever a political crisis arose between Austria and Slovenia, the Slovene politician Boris Kraigher would ring and say: "You know what, organise an exhibition, I need to meet up with their president."

And you then realised these "combinations"?

> Of course. We opened an exhibition, while the politicians resolved their problems. This, too, is part of curatorship, art management ... The difference between the way we managed and the way it is done today is that we did it for common social goals ...

Well, this is what curators today say, too. I've never met one, young or old, who didn't tell me that he worked for noble goals.

> You're quite right, but the position now is different. The custodian in the past mostly performed his professional work in regular employment. Modern curators are usually "freelance producers". The difference is in the economics.

But let's go back to what we were discussing; don't you feel that recently the exchange between East and West in the arts has drastically increased?

> No. For example, if I think of my late friend, art critic and philosopher Giulio Carlo Argan. After he became the mayor

of Rome in 1976, he visited many presidents in the East and West because he wanted to realise his idea that art in the East and West should be confronted and evaluated much more specifically and clearly. Not everything began in the famous Eighties: what did begin was a discussion about having to start everything from scratch and it was very difficult to acknowledge continuity. It seems to me that, in terms of functionality, such efforts were there at least most if not all of the time.

Tell me, were there any important protagonists from the East on the world or Western art stage even before the fall of the Berlin Wall? In spite of everything, you seem somehow a lonely "between East and West figure".

> Of course. But you have to also be clear about the opposite case: I personally got a retrospective exhibition of the progressive Slovene painter Marij Pregelj to Bucharest and it was well received there. Which means that there already had to be a new orientation, with all its artistic progressiveness. Dietrich Mahlow, the director of the Kunsthalle in Nuremberg and a very good colleague of ours, paid particular attention to the dialogue between East and West. In setting up a biennial of constructivist art he often took my advice, and this event in Nuremberg was very interested in looking to the East. For him, I chose a collection of works by Gabrijel Stupica, Janez Bernik and Vladimir Veličković.

Who in the West were the key advocates of art from the East? And why? On the basis of what did they advocate it?

> Definitely Argan, Pierre Restany, Ryszard Stanisławski, Will Grohmann, who played an important role as the editor of an excellent *Skira*, and others. They all advocated East European art on the basis of its quality. They did this on the basis of autonomy, whereby the social order does not alter quality, just as it doesn't change art, whether it is made above or below the table.

If we now talk about the art market in connection with the biennial in Ljubljana, I have for a long time been wondering about a specific matter. The award given to Robert Rauschenberg in 1964 at the Venice Biennial constantly reappears as a turning point in the change in power relations between America and Europe and between artistic criteria and the influence of the market on biennial exhibitions. To put it bluntly, the award is said to have happened

     Beti Žerovc

because American art dealers gained the upper hand within the management of the art system and ensured that Rauschenberg received the award in Venice. Prior to this, the artist was given an award at the Ljubljana Biennial in 1963. How and why? What is your comment on the award to Rauschenberg in the light of these assumptions?

> When I was organising that biennial, I found out that a certain "lady", who lived in America, but was originally from Vienna, was organising an exhibition of Rauschenberg, Johns, Oldenburg and another artist. She rang me from New York, told me what she was doing and asked me if we were interested. I said yes and she came to Ljubljana personally and brought all those things. The jury already included Pierre Restany, Werner Schmalenbach and Ryszard Stanisławski. We were already perfectly aware that this was part of a pop art trend. After a long discussion we decided that it was so impressive – the lady brought complete graphic sets – that we gave him the award. It is interesting that American and European journals immediately took hold of it.

So, you decided exclusively on the basis of quality and impressiveness, without any connection to the market or influence from an art dealer?

> It was a purely artistic decision, a professional one.

Was Leo Castelli already Rauschenberg's dealer when the latter received the award in Ljubljana?

> Yes, he was, but he didn't know that Rauschenberg would get the award. The lady who brought the works printed things herself. She had a small printing workshop on Long Island and that's where it was all created. We were not influenced by any Castelli, any Ileana Sonnabend or anyone else. But they made good use of this later at the Venice Biennial, where Rauschenberg had an exhibition at the American consulate, which was his big break. When we wanted to organise an exhibition for him in Ljubljana afterwards, he was already taken over by private art dealers and the price of transport and insurance became too high for us, even though Rauschenberg was very interested. In all the catalogues, his CV states that he received his first award in Ljubljana. This was really a new chapter and a very interesting one for our biennial. At the same time, we supported more established artists and

confirmed the high value of artists whom there were attempts to destroy or at least push to the margins.

And how did you experience the late 1960s, early 1970s? Was your personal world strongly marked by student demonstrations, radical philosophies, the rise of sociology, etc.? Did it touch you at all?

> It was perfectly clear that there were great shifts taking place. We tried to persuade younger curators to draw attention to the key names that were appearing within this new constellation. With regard to this, we also had very good cooperation with certain institutions, such as the British Council.

And what were your feelings in connection with exhibiting contemporary art when a figure like, for example, Harald Szeemann appeared?

> Well, Szeemann cooperated with us, too, at the beginning of his career, when he was still committed to traditional art. Of course, at documenta he broke away from that. Later, he became an advocate of the Eastern bloc, including Zdenka Badovinac and all the others. And we got new works precisely via these individual curators from other countries. When Jure Mikuž in 2005 worked as a curator for the Biennial of Graphic Arts and invited institutions to present their selections, he in fact used the same principle that we had used before. We would turn to individual museum employees who were involved in graphic arts and they would suggest names to us. Our own selection was thus always a "gold reserve", established names, while half of the exhibited material was obtained in the way I described.

Do you think exhibitions are an appropriate medium for political declarations?

> I think exhibitions have been taken over by politics too much. Especially as some curators are very well paid. When we were creating the biennial, we never paid anyone specially. We invited people to Ljubljana and gave them accommodation, but we attracted them on the basis of their interest, as the biennial was sufficiently interesting for them to simply want to appear in Ljubljana.

But you cooperated with the political sphere, too.

> Yes, but that was something else. It was us who were using politics through persuasion, not the other way round.

 Beti Žerovc

You think that is possible? To be stronger than politics, money ...

> Listen – I don't want to brag, but we managed it. I managed to convince a few people in politics that this was their future. I proved to these people that we could be a source of liberalisation, which is not brutal in the sense of socially tense situations, but that fine art can be an instrument of a slight liberal opening. That's how it was. You know, through establishing ourselves in art, the world wrote about us favourably, proclaiming that we were an open society. Then, for example, I was able to say to politicians, in this case to France Popit, even about Giulio Carlo Argan, who was practically a communist, that he was more important as a philosopher than an at-times politician.

Do you feel that the exhibition medium has changed? Exhibitions revolve around themes, curators can follow personal stories and impulses ...

> In our time, art set certain norms for itself in which a custodian would try to find what was best, of the highest quality. If always successfully, I don't know. But now, it's just the opposite. Today, a curator adopts the standpoint: "I'm God Almighty, I don't care about anything, I can do what I like."

Could a curator be an artist in the sense of a theatre or film director?

> Hm ... I remember when we were creating the exhibition *Dal pensiero al mano* [*From Thought to Hand*]. It was an exhibition of 130 artists from Picasso to very recent ones, each represented by one key work. What did the exhibition do? It established the highest quality, it was perfection, a condensation of an idea that was pure. Today, it's different – the difficulty is the relationship between the content and the packaging. The packaging can be a stronger factor that the content that the exhibition was created for. I was in this business for sixty years. If I were to create an exhibition now from that golden period, with the strongest artists I worked with – I don't know – perhaps I would have the feeling that I had climbed to the level of a good director. That doesn't mean that the brilliant idea that was the origin of the whole thing is at the same level, no, it's actually slightly higher.

**As you were designing these exhibitions, what were your
criteria for assessing the exhibits?**

> When I was creating an exhibition, I thought about whether
> the exhibition satisfied my narrow environment or whether
> the selection suited more global criteria. The biennial gave
> us the scope, we simply knew things. It's almost like the
> load-bearing calculations for a building, but where in the end
> you can't avoid subjectivity. Let's say that I added my own
> personal feeling to what was mathematically arrived at. I
> don't know, am I making myself clear here?

During your career didn't artists change, too?

> I think artists, by and large, conform simply in order to re-
> main on the scene.

**Probably not only to remain on the scene, but in order to
survive. Curators yield a great deal of power now and it
was the same in your case.**

> There was power, but it was controlled somewhere else. If
> I were a believer, I would say that we took the situation as
> something sacred. We felt that we served something, that
> we were doing our best to manage things in such a way that
> they reached the desired level. Now, on the other hand, I have
> a feeling that, if you're very skilful and you possess enough
> arguments and instruments, you can elevate things to a very
> high level, things that don't actually deserve it.

**Can you believe that curators who are now 30 or 40 tell me
the same? We are committed to this and that …**

> Which is why I am saying that these comparisons are really
> impossible. The time dictates a completely different ap-
> proach. If I were a philosopher, I would start wondering
> whether the period of social realism was closer to the philo-
> sophy as it was then than contemporary art is to the philo-
> sophy now, which is in fact a philosophy of success and
> money. I understand that you are saying to me that the
> younger ones are saying exactly the same. So everything
> needs to be analysed, left and right. But is that possible?

**A final question. A director, the chief custodian of a large
national institution, especially if he carries out this work
for a longer period of time, should not have any lasting personal preferences or love for a specific art. The problem is
that if he does not "abandon" the art that is closest to him
and his generation, he begins to hinder the next genera-**

     Beti Žerovc

tion. Or the opposite, if he abandons his own generation, he lets down his friends, probably his most intimate criteria. How can this Gordian knot that I see as the most frequent criticism of your work be cut?

> This is a very fitting question. It is, above all, a question of tolerance, from start to finish. Another thing is a feeling – I will express myself badly and I have been quoted extensively because of this – a feeling, which, like an ear for music, you either have it or you don't. It's just like in music, where someone who is tone deaf cannot play well. And the third issue is great discipline, even though no one can remove from himself everything to the extent that when deciding he would be able to see everything as if it were on the same level. You have to try to confront that which is closest to you with all that is good on the other side and know at the same time what's bad on this side. You don't succeed in this on your first day, but only when you have been in the business for a long time. Not that I'm advocating the length of my career, which was, let's say, at least a half too long.

Interview
with
Harald Szeemann

First published as "Making Things Possible: A Conversation with Harald Szeemann", *MJ – Manifesta Journal* (Ljubljana and Amsterdam), no. 1, spring/summer 2003, pp. 22–31.

 Beti Žerovc

In the 1960s and early 1970s, the Swiss curator Harald Szeemann (1933–2005) played a key role in the development and widespread acceptance of a different approach to curating contemporary art, and then maintained an active and prominent role in the profession right up to his death. An enormous amount has been written about him – he was very photogenic and media-savvy – from his first more ambitious projects and especially since documenta 5 in 1972, when he became something of a prototype for the new contemporary art curator. The treatment he has received since his death is not unlike that accorded famous artists. He has been the subject of dissertations and books, including, in 2007, a kind of *catalogue raisonnée* of his projects.[1] The late curator's intense popularity was evident in Venice in the summer of 2013: Massimiliano Gioni, who curated the Biennial's main exhibition, was working under the visible influence of his great predecessor; the Fondazione Prada, meanwhile, attempted a reconstruction of Szeemann's pioneering exhibition *Live In Your Head: When Attitudes Become Form: Works – Concepts – Processes – Situations – Information.*

Szeemann studied art history, archaeology, and journalism in Bern and Paris. During his studies he was active as an actor, painter, and theatre artist – when discussing this period of his life, he usually mentioned especially his "One-Man Theatre". He began organising exhibitions in 1957 and, from 1961 to 1969, directed the Kunsthalle Bern. After the controversial exhibition *When Attitudes Become Form* in 1969, which combined artists from different new trends in contemporary art in a new way and which Szeemann often described as a cathartic, watershed event for him personally, he left the Kunsthalle and became an independent curator. He left voluntarily – in his words, from a desire to work more freely without being tied to a single location and, in particular, so as not to be burdened by the various constraints inevitably associated with working in such a venue (the Kunsthalle was run by local artists). As one of the main reasons for leaving, he cited the need to escape being constantly involved in the cycle of setting and raising the value of privately owned property, a process he could not avoid as the director of an art venue.[2]

1   *Harald Szeemann: With By Through Because Towards Despite. Catalogue of All Exhibitions 1957–2005*, Tobia Bezzola and Roman Kurzmeyer (eds.), Springer, Vienna and New York, 2007.
2   Szeemann often explained his decision to work independently, for instance,

Other exhibitions, also considered paradigmatic today, soon followed – above all, documenta 5, where Szeemann presented a complex and attractive kaleidoscope of different kinds of imagery, not all of which was connected to the current contemporary art. Since, even then, documenta commanded the attention of the broadest possible international art public, the idea was clearly gaining acceptance that a much-expanded art exhibition, one that might include even non-artistic objects,[3] with the curator assuming an authorial role similar to that of a theatre director, had the power to offer convincing and interesting results. Szeemann began to define the exhibition as his medium of expression and to declare his own subjective view to be the best criterion for selection. Exhibitions were about the ideas in his head, his own obsessions, from which it follows logically that the exhibition exists (or may exist) primarily for the sake of the exhibition itself and not for the sake of the artworks.

In my interview with Szeemann, I wanted him to discuss the challenges and dilemmas associated with such tectonic shifts. The new approach to curating destabilised the medium of the (contemporary) art exhibition as an (at least outwardly) disinterested and, in terms of the message, non-defining tool for the presentation of artworks, one wielded by an objective expert. At the same time, in this new form of exhibition-making the new rules and the relations between the participants were not clearly

in the significantly titled book *Harald Szeemann: Un cas singulier* (L'Échoppe, Paris, 1995) by the French sociologist Nathalie Heinich, or in Petra Kipphoff's interesting interview with him, "Blick zurück fast ohne Zorn" ["A Look Back Almost Without Anger"], published in the Hamburg newspaper *Die Zeit* in 1972 (reprinted in *Museum der Obsessionen: von/über/zu/mit Harald Szeemann*, Merve Verlag, Berlin, 1981, pp. 78–86). Szeemann worked as an independent curator from 1969 on, his excellent reputation ensuring him prestigious invitations to curate exhibitions all over the world. In this sense, he turned himself into a kind of unusual entrepreneur and even had his own team of collaborators. Between 1981 and 2000, he held the position of "independent curator" at the Kunsthaus in Zurich.

3   This aspect merits our utmost attention. The art curator is, as a rule, trained as an expert in art objects, and this is what he is expected to deal with; that is the usual reason why institutions hire him. Given this context, when the curator began dealing with non-artistic objects, it marked a very big shift, especially because this possibility had previously belonged only to the artist – and even that had not been the case very long, only a few decades.

      Beti Žerovc

defined – such a situation was for many people disturbingly non-transparent.

My conversation with Harald Szeemann took place in the winter of 2002, when he came to Ljubljana in preparation for the exhibition *Blood & Honey – The Future's in the Balkans*, which he curated for the Essl Collection in Klosterneuburg, near Vienna. In 2003, right before the Easter holidays, I sent him an edited transcript of our interview, requesting that he approve it as soon as possible because of our publication deadline. Then, to my great surprise, for three days in a row during the holidays, he faxed me a section of the interview every evening. He reworked the entire interview, writing in changes by hand. While he kept the same questions and structure, he reformulated things more clearly but also removed the paradoxes and spicier bits relating to the not-so-attractive aspects of the curatorial trade.

———————————

The curator of contemporary art, as we understand the role today, became established at the end of the 1960s or the beginning of the 1970s. Could we see the curator as an agent of compromise between, on the one hand, critical art and active institutional critique, which were very strong at the time, and, on the other, the traditional art establishment, not only such institutions as museums but also huge recurring exhibitions like documenta?

> I'm an existentialist. You are thrown in the universe from somewhere and are, once here, responsible for your acts. But it's always a privilege to fall into a well-made bed. In this case, the Kunsthalle Bern in 1961. I had the privilege of two fantastic predecessors, Arnold Rüdlinger, who showed us the history of painting from the Nabis to Pollock and Sam Francis, and Franz Meyer, who paid homage to Matisse, Ernst, Giacometti, Schwitters, Malevich, Tinguely, etc., in the 1950s. So, when I started, I could concentrate on the present and the "new sensibility". Before directing the Kunsthalle, I was trying to do my *Gesamtkunstwerk* as writer, painter, stage designer, musician, and actor in the form of a one-man theater in 1956, which to my surprise was very successful. But this also means that I have always tried to personalise all my activities – the Kunsthalle, in a way, became my beloved mistress

and the exhibition my own medium of expression. I never felt like a critical person; I only show what I love – this doesn't mean that nothing else is good, but, acting as I do, it meant that I refused to criticise. Lyotard said once: non-judgment as a way of being. Everything your question evokes was, for me, not about analysing but acting with and within a beautiful instrument: the Kunsthalle Bern. And if you look at the list of my exhibitions between 1961 and 1969, you can easily feel that what I wanted to do through all these exhibitions, activities, events, avant-garde films and music, collaboration with the Living Theater, with new writers and young fashion designers, etc., etc., was to set up the institution as a laboratory, as a living organism, at the risk of possibly losing one audience but in the hope of creating a new one. There was no such compromise as you suggest; it was a perpetual going forward without fear. This was the birth of the curator as we understand the role today.

The historical moment, when the image of the creator/curator became conscious and evident, happened in 1969, when I organised *When Attitudes Become Form* and the artists arrived and installed their works and TV reports publicised it. Beuys put his grease on the walls, Heizer made a hole in the public sidewalk, Artschwager distributed his "blps" in the city, Barry put the building under radiation, Weiner removed a square meter of wall, Ruthenbeck ruined the wooden floor with his wet ashes, Serra threw melted lead against the wall, etc., etc. This was no longer perceived as an art exhibition but as an anarchic provocation – not one by the artists, but by the curator who allowed this.

It was this show, and my eight and a half years of activity in Bern, which convinced the organisers in Kassel to nominate me. documenta 4 had to a large extent lacked this new spirit and the artists that embodied it. For documenta 5, they wanted to be sure they didn't make the same mistake again and neglect what was most current. But maybe you don't know: although I was the sole person in charge for documenta 5, I refused the title "artistic director" but instead called myself "secretary general", like the head of the communist party or the United Nations. The new curator was naïve, provocative, and full of love, but not cynical or arrogant or domineering.

And what I was always looking for was to get rid of style; that's why I invented *individual mythologies* – a human right. **When Attitudes Become Form was sponsored by Philip Morris; some writers, such as Mary Anne Staniszewski, have already pointed out the strange connection between the first big exhibitions of conceptual art and the beginning of big corporate sponsorship for contemporary art. So do you have any idea why it happened that way? And could we see this simply as a way of calming things down in the late Sixties in the field of art, in the sense of opening the borders up a little bit, but of course with the aim of keeping the broader hierarchy stable?**

> Calming things down? Keeping the hierarchy stable? Certainly not. Actually when you read my foreword, it deals more with introspection and attack: to try to break up the power triangle of studio–gallery–museum, to free the creative process to create an attitude. Art = life = art was always a very strong motivation for what I did and how I did it.

And to continue with previous question, the "new" curator was just perfect for this, since everybody was "dirty": the critic, the dealer, the museum. So on both sides, the institutional side and the artists' side, to put it simply, the curator could be seen as part of the solution and not as part of the problem.

> "Dirty"? I think you should be more careful with this kind of judgment. There were pure critics, pure gallerists, pure museums, both then as well as right up to today, so a distinction has to be made. In my case, I had 60 thousand Swiss francs a year to pay collaborators, wages, our truck, the insurance. My salary was only 50 francs more than the housekeeper's. So there remained 2 thousand Swiss francs for 10 exhibitions a year. One of my methods was to create such an interesting program that my shows were taken over – exported – to get back part of the costs. I stopped making expensive catalogues and instead made newspapers, which ran ads that paid for the printing. And I convinced other museums to collaborate with me – mainly Amsterdam, Stockholm, and Düsseldorf. So we split costs. Amsterdam had a sponsor for transatlantic transport, so I was able to show American art as well, since I paid only for transportation from Amsterdam. It was all tightrope walking. In 1968, I invited Christo to wrap the Kunsthalle,

and that made international headlines, in the States and even in the Soviet Union, and attracted a lot of attention, including from Philip Morris. And so they approached me and offered money for an exhibition. I could do what I wanted; the sums were $20,000 for the catalogue, $35,000 for the show, and they paid for about 20 artists. My first idea was to present artists working with light from California: Turrel, Wheeler, Irwin, Cooper, etc. But my colleague from the Stedelijk Museum said, "This is my project." I was touring the Netherlands with him, and that's how I discovered Dibbets in the studio of Rainer Lucassen. Dibbets worked as his assistant and just poured water on his grasstable. And this gesture was the initial move toward *Attitudes* – the rest can be read in my oft-published diary from this period. It was an adventure. Actually, for Philip Morris, the exhibition wasn't good publicity. The PR man, Mr. Theubet, was demoted after the show opened.

Was he really?

\> Yes, *Attitudes* was a scandal in 1969. Only eventually did it become the model for *the* exhibition reflecting the new spirit in art. But in 1969, the entire art world, as well as the City of Bern, was divided into *pro* and *con*. The parliament got involved, with the usual pressure about taking away subsidies, and the artists' union was against me – they are the owners of Kunsthalle. I was attacked because my name was not Swiss; people were shitting in front of the door of our apartment, I could no longer get served in restaurants; and some art friends expressed the desire to dynamite me and my family. It was all quite entertaining. And poor Mr. Theubet! But a couple of years later, his replacement tried to make a popular exhibition about William Tell – a flop. And after this, Mr. Theubet got his old job back – the one he had before *Attitudes*. But I never again got any money from Philip Morris; although today, they are proud of the show. They even paid for a reprint of the catalogue two years ago in honor of the 25th anniversary of the Philip Morris Foundation in Germany.

I'm asking also because sometimes I find Piero Gilardi mentioned as a kind of author of the concept behind *When Attitudes Become Form*, one that you later abandoned. In what way was his concept different from the one that was realised?

> I met Piero in Holland. Through Dibbets, I met van Elk and Boezem in Arnhem and Piero joined us. Of course, I knew him from Paris, where he exhibited at Sonnabend Gallery and was very successful. Moved by the '68 student revolt, he started to have – like many artists – an ethical crisis. He gave up production and dreamed of an "Internationale" of the new spirit – he called it micro-emotive – as a kind of permanent discussion, a formation of new forces in culture. My task was to make an exhibition – it's my medium of expression – and through it offer a new type of exhibition – a laboratory of attitudes, concepts, information, processes, and works. It was not about a difference in concepts; I had no concept, I had only my intuition. Actually, Piero wrote a long text in the catalogue of the Stedelijk Museum; my concept was described as "romantic". But when I was visiting artists in Torino, he accompanied me on his motorbike on night to Mario and Marisa Merz's and we talked and drank all night.

But as far as I understand, from what I have read about it, Gilardi wanted some active revolutionary participation in the exhibition. Didn't he also write a petition where he accused you of succumbing to pressure from Philip Morris and American galleries and depoliticising the exhibition because they didn't want it to be some anarchic event?

> You are reading, I was doing. I don't know about his accusations. Maybe he was jealous because *Attitudes* was an anarchic event supported with money from Philip Morris. The question was never about being against something but about being 100 per cent behind what you show. To live it, even if only during the time of preparation and for the duration of the event. I'm not so interested in academic differences. I'm a naïve guy who wants to do the best for the people he shows, to give things the breath they need. And why is it, actually, that you are still talking about *Attitudes*? Because it was intense, and only what is intense remains in the memory.

Do you ever have the feeling that your shoes, the ones tailored through your work and example, are just too big for curators today? And on the other side of the coin, are you happy with the fact that today curators use many of your past and present methods? For example, they come to Ljubljana just as you have come now: they stay here for two days and talk with dozens of artists, 15 minutes at a time.

> To question a), I would say: everybody is free to do great things. To question b), everybody is free to use the information strategies I initiated. But for c), talking to artists is still the best way to feel their intentions and intensity. But, of course, once you choose an artist, then 15 minutes is not enough – you have to give all your time – which works to choose, modes of presentation, the verbalisation of visual information, the balance between autonomy and neighbourhood, and so on. But what other curators do is not my responsibility.

Of course not.

> I do what I have to do. I see myself functioning much more as an artist, without being an artist – one who has chosen the exhibition as his medium of expression. That's exactly the point. And I'm romantic; I like the idea of failure. I've never wanted to make my position into a power position. I always throw everything away before I start something new. I discuss everything, even with artists I'm not so interested in, in order to keep an open view. For me, it's a completely different way of thinking; it's really a medium of expression. I always say: things that are not really grounded become absurd. So you really have to do it as long as you live. You know, everybody asks me what other exhibitions I am interested in. But when I'm preparing something, I don't see a lot of exhibitions. I think about my next exhibition. And when I go to see an exhibition, my criteria are: Do I feel that it is made with intensity and love? And I'm not so interested in the rest.

So are there some younger colleagues and some exhibitions that you could say you found interesting?

> Well, for example, when I saw Hans Ulrich Obrist's exhibition *Cities on the Move* in Vienna, I was not so enthusiastic about the way the things were represented, but I felt the new atmosphere. Through kind of mixing up different things, the atmosphere was tangible, and I liked it. It was fresh.

But, if we go back to the question of power, you have explained in your articles that your power lies in making things possible for others.

> I said I would rather make things possible than be rich. That's slightly different. But it's true I'm better at making things possible for others than for myself.

How does that go together with your advocating the idea that the curator is responsible only to himself – even if we

 Beti Žerovc

don't take into account that, at the same time, the canonisation of works of art takes place through him, that the finances of the art world go through him? He's the one who can make the artist live, through scholarships and grants; he sits on the boards that are buying artworks, etc.

> You are forgetting all the battles that take place in everyday practice. Of course I'm responsible, but for the whole, and through the whole also for myself. I don't think it's forbidden to have an ego and a self even if you are only a curator. Canonisation? I can only do my best for a work in a temporary exhibition; I'm not the Louvre, the National Gallery, the Metropolitan. But of course, when I show an artist, it's important for him and his prices. I'm not denying that, but it's no longer my business. I don't touch a percentage of this plus-value.

The finances: in each new location, there is a different financial structure; actually, I do a lot of shows because I love to do them, even if they do not even cover my expenses. That is also my decision. Usually, I get only a fee and travel expenses, but the finances are not given over to me to do as I wish with. There is a certain mistrust on the part of the administration toward bearded guys like me.

Boards, etc.: I always refused to be on many boards, juries and the like. It takes too much time. I was 20 years on the board of the Stanley Thomas Johnson Foundation, but I was voting also about medical, Third-World projects, children and the handicapped, and in culture, too, about some art requests but mainly I was supporting films of the East and South, music, dance and art exhibitions and never individual artists, and we never made purchases. I learnt a lot about talking with medical doctors, distinguishing basic research from real help for human life. That's what I'm interested in.

Of course, there were some important people asking me to put a collection together. But I always made it a condition that they accompany me in looking at the works and that we discuss them, and not just send me a concept. So I was asking that they invest the same time as I do. Then a dialogue evolves, and sometimes a friendship.

But even in my country, I didn't belong to the upper crust. I'm actually the only one who was never asked to be part of the National Art Commission. But I was glad I was never asked. Too many compromises. When I look at my correspondence, it seems that everyday I decline to be part of some committee, jury, board, to talk at openings, to write forewords. Why? I want to be free for what I love to do.

In your texts, you talk a lot about your own self-realisation. In a way, it seems you really don't care when you are accused of using an artist for the sake of your own art.

> Well, artists like to be exhibited by me. And I respect the rules: I'm asked if I want to do a show, and I can say yes or no. Then I ask the artist, and he can say yes or no. If he says yes, we discuss it, and it becomes a discussion between two human beings. So for me the term "use" sounds too colonial.

So, in a way, do you think that if you do good work, you can somehow escape political and economic kinds of restraint?

> It's sometimes a balancing act, but I've always countered such restraints with my arguments: the more freedom you give to me, the more it's in your own interest, too.

You don't have the feeling that the touch of the institution or the art museum is like a Midas' touch? Everything loses its edge, becomes similar, and starts to perform for purposes that are different and contrary to those it had been made for.

> Yeah, but this is exactly why I never chose to become a director. This was my choice. I mean, if I see my sons ...

Your sons?

> Rudi Fuchs, Jean-Christophe Ammann, etc. They chose power positions.

So are you in a way critical of this?

> Well, I see how it functions. I mean, I never write articles against somebody, because otherwise I could become a fatalistic Islamic philosopher.

Something else interests me: a lot of curators start out as independent curators. But then, they all somehow end up in institutions.

> They sure do. You need a lot of energy to stay independent. If I think about when I last took a Sunday stroll, that would be 19 years ago. If you're independent, all you do is work. You work double, you pay the state double in taxes, social insurance ...

But isn't it, then, in a way, the symbolic capital you have as an important independent curator that makes it possible for you to live and work?

 Beti Žerovc

> Yes, symbolic capital I do have, and it's what gives me inter-
esting work. The other capital is less brilliant. Since I pre-fin-
ance almost everything, I still have debts of almost half a million Swiss francs. But I never took the secure way; otherwise,
I would have accepted all the offers from museums, institutions, etc. But you know, I'm rather unique. Mr. Messer of the
Guggenheim always called me an impostor. He said, "You are
a poet, not an art historian."

**Could you have foreseen, in the late 1960s, say, that the
curator would become such a major figure?**

> No! My ambition was not to become a major figure; my ambi-
tion was to have an intense life.

Then how do you see this development?

> Backwards or forwards. Backwards, I started with theatre;
forwards, I will end up doing more shows – no more docu-
mentas and biennials, but precise things like I did last year:
Duchamp in the Tinguely Museum in Basel, *Money & Value
– The Last Tabou* in Biel, *Aubes. Rêveries au bord de Victor Hugo*
in Paris, now *Blood & Honey – The Future's in the Balkans, The
Real Royal Trip* at P.S. 1, *The Beauty of Failure* in Barcelona,
a kind of a biennial in Seville, *Visionary Belgium* in Brussels.
Nothing mainstream, all exploration and adventure.

**Your exhibitions usually have very meaningful, beautiful
titles.**

> You know, I lived such a long time with all these works
labeled "Untitled" that I thought at least exhibitions should
have titles again. I especially liked the one I found for "100
Years of Polish Art" at Zachęta in Warsaw in 2000: *Pay Attention Not to Leave Your Dreams, You Could Find Yourself in the
Dreams of Others.*

>   *El viaje real* was Columbus's last trip to America, but he
brought the Native Americans syphilis and other Spanish dis-
eases. Now I come with art; that's why I call the exhibition at
the P.S. 1 in New York *The Real Royal Trip.*

**You have very often talked about your concept "Besitz
durch freie Aktionen zu ersetzen" [Replacing ownership
with free actions]. I wonder if you could explain that.**

> Well, it was a slogan from the '68 revolution and I adopted it
when I called myself "Agency for Spiritual Guestwork" and decided to no longer work in institutions as a dependent worker.
You see, with temporary exhibitions there is the possibility for

you to use the presentation, the nonverbal, spatial arrangements to reveal the spiritual non-value of the work, the part that can never be property. I'm always sad when I see works I once showed under such ideal conditions exhibited in a museum like a document. When something becomes property, there are other laws that take effect. That's why I do not collect.

You were very critical about this: that art today is more something commented on and less an experience.

> Well, the date of my statement is important. It was in the Seventies. Conceptual art was a fantastic liberator: the work could be done or not. Not materialised, it became a real trip of the imagination. But then, the conceptual also became academic. I was deploring the lost dimension of freedom.
>
> I like full-blooded artists.

What makes an artist full-blooded?

> This ideal mixture of action and thought that I find in the work of Richard Serra.

What about such artists as Santiago Sierra – whom you also invited to the Venice Biennial – who are, in my opinion, highly problematic, especially since they use other people in very particular ways? For example, in the project *Line of 160 cm*, with the tattoos on the backs of drug-addicted prostitutes whom Sierra hired at the price of a dose of heroin.

> It's interesting you mention him. He started as a sculptor and wanted to be as tough as Serra. And then, living in Latin America, he moved on to social problems, which he attacked in the same tough way. You find in his work protest against social discrimination, misery, misuse and exploitation by working with human beings as living sculptures. And paying them on a regular, pre-agreed basis according to their needs: money or drugs.
>
> It's ambivalent: exploitation to make people aware of exploitation. I wouldn't say that he is full-blooded in the sense I said it for Richard, but he is a very intense artist. And I like intensity.

When you're meeting all these artists, do you enjoy your power of consecration? You can make art from no matter what.

> Well, I'm conscious that I'm not a guarantee; I can only try to give people something intense. For me, you talk too much

about our power – consecration is a long historical process. Thank you for the compliment that I can make art from no matter what. My poetics of free association hopes for this, but like everybody else in the world, I depend on others, and if they think it's art, that's OK with me, if they think it's rubbish, that's also OK with me. As I said before, my interest is to create temporary worlds in the form of exhibitions.

But still only temporary?

> Well, when the exhibition is closed and the spatial dimension lost forever, it's over, it's finished. It might survive in the memory of others. That's why I say I'm for a society without classes, but I have to admit at least two: the ones who saw my shows, and the ones who didn't. And now there is a third class: the ones who didn't see my shows but still talk about them. I like this magnetic field of production and the consumption of negation and recognition, which is never really tangible, like the collective memory, a whole composed of capricious and serious individual memories.

Sometimes I have this feeling that curators really get more enjoyment from the process of picking people, from their own power and importance, and so on, than from the art itself. In contemporary social theory, many renowned scholars speak of pathological narcissism as the dominant form of subjectivity in recent decades. Since the role of the curator developed and flourished in the same period, couldn't it possibly be a profession specially tailored for such a "human state"?

> Of course, it's a big pleasure to discover artists, but it's also a big pleasure to have long-lasting relationships. Is evolving together "narcissistic"? Some curators may be narcissists, others not. Some are taking curators, some are giving curators; most of them are both, a mixture. But to take the curator as a specially tailored image for the narcissistic "human state" is, for me, a little bit "short–circuited". But again: everybody can think as he wants. For a long time, I protested against being called an artist. Today I say I don't care. I extend this attitude to the charge of "narcissism", as well.

So in a way, there are also full-blooded curators?

> Well, in my case, I would say yes.

Interview
with
Daniel Buren

First published as "An Interview with Daniel Buren", *MJ – Manifesta Journal* (Ljubljana and Amsterdam), no. 5, spring/summer 2005, pp. 160–175. The version published here has been abridged.

 Beti Žerovc

In his artworks, the French artist Daniel Buren (born in 1938) regularly employs a pattern of evenly repeating, 8.7-centimetre-wide stripes in two colours. This is the pattern traditionally used, in everyday life, on the sturdy canvas that covers the canopies and awnings of France's famous bistros, among other things. The rationale for this art practice comes from the late 1960s, when the group BMPT, to which Buren belonged,[1] expressed their opposition to traditionalist art tendencies and the art system by producing only the simplest, most basic elements of painting, for example repeating lines or brush marks of equal size (dots). In the spirit of the time, these young artists produced this work as live actions, as displays in non-traditional places for art, and the like.

Eventually, things took a peculiar twist (which is hardly rare in art): Buren continues to apply this same pattern to all sorts of things, but the content and connotation of his work has significantly changed over the past decades. If, at the beginning, his use of a common industrial cloth pattern in the context of exhibiting art may have produced surprise, uncertainty, and thus critical questioning in spectators, today "Buren's stripes" are primarily a recognizable brand, something that affirms the system and tells viewers they have come to a first-class art exhibition. Buren himself says he realises he has, in a way, gone from deliberate reduction to an expansion of the painting field, but at the same time he insists that an encounter with his work should still cause viewers to think about the origin, mediation, and evaluation of art and to reflect critically on the museum context and its inevitable formatting role.[2]

Buren can be a very frustrating subject for art historians and others who write on art, since in combination with this elusive art production, he is also a formidable writer and thinker. It is difficult to interview or write about him, since he can never quite be pinned down: he has already considered everything – and often written about it, too. He has examined all his own issues and considered the contradictions. He is also a vocal critic of the Western art system, and even his now decades-old articulations of its problems remain relevant and fresh. He also noted

---

1   The name BMPT derives from the initials of the four members' last names: Buren, Olivier Mosset, Michel Parmentier, and Niele Toroni.

2   Daniel Buren, "Dekonstruktionen", in *Daniel Buren: Erscheinen. Scheinen. Verschwinden*, Thomas Heyden and Dorothee Jansen (eds), Richter Verlag, Düsseldorf, 1996, pp. 96–104.

the emergence and significance of contemporary curatorship at a very early stage. Writing about Harald Szeemann's documenta 5, he was among other things critical of the obvious way it made the curator dominant over the artist and saw the exhibition's clear aspiration to be an artwork. The basic objective of my interview with Daniel Buren, then, was to articulate as clearly as possible how the artist experiences the great "period of curatorship".

Our conversation was recorded in Ljubljana in the early summer of 2003. The artist and I sat "inside" the installation he had just completed for curator Zdenka Badovinac's exhibition *Form-Specific* (Museum of Modern Art). I think he was the only one of my interviewees who, in contrast to the usual practice of later cutting or softening problematic passages and statements in the interview, in fact made some of his already fairly sharp opinions even sharper.

Would you agree that the curator of contemporary art, in the current sense of the term, first became really present and powerful in the art system in the late 1960s?

> In 1972, at documenta, I wrote a text that said we have to take care as artists. I saw something that I think today is much worse than it was at the time, where the artist is invited by the curator and in fact the participating artists are just used as objects. We see that to a great extent in most of the big group shows today, which proves that artists have lost the quality of speaking for themselves. And the artists don't care, because today they are in one show, the next day they are in another show with another curator, who does a scene that is exactly the opposite of the one before, but with the same artist. It has become like fashion. So, artists – including myself, of course, even though I always try to fight against it – they are merely used as objects. That's all. What they do is good just for the discourse of the organizer.

Yes, but nevertheless, I think you've always been very much aware that an artist is not, and never has been, autonomous.

> First of all, I spoke about a work being produced, not about the one who does it. It's been said before, I'm sure, that it's always a balance or a fight. You know, for example, I was part

of the generation that really made the museum change a lot. But it's not that now that the museum has changed we can be satisfied with the result. So either many of our questions were stupid and they built this kind of stupid museum, or we have to fight against something else, because the museum immediately formalised such ideas, and these ideas are not valid any more. And I must add that there were also some art directors or curators who were completely in accord with the artists who wanted to broaden the institution. So these people were very interested in the artists who wanted to blow up the institution and they invited them.

Which curators and directors were like that, who were prepared to blow up the institution?

> In the 1970s, there were many. They wanted a change; they shared the same ideas as the artists. I think the most famous was Johannes Cladders, the former director of the museum in Mönchengladbach. Before absolutely anyone else in the world, he invited people who were really the most, let's say, marginal or aggressive towards the system as it was then. He invited Joseph Beuys and many people who are now quite well known but at the time they were all making certain kinds of work, each one in his or her corner, in order to defeat the institution as it was. And he helped all these people do it. He was surely the most typical example of someone having the power and using it more or less against whatever put him in that power. And he was not the only one. Well, now it's all academic; if you still do that, it's stupid.

But, you see, the art pieces that really survived, became known or even popular, and got a place in history, are exactly the ones that stayed and participated in very classical frames of exhibiting inside the institution. It doesn't matter that, in that period, there were probably opportunities or initiatives to do it another way; they just didn't survive in our memory if they were not accepted by the traditional system. So could we say that the contemporary art of that period which survived would be exactly the art that was prepared to agree on a compromise?

> That's true in the most general way. But there are works that can resist this kind of formalisation or acceptance, in that there is still something in these works asking the same question, without being completely erased by the success.

Daniel Buren

What would be an example of such a work?

> It all depends on each individual. For example, many people whom I knew very well and who are more or less my generation and did a lot of the so-called conceptual work, transformed their work into photography, or whatever that is. I think as soon as they did that, they were absolutely out of the game of fighting against art history or the institution. I've always said this is the wrong way to go. Even if it's the best way to get some money, it's the worst way. And today, it's very clear when you see some of these artists with only pictures on the walls, etc., that they were not strong enough to say, "You have to accept my work there, and you have to go halfway up Everest to see it." But they came back from Everest with a photo and they put the photo on the wall. So, for short periods of time these photos were more or less half-documentation, half-work, but they became works as soon as they went on sale. The success of many of these artists was achieved by the *ersatz* of their work, which means: by work that was struggling to go inside the museum as it was, with no change done within the museum at all. And it was accepted as a traditional object without any problems. I'll give you another example: you have a piece of grease in the corner done by Joseph Beuys and you want to sell it – and you even can sell it, because someone in a museum is crazy enough to want to have such a thing. And what happens? Of course, the thing decays, smells, it's disgusting, and after a while you have nothing left. If Beuys was really strong, he would have said, "You buy it, you keep it as long as it lasts, and when it's finished, it's finished. Forget it." Instead, he allowed a museum to make a *moulage* with plastic – dead! He himself killed his work for some ... It's not even a compromise. A compromise might just be something intelligent; this is complete abashment, and at that point, such a work has absolutely no more meaning whatsoever. And I'm almost sure that with time, maybe 50 years from now, every one will see it like that, like something which is, as a piece in itself, totally meaningless. So in that way, you have people who have been the initiators of this fight against the institution, but who were also the very first to withdraw. And after that, there's total confusion because everyone is playing with this ambiguity, etc. In Paris, I saw the show of Beuys's works by Szeemann and it was

          Beti Žerovc

one of the worst exhibitions I've ever seen. Everything you can imagine, from Beuys's work with the broken table, etc., was redone as closely as possible from photographs. For me, it was totally meaningless; it lost everything. I would even prefer to look at a photo in a magazine from that time. I'm also sure you can sell your work without compromising, so it's not a question whether they sell it, but how they sell it, transforming the work into, I think, something else, which is much less interesting. But you have people who resist that, still posing the question from the very beginning of the work. I think these works still play in a kind of funny contradiction with the system. But they are very few, and, in relation to this first kind of tendency of works, any traditional painting, even if it's done today, will win, of course. Why? Because you make that painting, you don't cheat anyone. It's good or bad; it's new or it's not new, but, you know, it's a painting, it's nothing else. But if you say, "I am going to spoil the floor because that's my work," and then you put a photo of that floor having been spoiled nicely framed on your wall, or something like that, it's finished.

In this period, when art became a place for public debate, social questions, problems of politics, critique, etc., it became at the same time also a place where some big capitalist could very easily turn into a good, conscientious leftist for half an hour, because he was not buying traditional fine art but rather sponsoring some politically correct conceptual work. That's very confusing for me. The problem I see, too, is that the critical potential that could be harmful for somebody like that in his real life is in a way lost when it's placed in art; it loses power because, through its realisation in the art field, it becomes in a way unproblematic.

> I agree completely. I think it touches much more people who do political kinds of art. I think they are the first to be immediately driven into contradictions, much more quickly than someone who positions his work, funnily enough, in dialogue with art history. The only ones who are very correct when they do such a thing are those whose production is really like a flag with a political-ideological meaning, like, for example, "Vive le communisme!" or "Vive la société libérale!", etc. Which means that after its time, it's finished. But you know, the art world is a very strong machine, in everyone's mind,

even. So if you have a feeling that you are a good artist and you did something even politically very advanced, it's very difficult to forget that. So you want to keep it, and you keep it as an art piece, and this art piece, I would say, 99 percent of the time, if it's still visible, will lose all the political aspect that maybe existed at the actual time of that piece. So it's a failure, it's a terrible failure. After a while, no one will know why such a piece ever caused such a scandal.

For me, if you do something extremely involved in daily life, as with politics or something like that, it's either propaganda or it's a masterpiece and then it's no longer propaganda; it's become a masterpiece forever, with no political background. If you take *Guernica*, it's a fabulous piece, and today it's one of the so-called best works of art from the 20th century. But for most people, even those who know art, if you say *Guernica*, they will think, "Oh yes, that famous work from 1937, Picasso, etc." and not "Oh yes, the German bombing of Guernica before Second World War, bomb-testing, etc." Who is going to say that? Maybe the people from Guernica, but not the public in general, because it has become such a famous painting that it's a famous painting *per se*. So immediate political art is, of course, possible and may be extremely interesting, but it balances between that and the masterpiece.

But still, if I may go back to what I was asking before, what do you think about the fact that administrative and managerial bureaucracy is financing politically and socially conscious, committed art, partly because it's convenient for them that political and critical forces be dissolved in art and not in real life?

> I don't think it's impossible to fight against that, but it's one of the very sad realities. And also, if you take, let's say, an abstract painter of the 1950s, who was making the so-called (it's true somewhere!) revolution in art – even at that time, most of these people were personally and politically committed. And that was the time of the Cold War, and being a communist for most people in the Western world was a dramatic thing. But how can you explain, then, that Rockefeller bought Picasso and all these people? They were heralds of the communist party! And they were mostly bought by big capitalists.

At the same time, they were a fascinating ideological trap for Eastern artists, in the sense of "See the freedom in the

West, the artists who can do what they want," etc.

> But I never, not even for a second, believed that. I never believed in this freedom. I wrote many texts about that. I said Western artists were the result of the society. There exists a relation between pop art in America, supposedly free, and socialist realism in the Soviet Union. There is no difference. They all worked for the government; they were not free, either of them. They just illustrated, as well as they possibly could, what was good at that time for that society. I never saw any critical result from pop art. For me, pop art was the absolute image of what I hate most in our society, and that's the stupid race for consumption. So, one part was showing who leads the society, for example, the peasants, the workers, and the portraits of great leaders such as Marx, Lenin, Stalin, and so on. On the other hand, the capitalistic counterpart was showing the "beauty" of the object done for more consumption, pushing people not only to use it as much as possible but also to admire the beauty and the success of such "beauty". In both cases, it was just a reaffirmation of the strength of the regime, nothing else. There's nothing there that's a critique of either society.
>
> So, if you think this is freedom, you are crazy. You know, there is also a complete mythology about the artist, about him or her being free, because he can wear a hat with a lot of colours and people will say, "Oh, that's good!" because he's an artist. If he were a normal guy, he would be in jail or in an asylum. That was my critique against *When Attitudes Become Form*, where I was not invited but where I did participate in my own way.

Of course you were! Outside, you had ...

> No, no, I did this without being invited.

Oh! But now we read in books that you were there!

> Sure, I was there, but not as an invited artist inside the exhibition. In fact, I invited myself, and Harald Szeemann, who didn't want to see me there at that time – otherwise he would have invited me – was really furious. [*Laughs.*] So, I did this entire thing in Bern and then I had my night in jail. This is almost an anecdote. I was really against that show, saying, "This is the worst political show because it gives artists the feeling that they are free when they are just like a bear in the zoo." And it's so true that as soon as you do a little thing in the

street, you go to jail. So I said, "This is a demonstration." Theoretically, I knew that what I was doing was showing freedom – not in the museum. And finally, I really showed it because I was in jail, not free, and all the others, with a piece of shit on the floor or whatever, were free to do that – inside the museum! And then you see exactly what this kind of freedom is. It's freedom you can really control, so it's not a problem – you can do anything there, of course.

When I was talking about that with Harald Szeemann, he told me that with *When Attitudes Become Form*, the curator really became this new creator that we are talking about now, because everything became his responsibility, everybody blamed him because he let those things happen, etc. You obviously wanted to keep your responsibility to yourself.

> But I was so responsible that he did not even defend me. When the police called because I said that my work was parallel to this big show, Szeemann said, "I never invited this guy, so forget it. Don't call me, I have no responsibility."

Well, but in a way, he's very right about responsibility …

> Yeah, but that's exactly what I said in my text for documenta two years later, where I said that if the organiser was going to be responsible for everything, that means the artists have no responsibility any more. And the one who was going to be criticised or applauded was the organiser, and only him. So when he said he was responsible, that was exactly what I said. Exactly. And it's very logical when you really get to be that strong, manipulating for your own ideology. I must also add that he never said such a thing at the time. He even told me that my book about this problem, *Reboundings,* was much too exaggerated. Now, taking advantage of the new regression of artists, organisers are very proud of being the "authors" of exhibitions, as Szeemann, too, calls himself today. In the late 1960s, or during the 1970s, if any organiser had dared call himself or herself an "author," the participating artists would have withdrawn from the show immediately! Today, no one even moves! The situation in this respect is much worse than 25 or 30 years ago!

    What I mean is, if I am invited and I totally agree with the idea of the curator, I have absolutely no feeling of being manipulated because I am just following my own way with something. And that's happened, too. But, if you are invited and you have the feeling when you read everything that the show is a problem for you and your work, either you fight with your work, or you fight with your work and the text, or only with your text, or you go out. But if you stay, saying nothing, doing your work as if nothing happened, and you go, like many artists, to a bar and say, "Oh, this is a piece of shit, this show is terrible," then, I think, that's really scandalous, and that's why the art world is getting to be so bad. Because of the lack of responsibility by the people who really see that it's wrong but don't care; and they don't want to move because they are afraid that it will be bad for their career or something. And it's true, it's a little risky to fight with the curator. For many people, that seems to be a very big problem, because they feel that this guy is going to do all these things and if they are too critical, they will never be invited anymore. And I understand that; I am not joking. But at some point you have to take responsibility. I did something in a big show done by my friend Jean Hubert Martin 15 years ago, *Les Magiciens de la terre* [*The Magicians of the Earth*]. I was really critical about the show. Not at first – his idea was pretty interesting. But then, little by little, I saw the idea emerging in the worst way, like a complete new neocolonialism, etc. So my participation was a total critique of the show, and when he received my text, he called me and said, "You know, I cannot accept such a text, so you have to withdraw it." I said, "You are crazy. I will never withdraw my text." And then he said, "OK, so I will censor it." I said, "You do whatever you want, but believe me, if you censor my text, you are finished." So he did not dare censor the text, and it is in the catalogue. He never invited me after that. Ever. So that's a personal experience, and I understand why so many artists don't do anything. Because they are afraid of what might happen later.

But you've been working with curators for almost 40 years, always somewhere near the top, so you really must be great friends with them. You must have a very good way of communicating with them since you're invited to all the important places, biennials, etc. Could we not see that as an award for being a loyal and diligent servant within the system? Usually, you're very critical about the system, curators, museums, etc., but getting those invitations means,

"They like me, we're friends!"

> I've heard that many times, and I really think it's superficial. If you look at what has been done and then you get that feeling, you may be right. But if you only connect the facts that I am in this show or that one, it's not enough. If you don't know what I did, what you said is meaningless. And if you know what I did – not only the story, that is an anecdote, but the text I wrote and the piece I did – you cannot say that anymore. Because my position there was, first of all, written in black and white. It's my feeling about such an exhibition, which is still valid today with all those exhibitions that followed *Les Magiciens de la terre*. It's like fashion. So, even my friend Jean Hubert Martin – who was shocked by the critique, and in fact, the show was not such a success – today, he has the feeling that he invented the moon. But if I were in his shoes, I guess I would have the same feeling because I see each and every new curator doing the same show! Exactly the same! So this means 15 years of fashion, where you get as exotic as you can. And you show people from everywhere. So I think this is a dramatic success. It shows that society is going completely wrong, certainly that it's going back to a new kind of imperialism, colonialism, and all that. I want to add that, with very few exceptions, you should also see that, even if I was often invited, the people in charge are not always the same. So, I am still being invited by new people. The ones I have had big conflicts with, like Szeemann, Martin, Fuchs, etc., never invited me after the fights. At least not so far!

There are probably also positive things that happened during your career? If you had to name some positive changes in the museum, or in doing exhibitions, etc., what would you say?

> Physically, the big switch has been the possibility of using the walls of the museum almost like material. Before, you never saw that, ever. So that's an objective difference. It's not so big, and I don't even know if it's so good, but at least, if an artist comes to a museum and starts saying he wants to have a window there and it does not exist, if there's money, they will do it; it's no longer completely impossible. No one thought of such a thing before 1965. And again, I am afraid not too many things have changed, and I don't even like all these changes. But to reply to your question, I will say, physically, it's the use

 Beti Žerovc

of the space of the museum by artists before 1968 and after 1968. Let's say, from the mid 1960s till today, the museum also lost its authority. So that's a big change.

In what way?

> Let's say, for an artist, a living artist, to show in a museum was almost like proof of his or her quality, and it was also proof of what they called "consecration." Today it's not, because there are so many museums.

So canonisation, or consecration, is happening in what way? Who is canonising the artist?

> No one. There are no big artists. I am speaking about real artists, like Picasso or Matisse.

OK, but there are also some real stars, and they've been here for quite some time – at good prices ...

> Yeah, but that's not done by the museum, it's done by commerce, the market. The big stars today are the ones who are the most expensive. In a way, such a criterion is new!

But you know, the artists who are now "the stars" are in many cases exactly the artists who, in a way, don't really sell a lot in the market, or only do so very late in their career, but they are artists who move constantly from gallery to gallery, from museum to museum, from institution to institution, doing projects. And they get paid for that by money from different funds, public money, and so on. So they are maybe even less connected with the market than artists were before. They are more connected with institutions and curators, and through them, with all kinds of private or public funds.

> Hmm, I think what you said is true in most cases, but for someone like myself, if I can dare to view myself as a star, it does not work like that. The stars who really count for the magazines, etc., are the ones who sell for the highest amounts of money, whatever the quality of what they are doing. In fact, the real "quality" today is to have works that are extremely expensive. People now think that if a work is not really expensive it's because it is not really of high quality! That's of course not true, but it's more and more perceived like that. Such a situation puts the so-called "stars" in a very fragile position, because if the mood of the market changes, the "stars" who are maybe not so flexible will fall with the failure of the market, which is also immediately ready to support another

type of work to make a new group of "emerging stars." The market is always craving fresh flesh again and again. Where is Sandro Chia? Where is David Salle? Where is ...?

Returning to the changes I was asking you about, a big change in exhibiting contemporary art is, probably, that now you have many more possibilities for the public financing of projects than you had, let's say, in 1965, when there weren't as many.

> Oh no, that didn't exist. It's not because I was too young; it's because it did not exist. This is very new, the idea of giving the artist the possibility of doing something in the street or in a public place for permanent exposure. It started in the early 1980s in France and spread around the world. It is a new aspect of the possibility of doing work which did not really exist before in the 20th century. If it had existed, it would have been fabulous; we would have had incredible works, when you consider the number of quasi-art-geniuses in the 20th century. If there had been municipalities asking people like Marcel Duchamp or Picasso to do something, we would have had fabulous things! But we have nothing – zero.

So, these new ways of financing art and artists – do you find them positive, or do you think that because of them the artist is even more caught in the net of the curator and the people who are offering the money? Because money is always given by somebody. It seems that these ways of financing art give the curator ultimate power over the artist.

> True, but I don't know a lot about that because I don't have these kinds of relationships or connections. But this tendency of the curator-organiser to become a manager is certainly very intense and much more frequent than I even know myself. It's logical. But again, everything certainly depends on the quality of the people who are doing it. So we have all sorts of possibilities, like everywhere else: someone who does this and really makes a big step, and more people who don't care and just make money. That's again another way of making money. But it's the same with artists: you have artists who are just making money – when they find out how to do it. And there are others who do not do their work just to make more and more money. But you've had such types of artists most of the time. You really can see it. If you take someone like this French artist living in America, Arman, you see that his work

is only done to make money. Even if, I guess, at the beginning he was not a bad artist, he just became nobody when he
found a way to sell his works and did it just for that reason.
Why not, of course? The problem is only not to show such an
attitude too openly. In his case, unfortunately for him, just
such an attitude started becoming obvious, and the decay in
the quality of the works visible. As an artist, I guess that today
he might still be economically important, but that's all, and
that will not last forever because the real quality of the work
disappeared a very long time ago.

**Do you know what is interesting? Everybody I talk with
about these things, they always make a small exception in
this terrible art system for themselves, where they are the
ones who survive with dignity and do their work properly.**

> Oh but I know many artists who are really like that. Many. I
mean we all have the same problems, but we don't solve them
the same way. One after the other, all these problems are true.
They are everywhere, and there are more and more of them.
But the way you solve them; that's what makes the difference.
A difference that is also visible in the work. That's absolutely
true. You cannot see it at the beginning of the work, but you
can see it easily after 15 or 20 years. You really can. You never
get a good artist until a lot of years have passed. Unless they
are an exception, but that's very rare in the art world. Very
rare. The only difference today, which is really new for me, is
the existence – since the 1980s and it's still going on today –
of something that is absolutely disgusting and I think a very
bad sign. I'm talking about the possibility, available only to a
very few people of course, of making so much money by what
they do; this is something we've never seen before. Except
maybe with the *pompiers* in the middle of the 19th century.
But except for them – because we know these people were
making piles of gold – since then, not even Picasso ever made
so much money, especially not at such a young age anyhow.

**So you think that *juste milieu* is getting very strong now?
I'm very interested in that, since that's also my thesis.**

> I don't know; I don't want to go that far. What's happening in
the same way is the consecration of the same type of artist.
[*Laughs.*] I mean, artists have always been, when they were
successful, more or less rich. But to make so much money almost without working, this is new. This is completely new.

And, I think, a very bad sign. It's not healthy.

The other aspect of this, as I've said, is about the museum, the explosion of museums of contemporary art, which I think has a lot of good meanings. One of the good meanings is the fact that the museum destroyed itself with this explosion of spaces. And I think this is pretty good. [*Laughs.*]

Because of the inflation?

> Yeah. For that reason, the museum – and I'm speaking only about museums of contemporary art – has lost its authority. Which is good, I think, and not because I like to make funny remarks; it's just because I think it completely lowered the kind of respect people used to have when going to a museum before. I think now you can go to a museum and you know that just because something's placed there doesn't necessarily mean it's a masterpiece. Sometimes even they themselves show clearly that they can't be sure about the kind of experimental works. So even if you are not really aware, you get the feeling that it's no longer something where things are stabilised forever. So I think this is a very good aspect of the change in the museum, which has nothing to do with what the artists who wanted to change the museum were thinking about. In a way, people are no longer so shy inside the museum. They know that it's not a place of consecration anymore. That's what I've said: the museum is not the site of consecration. Today you still have maybe three museums in the world that place themselves a little above the others. That's maybe MoMA in New York, the Tate Gallery, Pompidou, and, let's say, two more ...

And of course, then you have the important biennials, and such things.

> Yes, but that is more automatically ephemeral; you don't get the same thing.

You think so? I think that now it's very important to be in the Venice Biennial, to be in documenta, to be in ...

> Oh but that's always been important. documenta, of course, is younger, but since maybe the second one, it's been a place to be, too. It's just bringing more people today. But if you take the biennial from the biennial, the documenta of Szeemann's, and you take the last documenta – the fall has been really gigantic. The fall has been enormous. To my mind, at least.

So the documenta of Szeemann was good?

>   Compared to that, I'm sure it was one of the best.

But still, you were so critical about it.

>   I was critical about the role of the curator. But it was certainly
    the best documenta. I did not see all of them. I saw the first
    one in 1968, and then I saw all the others. But since 1968,
    which was still like the one before, Szeemann made a break,
    something very interesting. After that, it was more or less in-
    teresting or really completely mediocre. Don't forget that as
    much as his position can be criticised, Harald Szeemann was
    the very first curator of his category and he invented the role
    of the curator becoming an artist, and by far, in doing this, he
    was the most intelligent of them all. Everything with such an
    attitude that we have witnessed since is just a pale and weak
    imitation, including his own things whenever he tried to im-
    itate himself!

Networking, Curatorship and Social Capital[*]

First published as "Mreženje, kuriranje in socialni kapital" / "Networking, Curatorship and Social Capital", *Maska* (Ljubljana), vol. 23, no. 115–116, summer 2008, pp. 35–44.

     Beti Žerovc

To better understand how the art system is structured as regards curatorship, and to be able to more easily follow curators' professional pathways, we are going to reimagine the system and its functioning in a simplified and schematic way: as an irregular network structure that expands internationally and accommodates constant exchange and presentation of various segments of contemporary art at a global level. The curator is a vital part of this circulation, most often functioning as a nexus between the local community that hired him and the most topical information about art available outside this community, the most significant international contemporary trends, and so forth. At the same time, the curator also ensures that the community's own production successfully enters broader circulation in respected social circles.

If we simplify things even further, the key or logic of this network is that it (the network) includes institutions, groups, and individuals from various *milieus* who are collaborating and supporting each other within the network. Inclusion in the network enables them to secure, for themselves, the possibility of working internationally in the very "official" mainstream of contemporary art that is at the same time established and legitimised by this network. For the participant, being included in this system means gaining special status and broader relevance in his own environment (if this environment takes the network into consideration, it is an excellent source of funding that enables inclusion in the broader network) as well as internationally – anywhere this network shapes the criteria that determine what constitutes relevant contemporary art.

Inclusion in the network, of course, does not come about by simply filling in an application form, but rather through: activity, which needs to be as intense as possible and in harmony with the functioning of the network; recognition of the authority of influential players in the network (institutions, art journals, curators,

---

* The following essay is an abridgement of the second part of the chapter "Mreža" ["The Network"] from my doctoral dissertation, *Umetnost kuratorjev: Vloga kuratorjev za sodobno umetnost* [*The Art of Curators: The Role of Curators of Contemporary Art*], University of Ljubljana, Ljubljana, 2007. Its first part explores the strong faith that contemporary societies share in relation to art and its positive dimensions. This is, among other things, the basis for considerable increase in support for fine arts, which has been evident in various phenomena over the past few decades, including the thriving of curatorship.

Networking

artists, etc.); intense networking with these influential players; and other such activities. The trend among the participants in the network is to try to secure for themselves the best available position; both the efficiency with which the participant might be able to place "goods", ideas, and activities into the network as well as the possibility of exerting influence over the network is all usually related to the participant's status in the network's hierarchy.

From the network perspective, then, the maximum achievement of the curator (as well as the artist) is to get as high as possible in this hierarchy and to secure for themselves the most stable position available; in so doing, the curator/the artist can best justify the local community's investment in them and ensure the most efficient circulation of art in both directions: prominent exhibitions at home and a good international placement of local or national art. In agreement with these observations, curators today present themselves to the public and most effectively demonstrate their competence with impressively extensive *curricula vitae*, which testify to their hyperactivity and connections with the most prestigious nodes in the global network. An extensive and distinguished CV points to the potential "winner", a person who understands well and recognises the key events and nodes in the network and is able to access them at the right moment.

This brief description highlights some key discrepancies between the functioning of the network and the declared principles of the field of fine arts, such as the exclusive status of art and quality, or the equity of inclusion in contemporary art – if it is to be taken as unified and global. The system, however, is very inequitable considering its actors have very different starting points and opportunities, many of which depend on various factors, such as their place of origin. The system is still, above all, the Western art system, which has spread to all corners of the world, and actually, the participants who are most effective are the ones who are working under conditions that are most like those in the West. The other problem of the system is the fact that the described circulation produces conditions in which a curator's statements and activities gain value and currency not so much due to their theoretical consistency and imaginative shows but, rather, in proportion to (the extent of) their inclusion in the Western art system network. Artistic activity as such seems to, all too often, come second.

     Beti Žerovc

Since contemporary curators are the youngest product of this system and it is precisely such a system that ensures flexible and relatively unencumbered conditions for their work, they usually avoid considering the long-term consequences of such functioning and implementing actual changes, despite the incessant and loud debates about these problems. These curators understand their own tasks and their reformist tendencies as, above all, modelled upon the system. This situation reinforces the system, which is why it increasingly appears to be the only possible system. Even when curators seem extremely conscious of the situation, supportive of art and critical of the system, they never lapse; they never cease to "believe" or stop delivering. They are well aware of the fact that they are the lucky ones, recruited from the horde of potential candidates, and could be immediately replaced; they know very well that the network quickly demotes and excludes the truly critical ones, those who demand changes. Or they exclude themselves, for to be out of line with the specific conventions of a field – especially those that enable one to make one's living – is to commit professional suicide. The network functions in such a way that the person wanting to enter or be promoted within it must accept the established hierarchy and rules, for the network recruits and promotes precisely those individuals from the mass of potential curators who most passionately display their faith in the network's values and procedures; who demonstrate this most obviously by delivering events, social connections and capital; and who quickly establish a system – a miniature network – around themselves.

The principle is simple: at all levels of the network there exist mechanisms of control implemented by those who provide for the network's funding. If a curator wants to be successful, he must establish a successful connection with those who facilitate and fund his activities. Smaller and bigger venues and events are pretty much the same in this respect; the curator experiences identical situations from Ljubljana's Škuc Gallery to New York's famous MoMA. In the era of transnational corporate sponsorships, it is even quite likely that he could be supported by the same sponsors in both spaces. Because, as a rule, if he is successful of course, the curator moves from smaller to ever larger and more prestigious spaces, and within these to higher positions; so it is only the most tested who reach the truly important venues and positions.

Approaching the field of art through the prism of networks is hardly a novel idea, yet, it is very useful in our case, for it enables us to trace the relationships and connections between various actors; it enables us to see their movements clearly. It is a good tool for our purposes, for it draws our attention away from individual viewpoints about the system, which has its own direction and ensures its own constant supply regardless of the occasional loss of faith in art or ethical scruples – something that can happen to people. The force of the shift – away from individuals and towards longer-lasting confluences that tighten the links of the network and a range of institutions and established pathways – makes it clear how very dispensable the individual is. In addition to showing that the show indeed must go on – at any cost – it also reveals that art itself can be a very minor and marginal business in this gigantic system of connections and relationships.

The network is particularly helpful in that it does not direct our attention towards lofty beautiful intentions and it does not miss the specific way of forming and shaping the links and nodes in the network. For every node, for every institution, exhibition, etc., there must occur, literally, a confluence of interests for both artistic and non-artistic parties. If the initial interest in art institutions and exhibitions seems to concern the artists and the field, the realisation of projects, as a rule, always requires a compatible interest from external parties. Things happen only after the usual partners of art, politics, and private capital have worked out that a certain project holds interesting potential for them; if it does not offer immediate material profit, then at least it should enable the accumulation of social capital. Since the basic speculation always concerns the desire to get the most for your money, the ultimate gains from such connections today are obviously high; otherwise, the development of the field of fine arts would not be as rampant as it is.

Politics and capital are becoming increasingly indistinguishable as regards their strategies and desires; this is a claim that probably requires no special elaboration, for capital is increasingly controlling politics, and to say that the two function in harmony is to state the obvious. They both aim at securing maximum prosperity for themselves, which they both, of course, see

 Beti Žerovc

predominantly in terms of economic and financial surplus – "the greatest possible economic growth" has been a global *motto* of sorts for years – and which is why they both subordinate everything else to these views. That the differences between final cultural products financed by either of the two are small – although they still exist – has been noted for a long time. For instance, classical analyses of cultural economics by Bruno S. Frey and Werner W. Pommerehne in the 1980s showed that American and European opera houses have virtually identical programmes, despite the fact that the European operas usually draw their funding from public sources. Frey and Pommerehne mention the influence of public servants, who allocate funds and dislike risks (such as those involving support for more audacious art programmes), as an important cause of such a state of affairs; their subjective tastes are obviously quite similar to those of American private investors.[1] That art professionals themselves – artists, curators, art directors, etc. – make little attempt to differentiate between the two sources became obvious in the 1980s (as well as later), when many public funding sources for culture were abolished and art institutions, without significant upheavals or programme changes, started receiving money from private capital and corporations. Even though it was precisely the very tax cuts that they themselves extorted from the state that brought about the impoverishment of the public sector – especially the cultural sector – private capital and corporations in fact acquired the virtuous image of saviours who were concerned about the future of art.

The curator often comes across private philanthropy and meets social groups who practice such activities. Because he needs to please them and be in harmony with them, let's have a quick look at some conclusions regarding these activities offered by Francie Ostrower. Ostrower's study analyses American philanthropy, which is very well developed; however, her conclusions can be applied more broadly, for philanthropic tendencies such as these are emerging virtually everywhere nowadays. Philanthropy is an integral and defining element of elite culture; it signifies membership in the upper social classes and is an important socially

---

1   Bruno S. Frey and Werner W. Pommerehne, *Muze na trgu. Odkrivanje ekonomike umetnosti*, Pomurski akademski center, Murska sobota, and Ustanova za podjetništvo, Kranj, 2001, pp. 36–41 (*Muses and Markets. Explorations in the Economics of the Arts*, Basil Blackwell, Cambridge, Mass., 1989).

stratifying factor, for it contributes to the definition of cultural boundaries and to the maintenance of the organisational boundaries of elite life. It is one of the ways by which society creates its bonds, enabling the cohesion of elite groups and the creation of a homogeneous elite environment.[2] Of all kinds of philanthropy, the funding of culture is especially popular and common, for it provides the strongest link between the richest and the most powerful elites. It enjoys the highest status, contributes to a specific lifestyle in the most conspicuous way, and offers the greatest number of opportunities for encounters wherein social links can be forged and consolidated. If we add Ostrower's decisive claim that people practice philanthropy to gain something, we reach conclusions that are difficult to connect or reconcile; just think about the history of the museum or the stories about philanthropically conceived and curated shows and their assurances that art belongs to all people and works towards a better world based on equal rights for all. What becomes obvious in this confrontation is, above all, the specific quality of this field, in which conflicting interests and parties reside side by side in a tolerant manner, without hassling one another.[3]

Even if, in the end, the art put on display at the exhibition does not appeal to those who financed the event, they seem to be very well aware of other related gains and the latter are obviously more important in this equation. Besides, it seems that there are more and more philanthropists who are keen to interrupt their daily routine of ruthlessly pursuing profit or simply enjoying their wealth-based prosperity by being (at least for a couple of hours) as "avant-garde" and "engaged" as possible. In one aspect of their manifestations, the avant-garde and critical social engagement have long been popular and easily bought fashion

2   Francie Ostrower, *Why the Wealthy Give: The Culture of Elite Philanthropy*, Princeton University Press, Princeton, NJ, 1995.

3   For instance, official politics subsidises an exhibition that depicts art as sympathetic to anarchists. Despite there being projects included in the exhibition which are critical of a certain multinational corporation, the latter pays for the exhibition catalogue. The venue for the exhibition is provided by the local tourist office, which can expect that the show, despite the content that is related to weaker social groups, will draw visitors with greater purchasing power and thus create profit. And so on. Of course, this is an invented scenario, yet, one that is not far from the reality of documenta and similar large shows.

accessories that can be put on or taken off at any moment, depending on one's "image" at the time.

How are such disharmonious coexistences even possible? How do they unfold in reality? What kinds of profits and benefits does the funding of culture entail? Let's consider these questions by means of a concrete example, drawing on the enthusiastic statements by Marilyn Laurie, one of the former heads of the AT&T Corporation, who wrote about philanthropic activities in this corporation.[4] Since Laurie, a famous public relations figure in America, has very generously supported art all her life, she has obviously also carefully thought through the reasons for doing so. In her article, she considers philanthropy to be comprised of a range of ways of supporting culture, which always, in one way or another, bring positive returns to the investing company. She makes it very clear that companies no longer donate money or sponsor projects for the sake of art or community; in her opinion, even the donations to the most newfangled and, for the company, least attractive projects should be gainful. The gain in this case is particularly appealing, for it leads to the pleasant situation in which the company is "caught red-handed doing something good." Regarding aims and gains, Laurie makes the distinction between sponsorship and donations and enumerates a long list of benefits for the company that regularly supports art while at the same time demanding intense branding in exchange for its money – from the establishment of a clear publicity link (if the consumers have a positive opinion about the corporation's contribution to their community, the opinion is usually extended onto the corporation itself and its products) to the establishment of profitable business links. Laurie commends the CEO of the DEC Company, who wisely started supporting dance – which was a branch of art in the United Kingdom that was sorely neglected by sponsors. By doing so, his company spent less than a million pounds a year meeting and entertaining 75 per cent of the key British people who make decisions about computer systems used in their companies. Laurie is clear and confident that companies today do not care about geographical allocation of funds,

----

4   Marilyn Laurie, "Corporate Funding for the Arts", in *The Arts in the World Economy: Public Policy and Private Philanthropy for a Global Cultural Community*, Olin Robison, Robert Freeman, and Charles A. Riley II. (eds.), University Press of New England, Hanover, NH, 1994, pp. 67–76.

however politically incorrect this might seem. Business invests money only where its business interests are. Laurie emphasises another important thing, to which we shall return later – namely, that corporations do not support individual artists but rather, usually, institutions.

Having answered some questions about philanthropists' benefits and gains, we can move on to the issue of how this gels with, say, newfangled or hermetic art. Marilyn Laurie reports unpretentiously that her company always gains from financially supporting culture, regardless of how avant-garde, hermetic, classical, or even popular and appealing to the masses the supported event is. In simplified terms, if the event is avant-garde or hermetic, they enjoy themselves, for they really are *aficionados* and *connoisseurs* of contemporary art; at the same time, they also "make a good impression", for they appear useful and acquire the reputation of being *connoisseurs*, especially since, as a company that deals in high-tech, they want to be seen as contemporary and innovative. If the event is classical, they make a lot of useful business connections, they gain more publicity and, again, they are enjoying themselves, for such events usually comprise the cream of cultural production of this kind. In short, the financing of avant-garde art as well as the financing of classical art are "good for business", while also being sources of pleasure and satisfaction. Laurie, a veteran philanthropist, insists that this is a win-win situation, and unless you are incredibly dumb and inept – which is something that people with money usually aren't – it is also sheer pleasure rather than a bothersome way of minimising taxes.

What does this mean for the curator? His conceptualisations of exhibitions and, above all, the exhibition plans of the institutions where he works must appeal to the financiers, otherwise his projects will not see the light of day. The larger and more ambitious the project – which also means the more effective and visible – the more appealing they need to be. If an interest appears for a large manifestation, such as the itinerant European biennial Manifesta for example, it needs to be resourcefully inserted into the interests of politics and capital and its benefits for the two must be skilfully laid out. Regardless of what the actual exhibition involves, the curator and the institution must offer an interpretation of the event that successfully draws the attention of politics and capital. It is an incontestable fact that exhibitions are conceptualised in such a manner, and it is also obvious that the sponsors can be sympathetic and open to anything – as long as the exhibitions are set up in a way that ultimately confirms their narrative.

Our discussion thus far has had a local focus, demonstrating how the financing of culture produces a good "image", facilitates the homogenisation of the rich and the establishment of business connections, and so forth. It is now necessary to stress that this constant and increasingly global circulation of art works and events also creates global effects that are beneficial for the sponsors. This is especially true with the increasingly strong "philanthropy" of multinational corporations. Thus, global elites are formed, who enjoy the classic effects of philanthropy, while also contributing to the global universalisation of values and thinking patterns – hundreds of events all over the globe can result from this. This is part of the formation of a more unified – and thus more easily controlled – global market and, above all, the establishment of a global hegemony. In skilfully financing culture, global elites send uniform cultural impulses into the global arena that direct our consumer desires towards the same things and spread the ideology that is in the interest of transnationally operating economic and financial elites from various spaces. Since this process is difficult to grasp theoretically, because of its contemporaneity and exceptional extensiveness, its effects and links have not yet been clarified in detail. However, some trends are obvious. The amalgamation of multinational corporations and national politics is becoming increasingly common, especially in the context of large cultural events or even clusters of events, where multinational corporations and national politics more and more often work in harmony and collaborate as co-producers. It is obvious that the same, or at least very similar, events and narratives appeal to both financial sources.[5] With the

5   This is far from the only commonality between politics and capital; numerous others exist at all levels. One of them, for instance, is the following trend: in exchange for their collections, politicians build exhibition venues and mausoleums that carry the names of rich private collectors. This is a clear demonstration of mutual trust, in which both sides strengthen their

increase in the number of sponsorships and the transition from the local to the global, various scruples concerning the exploitation of art grow weaker and art is increasingly becoming a means of generating publicity. We are witnessing the appearance of purely politically or economically motivated art events that – despite creating profit for the groups that support them – always feature totally contradictory messages, such as the promotion of the common good. Therefore, there are more and more events that are not only part of the branding process but are also planned by the strong public relations offices of large companies along with various state and local authorities. Yet these events are disguised and presented in accordance with artistic conventions and current socially desirable ideas.[6]

If we return to our network of contemporary fine arts, it is clear that the network is affected by everything discussed above. When the "big guns" show interest, the network can light up anywhere in the world, in hundreds of places all over the world, as if someone waved his magic wand. And the stories and the intentions of these little lights are in agreement with the "magic wand" that conjured them up, even when the "hand" waving the "wand" is nowhere to be seen. The "always starved" Western art system fits perfectly into these economic and political tendencies, for they suit its expansionist tendencies; the system can claim practically any circulation or exchange, and it can justify them as positive to itself and, most importantly, to the critics.

One of the aspects that can be linked to these processes – one that we are going to examine – is the following: in the name of

positions – and it is a clear indication of the two forming a unified, invincible bloc.

6   Brian Wallis, for instance, has shown how various countries, particularly Third World countries, and multinational corporations collaborate in the organisation of large state manifestations in the USA, which usually take on the form of mass cultural events, such as the Indian festival, the Mexican festival, etc. They focus on the presentation of the visiting state as a democratic country that is suitable for economic collaboration, a desirable tourist destination because of its beauty and culture, etc. Wallis argues that, under the sophisticated aura of culture, such events facilitate the establishment of new partnerships and connections between First and Third World elites, who control natural and economic resources as well as trans-border cultural configurations (Brian Wallis, "Selling Nations: International Exhibitions and Cultural Diplomacy", in *Museum Culture: Histories, Discourses, Spectacles*, Daniel J. Shearman and Irit Rogoff (eds.), University of Minnesota Press, Minnesota, 1994, pp. 265–281).

democracy and equality, art actively participates in the colonisation of new spaces. To put it mildly, despite the impression that the flows within the network are omnidirectional and that art plays a pivotal role here, what also constantly transpires in this process is a "soft colonisation of new markets", which, in an effort to show their willingness for economic collaboration with entities more powerful than they are, impose on themselves even voluntarily. It is not only the Western art market that profits from and enthusiastically participates in this; because of its successful establishment of absolute global dominance in the field of contemporary art, there are numerous curators as well as other similar managing figures in the field of art who are constantly prepared for such tasks – of course, always with the best intentions. The hypothesis is that the network or the Western art system and the hegemony of transnational economic and bureaucratic elites spread in a reciprocal manner is not far from the truth.

Expansion in the field of fine arts happens gradually, with the help of many "gifts" (which should be contributed to the development of less developed and undeveloped areas) and the gradual introduction of new candidates into the circulation of the network, particularly through one-off exchange events such as assistance in the organisation of local biennials. After the aggressive demonstrations of international cultural cooperation and the cultural "adequacy" of Third World countries in the 1970s – such as the "entirely artificial" museums of contemporary Western art in Tehran and Manila, where the latter was apparently put together in a matter of weeks to impress important Western bankers who were visiting the city to attend the International Monetary Fund conference – this appears to be a much more effective option.[7] In the global arena, the two museums, which were established in collaboration with Americans and which were supposed to demonstrate the modern liberal nature of their non-Western environments, brought indignation and scorn to their founders rather than respect or benefit. Art is an environment with very complex conventions, which is why gestures and moves that defy these conventions without an appropriate justification can end up being very painful *faux pas*. Since

---

7   Carol Duncan, "Art Museums and the Ritual of Citizenship", in *Exhibiting Cultures: The Poetics and Politics of Museum Display*, Ivan Karp and Steven D. Lavine (eds.), Smithsonian Institution Press, Washington and London, 1991, p. 89.

they can appear as caricatures not only of themselves but also of the system as such, they are highly undesirable and likely to be sanctioned by the system. If a museum can be established only as a result of the noblest impulses in a society – usually, the most visible actors in this society need to join forces over an extended period of time in order to facilitate its formation – it is impossible that a practically identical structure would be established within a few weeks as a result of a whim of a wealthy shoe fetishist.

Today's approach to these things seems to have recognised and rectified the aforementioned mistakes. The West is no longer forcing its own art on other cultures as the absolute climax; rather, it pays a lot of attention to local contemporary productions all over the world, and it supports and cultivates them. It approaches them with an invitation to become involved in the network of world art, which represents a very desirable opportunity to enter the canon of world art, which is still controlled by the West, and an assurance about all the sorts of benefits such a collaboration entails. Collaboration, of course, often leaves the sphere of art behind and turns into assistance in the establishment of a "healthy" democratic society, various forms of socially beneficial political consciousness raising, etc. It is precisely in contemporary critical post-conceptual art, which is favourably disposed towards all beautiful options – minorities, the threatened, the impaired, etc. – that this collaboration finds an excellent starting point for justifying its operation and a perfect partner for its realisation. Thus, the network expands more easily under the guise of being interested in equal exchange of art worldwide, despite the fact that it is actually controlled and directed by the Western – or at least Western-educated – curators and their colleagues whose speciality is the art market.

If we look at this from a different perspective, we can see that new nodes and links are being woven into the network as the curators – just like some other cultural mediators guided by the economy, politics and the direction of their financial funds – travel the world and kindly invite various cultural workers and artists to enter the circulation of the dazzlingly well-organised Western system. In so doing, they usually connect and align with local interests and the local scene, which – at least one of its segments, usually because of a previous influx of Western scholarships and funds – is already ready for collaboration and wants to be included. A Western-style management of art is thus set in motion, and the chosen representatives, usually as visiting artists, travel to the big centres in the West. In this aspect, the curator's activities today click with the environments that take the possibility of approaching the West by means of art as a serious option and use these mechanisms to present themselves as democratic, "civilised", compatible societies. In this case, the curator's activities are supported by local and state politics as well, regardless of how perplexed or shocked about their choices the local public servants or *connoisseurs* may be.

The curator is thus one of the agents of contemporary "colonisation", while he usefully illustrates the process and justifies it ideologically. With the sheer enthusiasm of his collaboration in this trend of "mundialisation" of contemporary art, he confirms the sensibilities of the global expansion of this basically Western network. The notions of equality and the shared flows of contemporary art in the world are confirmed through a reinforcement of the illusion that the curator's knowledge and interests truly encompass those of the whole world's. This is occasionally confirmed by aggressive demonstrations, such as the exhibition *Les Magiciens de la terre* [*The Magicians of the Earth*] in 1989 or the mass of Chinese artists at the Venice Biennials in 1999 and 2001. With this and the exhibitions that are conceived as political manifestations, perfectly harmonised with the current desirable socio-political views, today's curator contributes significantly to the field of fine arts being politically positioned in such a manner, that it presents itself as a field with a strong social commitment, which propagates and supports democracy and human equality, even if these noble goals ultimately produce unpleasant or even opposite effects. While they indeed encourage the inclusion of those that have been "marginalised" (until recently), they authoritatively legitimise the Western art system as the norm of the entire world production, and they, more broadly, reinforce the capitalist ideology. They disseminate ideas that – of course, safely packaged in the form of exhibitions – are not the direct ideas of the ruling groups, that international jet-set of the most financially powerful people, but that are crucial to the establishment of a climate wherein these groups can function without interruptions or complications, not only maintaining their dominant position but even strengthening it.

The Curator and the Leftist Politicisation of Contemporary Art

First published as "Kurator in levičarska politizacija sodobne likovne umetnosti" / "The Curator and the Leftist Politicisation of Contemporary Art", *Maska* (Ljubljana), vol. 21, no. 101–102, autumn 2006, pp. 112–126.

 Beti Žerovc

If the basic question of my thought is whether art may be used today, and in the existing circumstances, for doing active political work and bringing about positive social change (justice, equality, and a better life for all), then here I will confine myself to examining the curator of contemporary art as currently one of the key practitioners of this trend, which we may call *the leftist politicisation of art*.[1] He is, at the same time, the one who most persistently generates the discourse in which such views and efforts are presented as realistic, useful, and reasonable, as, indeed, an effective option for bettering contemporary society and the relationships within it. He often advocates even the "most radical" viewpoints, in which, along with other figures in contemporary culture, he goes so far as to present art as virtually the last remaining field not completely subject to the logic of global capitalism; because of this, he says, art in particular offers real possibilities for experimentation, the activation of society, and political action.[2] Thus, despite the sobering lessons such "functionalist" views of art regularly received during the 20th century,

1   This description is a somewhat rough generalisation of the current state of affairs. The modifier "leftist" refers to the traditional political division into left and right. Contemporary art curators are, in fact, so inclined to leftist views that we can even say that the curator is, as a rule, a leftist. The question we address in this essay might, in fact, be posed somewhat differently: How and why did leftism – at a time when it does not necessarily carry much weight elsewhere – end up as part of the curator's standard job description and thus, in this field, can be part of an exclusively personal career strategy?
2   One very vocal advocate of such "possibilities" in the art field is, for instance, Charles Esche. See my interview with Charles Esche, pp. 148–164. Along the same lines, much support for the politicisation of art also comes from many of today's "leftist academic lions" – such as, for example, the currently very popular Brian Holmes. These academics can be very closely tied to curators, since they can disseminate their ideas through the art infrastructure – exhibition catalogues, symposia about art, gallery lectures, and so on. I mention Holmes in particular, because he discusses the art exhibition as a revolutionary medium that today lets us see, realise, and perceive things in a way that formerly belonged to the work of art. For Holmes, the exhibition, by telling its public something concrete about the mix of historical, cultural, and economic relations in which artworks originate and are interpreted, might, in a real way, "help its visitors to better grasp the political essence of conflicts in the world today," to interrogate the relationship between economic globalisation and cultural exchange, etc. (Brian Holmes, *Hieroglyphs of the Future: Art & Politics in a Networked Era*, Arkzin and WHW, Paris and Zagreb, 2003, p. 41). In such views, he is in agreement with curators, who similarly tend to treat the exhibition as a medium that is itself unburdened by the specific conditions of its origin.

we can say that this has been the dominant trend of the past decade at the institutional level, and that it has global dimensions, since the most prominent people in the curatorial profession, and therefore also in the contemporary art scene in general, are part of it, as are the most visible art events, including the last two documenta exhibitions (in 1997 and 2002). Although many differences, variations, degrees of commitment and radicalism, etc., can be seen between the separate views and discourses of curators, what unites them is the clear assumption that art can certainly play a positive role in relation to contemporary society: that it is an effective means for reducing social differences and inequalities, achieving justice in the world, and mediating on behalf of the weak and marginalised, and especially that by spreading information and combating misunderstanding and ignorance, art can make an effective contribution to social awareness. Such thinking is actually a kind of derivate of the old leftist idea about the subversive function of art, which exposes the contradictions and conflicts of society and thus pushes things in a positive direction or helps to resolve them. That is why even in art criticism curators and exhibitions are today assessed in this light; for instance, Okwui Enwezor, who curated the most recent documenta, received much praise for the way he so precisely delineated and displayed the geography and content of the world's political, social, and economic problems in the exhibition – which for an art show today is an entirely relevant compliment.

This trend can be seen on all levels of the curator's public discourse. Besides his exhibitions, which in one way or another tend to be reflections on the pressing political and social issues of the day, the curator's politicised writings, statements in interviews, and discussions at symposia vary from "old-fashioned" revolutionary zeal to sad concern, comments, and suggestions for improvements on every level of modern life anywhere on the planet.[3] In all of this, he presents himself as motivated solely by

3   The exhibition catalogue deserves a separate discussion in this regard. As a rule, the catalogue that accompanies a contemporary art exhibition is entirely conceived by the curator, and increasingly, instead of simply presenting the exhibited art and artists, it serves as a kind of calling card for him, a demonstration of his political awareness, orientation, ideas, and so on. Along with the fact that exhibitions today boast an ever-increasing amount of accompanying material (what was once one catalogue per show can now sometimes be several), the most important change in this area is, indeed, this new understanding of the catalogue as a reasonable vehicle for pro-

a desire to see a better common future, to bring about change for the common good, etc. – in other words, he is motivated by his personal, independent commitment to some noble political conviction. And although he is, as a rule, always preaching to the choir (for instance, in catalogue texts intended for a like-minded art public) or demanding an increase in funding or some other way of improving the potential of his work, his discourse is often structured as the voice of an aggrieved, marginalised opposition on the edge of survival. It is as if he is permanently engaged in a momentous, unequal battle with conservative forces and the capitalist system and his defeat could lead directly and swiftly to the collapse of human rights – even though his words, in their most immediate short-term effects, normally do little more than win him merit points and success in the art field.

Discourses that might actually try to refute the curator or engage him in serious debate – whether from conservatives and the far right or from those who insist that it is high time that critical art move from its now-traditional status as an eternal, potential left into an actual left that operates in concrete ways – such

gressive and critical thought. For instance, in the catalogue *Who If Not We Should At Least Try To Imagine the Future of All This?* (which, in fact, covers seven exhibitions at once), we find an enthusiastic explanation for why we are being presented with a whole pile of texts to digest: it is because the organisers believe that "creative and critical thought can provide a framework for concrete political participation" and hope these texts will "encourage the development of a fresh debate" on the most diverse topics, and the like (Jill Winder, "Introduction to the New Texts", in *Who If Not We Should At Least Try To Imagine the Future of All This? 7 Episodes on (Ex)changing Europe*, Maria Hlavajova and Jill Winder (eds.), Artimo, Amsterdam, 2004, p. 149). This kind of thinking shows a serious lack of understanding about the medium itself – the exhibition catalogue and, especially, its readership – as the authors fail to give enough consideration to such questions as: Who are they actually addressing? In whom do they wish to awaken all these fine processes and changes? Will the catalogue ever really reach the people they perhaps have in mind? And will these people have the time they need – several entire days – to read even half of these texts?, and so on. It would appear that, in general, curators do not sufficiently weigh the consequences of such an undertaking, consequences that are quite different from, even in opposition to, their purposes. For when they publish all sorts of political and "revolutionary" texts in exhibition catalogues, they are, in fact, separating these texts from life in the most efficient way possible: they are now locked away in books that are hardly ever read, since these books are not meant to be read but only browsed (as their design and format indicate), and then stored as fashionable decor on shelves belonging to people who often have no wish to see the kind of changes these texts celebrate, demand, and promise.

discourses are today few and far between. They also seem to lack a financially healthy platform that might cultivate them the way the visual-art infrastructure, and the broader cultural infrastructure, do the "potential left". Indeed, it is this striking aspect of "leftist" discourse – namely, the fact that, in most cases, those who so kindly cultivate it financially are the rich and powerful of society – that compels us to the persistent and constant examination of why and in whose interest this "leftist conviction in art" occurs, what its long-range effects are, whom it really benefits, etc.; even if we would prefer to accept the discourse of curators as "plain and simple fact" and, especially, if we would like even more to be able to ascribe to art, without reservation, the potential for at least positive, if not entirely revolutionary, political change. Not only is it strange, it seems a total paradox that leftist ideas that have been ostracised from actual political life now find a comfortable home and safe haven not merely in high art but in the art system itself, which is a direct satellite of the world of the rich and powerful and which practically everyone involved in it says is deficient, corrupt, and biased in favour of the affluent West.

Here we find ourselves before some of the most pertinent and intractable criticisms that plague today's art system and its representatives. But they are not the main topic of our discussion, at least not in their "standard form"; our focus is rather on a somewhat different question, namely: how serious are curators themselves in their commitment to the social and political project they espouse? Based on curators' own attitudes, as realised and demonstrated in what they do, the way they solve routine problems, their championing of positions on various levels, etc. – and not only in the more visible aspects of the final product on display – we will try to uncover the curator's actual attitude toward the ideas he so ardently proclaims in his words and exhibitions. Does he try to realise these ideas in his own life as well, in his day-to-day professional practice, or are they merely beautiful ideas for the public's amusement, to which he feels no commitment in his everyday behaviour? And if it is difficult to offer a single and sufficient answer to this question, then we will at least try to clarify what he is more committed to: the realisation of positive political change for the good of all, or the "realising" of social events for only the few?

Although many insist that such qualms are inappropriate, childish, and even a disservice to art and not worth discussing, it is irrefutable that art – if we take the position that it is, in a way, the last refuge of leftist political action today, that it can open people's eyes and make them critical thinkers, and that it contains the potential to effect real change for all of us – is also much too important for us not to ask who is running it. Is it someone who is highly ethical and independent, who has clear ideas and understands the consequences of his actions, someone with sufficient command and knowledge of politics and the social and ideological processes to know what is right? And we must further ask why and how it is that we expect such qualities in people whose work is otherwise not in the least connected to social activism or anything similar but who, apart from designing the conceptual/artistic structures of exhibitions, are mainly producers and organisers of art events for people who in every respect are privileged. In other words, curators are in a distinctly non-autonomous position, since if they wish to create anything at all, they must at the very start find someone outside art whose interest is compatible with their own – their concepts must first be acceptable to financial backers and the people who run institutions. They are the ones whom the curator must first convince that his project contains something useful for them as well, and that they can't get it anywhere else for the same price.

So why, in such a complicated situation, should we necessarily and automatically ascribe the curator's words solely to his commitment to ideals and political change? And if we are not particularly concerned by the fact that art is happening in such a framework (since we're used to it and it's how things are done now), then do we perhaps care whether what is happening in this framework is "leftism"?[4]

We can get an idea of how serious the curatorial community is about its progressive political views by analysing the way it raises

4   We might possibly view this phenomenon as one of the ways the left in general moves from real life into what we could call protected reserves or hothouses. In the otherwise increasingly capitalistic and oppressive conditions of the United States, for example, are not leftist views being most successfully cultivated behind the walls of universities and college campuses?

its young, the advice it feeds them, how it trains them to work in this demanding profession, etc. Curatorial training is a particularly suitable topic for our discussion partly because it is very young – even younger than contemporary curatorship – so the discourse that accompanies these programmes is not yet fully articulated to the point where their professional behaviour is beyond reproach; as it is, the contradictions are obvious to anyone. But such training is interesting mainly because here, it seems, the two essential, if contradictory, forces in the curator's work and life necessarily converge: the practical part – which imposes negotiating, bureaucratic, and entrepreneurial obligations on the curator and ties him to social groups that one might think would be disagreeable, even odious, to him (wealthy philanthropists, dealers and collectors, government bureaucrats, corporate PR people, etc.) – and what we will call the artistic/demonstrative part, which obliges him to present himself creatively, to execute beautiful concepts, to change the world, and so on. Clearly, training and education cannot escape the fact that the curatorial cub must learn both parts in order to survive. And from the way this dichotomy is presented to such cadets, we can interpret both the curator's stance toward it and his attitude toward political responsibility, both of which will perhaps be more genuine than the revolutionary slogans "transmitted" on paper in his catalogues.

Also, since curatorial schools are structures without a long tradition and were founded and shaped by curators themselves over the past ten years or so, they are of interest because, in accordance with the ideas curators constantly promote, they could, or should, be living examples of a new approach to art, the development of independent and more democratic practices, attempts to introduce alternative economies, and a rejection of the old system.

So let us look, first of all, at curatorial schools, all of which in theory place a high value on social commitment, critical thought, etc., and we will try to answer a few questions by analysing how they actually operate.[5] Do they really produce individuals cap-

5   My conclusions are based on these schools' own promotional materials, as well as other writings on this topic (which so far have come mainly from people involved in such training), interviews and discussions with students and teachers of such programmes, and a more detailed examination of one programme in particular, namely, the 2002 edition of the very popular

able of dealing with politicised art and prepared for a critical and active social role, or bureaucrats who are more prepared for compromise and who organise events in line with the grant requirements set by state policy and capital? Are they taught to contemplate and try to resolve such tensions in the profession, or to overlook them and even cover them up? Are the students encouraged to change an art system that has come under such intense criticism, or to preserve it?

Taking the last question first, we can say that students are certainly not taught to change the system – at least based on these schools' manner of operation and already obvious results. They give the existing system concrete support by teaching the most conventional ways of working in it,[6] and not, for instance, some more politically correct alternatives. Thus they are even propagating the system by training a work force that will then go on to work, uniformly and universally, around the entire globe. I say this because one of the typical consequences of such training is that curators from around the world, after being educated in Western centres,[7] return to their home environments and so

Curatorial Training Program that is offered each year by the De Appel Foundation's Arts Centre in Amsterdam. I am grateful to Nataša Petrešin for kindly providing me with a great deal of information, and a wide range of materials, from this programme.

6   If we take, for instance, the De Appel programme, this is attested to by, among other things, their selection of mainstream exhibitions for more detailed analysis, as well as the very method of teaching curatorial practice, in which students are encouraged to work "by the rules" – the kind of work procedures that all contemporary mainstream art institutions follow (or at least try to follow). What we see here, then, are not different and alternative forms of curatorial practice, but rather an attempt to reach the highest level in accordance with existing standards. A student with such training is a valuable asset for any institution, not because of some deep social commitment or anything similar, but rather because he brings to the institution an already established network of contacts and knows how to ensure success and good media coverage for projects, how to win prestigious sponsorships, and how to present it all as attractively and stylishly as possible. Indeed, we know that De Appel's students receive very desirable jobs in the art field and that De Appel is extremely proud of this, for they tell us so at the end of the school's Web presentation, where the careers of former students are described in great detail. See the website for the De Appel Arts Centre, Curatorial Training Program, http://www.deappel.nl/english/curatorial/main. htm (accessed early 2005).

7   Only a few Western schools really count as internationally important references on the curator's CV. Such, for example, are the curatorial programme at Bard College in the United States, the De Appel programme, and the

effectively "disseminate" the system throughout the world, even where it perhaps does not yet exist or at least is not well established. A young curator of this sort will, if only for his own position and profit, do all he can to make his local environment as compatible as possible with the Western system, since only such a setting will allow him to fulfil his own careerist ambitions. And clearly, the training alone does a great deal to confirm students in such ambitions – even their instructors, among others, have been dismayed at how students' zeal for work is inordinately supported by a drive for career success.[8] It would in fact be hard to imagine, let alone implement, a more effective means for the "controlled" propagation of the existing system, especially as, during their training, the young curators fully internalise the established international hierarchy. As part of the learning process, students become acquainted with as many of the big-name figures in the art system as possible – as well as their enviable status and the benefits it brings – and will do whatever it takes to plan their own careers in the exact same direction, to enter their orbit and stay there.

Because the logic of contacts, acquaintances, and social manoeuvring that leads to connections with the highest possible members of the art hierarchy is one of the most effective keys to success in the art system,[9] the schools make no attempt to

school at Le Magasin in Grenoble, France. It's one thing to have the curatorial school in Ljubljana on your *résumé*, but quite another to have the De Appel programme. Nevertheless, the programmes themselves are similar, since the easiest way for the "non-Western" affiliates of the curatorial schools to succeed is to be as much like their Western sisters as possible.

8   The excessive ambition among curatorial students has been described for posterity by Rainer Ganahl, for instance, as well as Pier Luigi Tazzi, who even cites it as one of the reasons he no longer teaches in such programmes. See Rainer Ganahl, "When Attitudes Become – Curating", and Pier Luigi Tazzi, "A Short Report on My Previous Activity Raising Little Monsters", both in *MJ – Manifesta Journal* (Ljubljana and Amsterdam), no. 4, autumn/winter 2004, pp. 43, 16–17.

9   This of course is not the only condition for curatorial success, although it is a fact that, given the kind of division of labour and work procedures the curator deals with, a large part of his success depends on being properly positioned in relation to his fellow players and certain other factors. According to Pierre-Michel Menger, who has analysed such connections in art, this means, in particular, that people who are successful in the art world have mastered the triad *savoir – savoir faire – savoir être* (Pierre-Michel Menger, *Portrait de l'artiste en travailleur: Métamorphoses du capitalisme*, Seuil, Paris, 2002, pp. 41–45, 81). For more on the economic aspects of this topic, as well

conceal their efforts to point students toward these patterns and behaviours – even as they preach about overcoming established injustices, love of equality and democracy, etc. On the contrary, they advertise their help in establishing such VIP connections as one of the major benefits a student receives from such training. We can say that a school's "prestige" and success to a large degree depends on its concrete ability to help interns rise through the existing network and build relationships. The stronger a school is in this capability, the more desirable it is. Take, for instance, the De Appel curatorial training programme, which has been very successful in this respect and, one supposes partly as a result, is besieged by applicants from all over the world. De Appel, indeed, promises such advantages right off in the introduction to its web presentation, where, despite the innocent wording, we are given what sounds like a guarantee that during the programme the candidate will profit the most precisely in the areas of social manoeuvring, meeting as many important people as possible, building personal networks of contacts and acquaintances, etc. Of the programme's most important merits, the one listed first is "the opportunity to meet a large number of artists, curators, critics and other professionals from the Netherlands and abroad in a very condensed period of time [!], and having the chance to exchange ideas with them, often in a very informal way." A few lines later, we are promised: "The group automatically forms a network, which will continue to function after the programme has finished. Through meetings and excursions, the participants are also able to work on their personal network throughout the entire period of the course."[10]

In short, the school will, quite literally, show students what success looks like and introduce them to the ones who have "made it" – the people they must socialise and collaborate with, and whose favour they must win, if they themselves wish to get there.

as a history of such connections in various areas of art and the reasons behind them, etc., see Richard E. Caves, *Creative Industries: Contracts between Art and Commerce,* Harvard University Press, Cambridge, Mass., and London, 2000.

10 De Appel Arts Centre, Curatorial Training Program website, http://www.deappel.nl/english/curatorial/main.htm (accessed early 2005).

It is clear that pointing students in such a direction leads to an overall conformism – and not just to mere conformability to the system, its successful reproduction, and less desire to change it – especially when this is linked to the second problematic aspect we will look at, namely, the weakness and incoherence of the theoretical knowledge offered in such schools. If today we know that, in a field such as art, meaningful progress, the kind that does not bend to external pressures (from the media, politics, marketing concerns, etc.), can as a rule be realised only by people who are rich in the specific capital and knowledge of the field,[11] then it seems a contradiction that curatorial schools do not strive to provide students with coherent theoretical knowledge. Instead, they enthrone as important curators people who in fact are not specialists in either of the two possible areas of theoretical knowledge associated with this training: the knowledge of art, and what we might call popular philosophy. At the same time, it seems, not only is the knowledge offered in these two areas insufficient, but also the areas themselves lose out, or take a distant second, to so-called practical knowledge (the acquisition of sponsorships, networking, bureaucratic work, and the organising of events – from exhibition security to the entire production of the catalogue, public relations, etc.). This knowledge is, as a rule, bound to turn the curator's attention away from art to other fields, such as the media and sponsorships, and, literally, prepare him to search constantly for connections in these other fields – and thus to subordinate himself to external coercion and pressure.[12]

11   On the question of autonomy in art and the different inclinations of individual figures in this regard, see Pierre Bourdieu, *The Rules of Art: Genesis and Structure of the Literary Field*, Polity Press, Cambridge, UK, 1996; as well as Bourdieu's *On Television*, Pluto Press, London, 1998. This latter work is notable for its analysis of the concrete pressures that an external field, such as the media, can today exert on other fields such as art.

12   So as not to stray too far from our topic, I will add the following as a footnote: It seems that the search and desire for autonomy in the visual art field – which the entire field should be continually striving toward as if to its ideal state – is lost and abandoned most profoundly where the curator appears. He is deeply involved in the changes in the development of contemporary art precisely on the level of its shift from its emergence in a narrow circle of artists and the most devoted art consumers to being, from its very start, the concern of such soulless financial backers as multinational corporations and possibly successful entertainment for the masses.

          Beti Žerovc

The first observation we mentioned is that involvement with art itself – that is, the detailed study and analysis of artworks and concepts, art theory, art history, and the like, in which the student would acquire a complex knowledge of this field – is not a priority in such programmes; they are too short and, as we noted, their focus is usually far more practical than theoretical.[13] Judging by what some of the students have said, they, too, during their training with its real if perhaps unexpressed emphases, came to realise that networking and logistical and bureaucratic activities were unavoidable in their work, while involvement with art and its messages was an area where they could cut corners (despite the school's fine rhetoric about the importance of being attentive to art and doing precise field research). A third thing that leads us to such a conclusion is the fact that these curatorial schools and courses almost always accept students from a variety of educational backgrounds, not only art history or visual art.[14] This could mean that the complex knowledge of art and art history required by the curator for his work is neither extensive nor difficult to learn – and so he must have other proficiencies.

Since in addition to this, and apart from instruction in mastering the "practical" side of curatorial work, a segment of the training is devoted to a wide range of popular theoretical discourses from the social sciences and philosophy, we can conclude that such schools are either encouraging curators to think about art in relation to political, ethical, social, and similar questions or trying to familiarise them with some sort of "mainstream philosophy". Given the quantity and variety of their learning materials, which can vary from year to year, I am inclined to believe the latter. While such a "cram-course" education really may not provide sufficient knowledge for any serious problematizing of the topics it presents, it can provide enough for students to learn the "correct" attitudes for their chosen profession and acquire some suitable ideas for their future exhibitions and projects. The question of proficiencies thus here becomes doubled. If those

13   This is not a key issue for our discussion, which is why I mention it only briefly. But the phenomenon of the art in "art" being given less priority than all sorts of other matters deserves our absolute attention.

14   In De Appel's 2002 programme, for example, in addition to four students who had studied art history (at least as their minor subject), there was one who had majored in political science and another who had studied graphic design.

with degrees in non-art fields will not know enough about art, then students who do have degrees in art-related fields likewise will not become proficient thinkers and researchers in, say, multiculturalism, as the result of a "cram course" on that subject either. They will, of course, be able to combine a specific philosophy with similarly oriented art projects and design large, politically focused, and politically correct iconographies, but they will not possess any deeper specialised knowledge – a knowledge that would also equip them with the requisite reflection on potential long-term consequences of such an enterprise. So we should not be surprised if the very events where this "art expert/world expert" (I don't know any term broad enough for this) acts with the finest of intentions as cultural mediator, advocate for marginalised identities, encourager of a healthy society, democracy, and much else besides – that is, events contributing to multiculturalism – we ought not to be surprised if they have as a consequence, in fact, neo-colonialism, with the offspring of the Western liberal hegemony being spread all around the world.[15]

———

I will not examine now the concrete effects of these activities but will sum up the previous section by saying that such training programmes show us that the curator's actual work and the way this work is presented to the world are two very different things. Based on the fact that these schools train a work force to perform work up to a certain standard, as effectively as possible, and within the existing structures, which has as its absolute goal the execution of a (well-reported) event, we can conclude that any simultaneous public criticism of the existing conditions is not intended to bring about genuine change in these conditions or to achieve any real-life effect, since curators themselves make no attempt to bring even their own field and activity into line with such critical thinking. Although such problems and contradictions as the marginalisation in art of economically disadvantaged people, the undemocratic processes of canonisation, and the like, are very visible and art exhibitions have presented these

15   A famous example of good intentions leading to negative effects might be the exhibition *Magiciens de la terre* by the French curator Jean-Hubert Martin (1989). Today, it is harshly criticised for its neo-colonialism, even by many curators.

    Beti Žerovc

problems to us hundreds and hundreds of times, these critiques seem nowadays to be standard, optional content that, to put it bluntly, appears only where we expect it, while in the most concrete and lasting displays of contemporary art (such as installations of large permanent collections), it is hardly to be found.

In light of this, the effort to implement political activism throughout the "art system" seems, then, a much less effective and realistic option (or a completely ineffectual and unrealistic option) than curators present it to be. What is more, it seems that, despite all their constant discussion and criticism, curators are hardly the ones who are able, or willing, to reflect seriously on this discrepancy, just as they avoid reflecting on other inconsistencies in their work. And this lack of critical thinking about themselves and their work and the perception of their own practice as not being defined by the conditions in which they operate are characteristics of this professional group that must not be overlooked if we want to understand how curators function, how they establish priorities among the various segments of their practice, and how they relate to the ideas they deal with.

In concrete terms, with regard to the issue of social commitment, these two characteristics appear as fundamentally problematic. Serious social commitment, which aims at real results, presupposes transparency in the conditions in which a person works and, first and foremost, the ability to reflect on one's own position within these conditions; hence, it is incompatible with a group whose members deflect such analytical scrutiny, minimise the conditional nature of their work, and try to persuade us that the conditions in which their exhibitions originate are neither important nor essential to the content and credibility of their messages.

Given the untroubled idealism with which many curators think about themselves and their position, it is clear that they do not view as especially problematic the double- or even triple-sided nature of their work – namely, the difference between, on the one hand, the professed ideal, and the image they try to align with it, and, on the other, the actual state of affairs (the curator is less the specialised expert in art than he likes to present himself as, and more art's impresario, populariser, and producer; he is less someone who actually thinks critically about society and the system and is more someone deeply and unreflectively social and accommodating on every side, etc.). To illustrate this assertion (while remaining on the topic of training and education), we need only turn to the anthology *Words of Wisdom: A Curator's Vade Mecum on Contemporary Art,* published in 2001 by the New York-based Independent Curators International as a handbook for young curators. Containing short contributions from 60 established curators, who offer advice based on their practice so far, this little book is of particular interest because from the curator's advice we can see how the profession's most successful representatives view themselves, their work, and their duties, and which duties or fields of work are given priority.

Apart from the rare critical voice, the advisers largely agree that the curator is a remarkable figure, since he must be, at once, a first-rate practitioner, an exceptional creator, and a careful, meticulous researcher. If it hardly seems possible to perform all these roles at the same time, at least more or less adequately, the curators clearly see tackling tasks and problems on all sorts of levels simultaneously as nothing more than a manageable challenge to their creative potential. Self-contradictory injunctions – along the lines of "Keep your feet planted firmly on the ground with your head up in the clouds at the same time," or "Be an exceptional diplomat and economist but also the greatest dreamer, risk-taker, guerrilla, anti-bourgeois, and social critic"[16] – which appear constantly in their discourse, are, to be sure, presented as hard to do, but mainly in the sense of the greater glory that goes to the curator who does do them; and far less is it about the difficulty of problematizing the consequences and limitations such work imposes on their exhibitions, the ideas they deal with, or even art itself. For example, the idyllically minded Rosa Martinez, the well-known Spanish curator who co-curated the Venice Biennial in 2005, writes:

> In my view, a curator should be:
> - a polymorphous being, but not a perverse one
> - an intrepid explorer with radar capable of picking up almost imperceptible signals
> - a diplomat with honed negotiation skills

16　See *Words of Wisdom: A Curator's Vade Mecum on Contemporary Art,* Carin Kuoni (ed.), Independent Curators International, New York, 2001, pp. 28 (René Block), 59–61 (Jane Farver), 73–74 (Thelma Golden), 116 (Andrea Miller-Keller), 150–152 (Paul Schimmel), and elsewhere.

 Beti Žerovc

- a guerrilla intent on promoting social change
- an economist capable of clinching the best deal in an exchange
- a therapist who can help change someone's perception of problems
- a "proposer" able to stimulate critical awareness
- a person willing to share both problems and success
- a bamboo rod, both strong and flexible, sensitive to currents without being swept away by them.[17]

There is no point, and no need, to explain in detail that we will not find such qualities coherently expressed in a single individual, and to do so would, I suppose, be taking Martinez too literally. We can, however, safely conclude, on the basis of hers and similar comments from many others, that the selection and canonisation of art is in the hands of people who clearly are much too occupied with everything but art. Moreover, such facts as, for instance, that curators are bound to various and mutually conflicting interests and options, and that this influences their selection and discourse, do not in particular attract their critical reflections, even if some of them take note of these things. Like Martinez, in such cases, they resort to related methods for idealising the situation – fine words and statements that can be read in different ways, and the portrayal of compromise as a kind of unavoidable, well-established curatorial *modus operandi* that has proved to be, for the good of all concerned, an acceptable and felicitous way out of all sorts of predicaments, even if the curator's independence and integrity must suffer in the process. Andrea Miller-Keller, for instance, tells young curators: "Your independence is your integrity. Keep a respectful distance from dealers and collectors. But know also when exceptions are appropriate."[18]

Because the book sounds so unvarnished, and because, with so many ambiguous and problematic statements from the most important figures in the field, the inconsistencies of these curators' work and thought can be seen very clearly and as a mass symptom, it is a good example of the curator's uncritical view of him-

17 Ibid., pp. 111–112.
18 Ibid., p. 116.

self and of the tendency of the whole group to present highly embellished pictures of themselves and their working conditions, instead of the actual state of affairs. Given that this is a compendium of thoughts by people who are in charge of the key assessments and procedures in the field, who dominate key contemporary art institutions – not small independent spaces but major institutions, the darlings of the philanthropists, with huge museum shops, etc. – it sounds especially strange and inconsistent when they expound *en masse* about their active social commitment and partiality toward marginalised groups[19] and describe their work as alternative, anti-bourgeois,[20] and so on. What may still sound plausible when each one speaks for themselves here turns into a farce in which the main players do not understand, or want to understand, either their own positions or why they occupy them and thus take full responsibility for what they do. Too often they speak as if they are entirely unaware of the fact that going to art shows and attending openings and art events at the highest level is a traditional form of bourgeois amusement, a pastime for the middle and upper classes – the same classes who finance art and supply it with abundant subsidies drawn from the public coffers of the entire population in a given locality.[21] Reading these curators' enthusiastic comments about their own marginal beginnings in alternative spaces,[22] it seems that, clearly, some of them have not really noticed that they've been "on the right side of the tracks" for a long time now, in places whose work plays an intensive part in ensuring the hegemony of the rich and the powerful and telling their stories. Despite the sociology so very present in these curators' discourse and catalogues, it is obvious that the sociology of leisure, which treats leisure time as a battlefield between various groups and assigns to "high art" and those involved in it a clear connection with the economic and political elites of a given society, does not particularly interest them. For instance, they never really wonder why traditional bourgeois strongholds, which are often extremely commercialised and,

19   Ibid., pp. 43–44 (Bice Curiger), 54–55 (David Elliott), 121 (France Morin), 153–154 (Jiří Ševčík), and elsewhere.
20   Ibid., pp. 26–27 (Carlos Basualdo), 44 (Bice Curiger), among others.
21   Another important source of funding for art is private philanthropy; on this subject, see my essay "Networking, Curatorship and Social Capital", pp. 110–123.
22   See *Words of Wisdom*, pp. 53–55 (David Elliott), 60 (Jane Farver), 159–161 (Susan Sollins), and elsewhere (see n. 16).

                                       Beti Žerovc

in many cases, have the area's biggest capitalists sitting on their boards of trustees, should be so very interested in these curators' "uncompromising" critical thought and social commitment.

We can see something characteristic to the nature of curatorial critical thought – as well as the fact that curators have a very superficial and arbitrary relationship to the criticisms they pronounce – in the techniques they use to maintain a "beautiful" image of themselves and their group. Apart from the most common one – the avoidance of unpleasant topics – the technique that serves them best is to express the most radical criticism possible of anything and everything connected with the art system and even themselves, but in such a way that the speaker ultimately exempts himself from what he is criticising. For example, if sociologists note that the divide between the commercial and institutional sectors in art is becoming ever more porous and that despite the constant talk about democratisation, equality, etc., the true power structure in art remains practically untouched, and that not only private collections but even those assembled by "critical" curators are designed both on a racist basis and in direct proportion to economic and political power, as they have always been,[23] the curator will be the first to acknowledge all of this and nod his head in concern. But there is not a hero among them who would confirm this situation loud and clear using himself as an example. The problem begins when practically everyone sees themselves as an exception; then things reach the point where conclusions they might otherwise most vigorously agree with are, in a sense, rejected by them as a group since they have exempted themselves *en masse*. To put it another way, because they are all exceptions, they no longer prove the rule. And what we get from all this criticism is a situation in which the matter

---

23   French studies in the sociology of art provide us with some very concrete and well-grounded research demonstrating, for instance, that in contrast to all the fine words about democratizing conditions in art, etc., there has been practically no change in the power relations of this field. One extremely instructive study is Alain Quemin's *L'art contemporain international: Entre les institutions et le marché (Le rapport disparu)*, Artprice, Nîmes, 2002, which began as an analysis of the conditions that led to France losing its pre-eminence in contemporary art in the previous century as well as a search for ways to restore France to its former status and glory. By posing the issue in this unromantic, very specific, and not really politically correct way, it soon became clear who the "real" participants were in these dealings, who had to be taken into account, who had the power to constantly impose their will, etc.

being criticised – something largely within the realm of human influence – all at once moves beyond the reach of human hands. Things so obviously wrong they cannot be denied thus go on happening without interruption, only now there are no specific culprits and no specific blaming. The key problem with such curatorial criticism, then, is that in the end its effect is often directly opposite to the intentions the curator ascribes to himself and to those ascribed to his criticism. In this way, curators preserve the status quo and help to preserve the very thing they criticise.

If not at the very beginning, then now is the time to consider certain specific aspects of the field in which the curator operates, since they explicitly define both him and his discourse, and to examine him in a way not usually done: as an ordinary figure in the art field who shares a discourse and strategies with his co-inhabitants in this field – instead of always exempting him from these relationships as an institutional expert bound to a different kind of truth or an independent worker dedicated solely to critical ideas.

Just as with the artist or the dealer – who of course does not sell work purely out of love and devotion to art, though this may be what he tells the public – so too with the curator we must accept the fact that he works in a field where concealing or embellishing the truth, hiding or only partly revealing one's intentions in a certain matter or project, obfuscating work methods, and the like, are traditional and quite legitimate standard operating procedures, strategies that are not condemned but rewarded.[24] Such strategies are linked, in particular, to the fact that this is a field that does not have an entirely normal economy; rather, economic issues are concealed and denied wherever possible. For this reason, too, the art field is always on the lookout for allied discourses that would facilitate these operations of embellishing and concealing certain impulses. And here, too, we might well find other reasons, besides noble intentions, to explain the connection with leftist ideas – reasons that of course will not be shouted from the rooftops. They range from the fact that this

24 See Raymonde Moulin, *The French Art Market: A Sociological View*, Rutgers University Press, New Brunswick, NJ, and London, 1987, pp. 3–6. In her introduction, Moulin expounds at length on the specific difficulties encountered by researchers in the art field precisely because of the peculiar attitude toward the truth exhibited by people in the field.

     Beti Žerovc

denied economy requires the constant construction of a beautiful façade to hide its economic/self-promotional strategies and transactions, to the fact that a segment of today's art system makes a good living precisely from trading in irreproachably "leftist-inspired" propaganda wares, with its customers being such larger systems as states and corporations. Understandably, in such circumstances there will be high regard for anyone who, wittingly or not,[25] does the most to enhance the "beautiful image" of the entire field, who can make sure that all these business deals are able to continually expand, without any real lull and without any annoying problematizing of the more "earthly" aspects of these operations, etc. And today it is clearly the curator who excels in these things. Indeed, with the excessive politicising and criticising, which he cultivates at every level, the actual political, ideological, and economic dimensions of the contemporary manner of exhibiting and dealing with art can remain in the background. At the same time, this constant criticism appears additionally as a kind of effective vaccine against the possibility of art directly serving the expansionistic ruling ideology – something to which, for instance, Western mainstream art succumbed in the 1950s.[26] In circumstances where the entire situation seems to be an object of constant critical scrutiny and reflection, it may be all the easier for certain segments of the art distribution process to be downplayed and for exhibitions to occur without anyone thinking too much about who set them in motion and why or what their ultimate ideological effect will be. And here it is the curator who, in the wide arc described by the exhibition, guides us so that we focus exclusively on the part we are meant to see.

Because the curator is encouraged to work in this way, including the strategic use of leftist messages, by the art field

25 It is a curious irony that both kinds of curators contribute to the "beautiful image" – both the one who is genuinely devoted to social commitment and tries to establish new models of work, and so on, and the one who sees his "pact" with leftism solely in terms of his own career strategy.

26 I am alluding here to the simplistic logic by which it would seem that, precisely because of its critical focus, awareness of ideological mechanisms, and the like, contemporary art might be able to avoid the negative (?) effects of its "being and existence" (such as contributing to an increase in social differences and inequalities, participating in colonisation, working to the benefit of the capitalist system, etc.) – in contrast to post-war abstract expressionism, for example, which tacitly and, because it rejected such critical discourse and self-reflection, seems to have almost willingly become, among other things, a weapon in the Cold War.

itself – which, fearing that its economic and procedural mechanisms might be shown in too clear a light, offers high rewards to anyone who helps sustain art's "prestige" – we must include this level too in our discussion of the curator's discourse. In such a schizophrenic field, constantly afraid of its "ugly" features being unmasked yet at the same time genuinely filled with a desire for the beautiful, the just, and the good – in such a field as this, the curator can be successful without any need for his discourse to be verifiable, applicable, or aimed at the realisation of the proposed ideas. It is successful if it is convincing and structured in a way that allows as many people as possible from the different groups in the field – from artists and sponsors, dealers and politicians, to the public – to pursue their own interests with the least possible hindrance.

If it was not obvious enough from our discussion of curatorial schools, then the curator's rosy, uncritical, and intrinsically unreflective view of his own position should at least make it abundantly clear that he can hardly be devoted body and soul to the service of progressive social change. If we keep trying to find in him some independent activist, we will be sorely disappointed. The evidence is too great to ignore, and if we persist in thinking this way, we will only misunderstand his position and social role and interpret his actions and statements in a false light. We have put the weight of his activities on the wrong side, and despite his assurances of complete dedication to the ideas he professes, we must at last shift this weight to his "producership", his organising of exhibitions – the events that also dictate his ethics and behaviour.

If, as we saw in our examples, curatorial education and training are intended primarily for organising an event, and the highest demands are made on the curator at this level – while such aspects as messages, the refinement of concepts and selections, etc., are areas where he can most easily and with the greatest impunity let things slide and be adaptable – then on this level too we must treat him and his discourse as conditioned by this. And we must also accept the fact that, since his primary commitment is to the execution of the event, he will adapt everything to this goal. So as long as they help him on this path, he will have no problem with either constant compromise – even if it results in things being the opposite of his professed desires – or perverted logic – by

     Beti Žerovc

which his very training both teaches him how to siphon money from rich sponsors and instils in him beautiful ideas about stripping these same groups of their power and wealth so they can be more justly and evenly redistributed, etc. If not before, then certainly after such training, the curatorial candidate's perhaps genuine youthful enthusiasm and social commitment can merge with his strategy, becoming mere forms, powerless to serve "the cause" – from the curator who, losing a battle with time, chooses noble themes for his exhibitions, themes about society and justice, simply because they are today's popular topics or are at least above reproach, to the curator who recognises that his winning strategy lies precisely in denying, ignoring, and masking the dualities we have discussed. He recognises that, in the existing circumstances, those who are potentially the most successful are the ones who have the ability to overlook this problematic duality[27] and so in their practical work are the most grasping and insincere, who are able to secure the most prestigious venues, the greatest media attention, and enormous financial resources, and who at the same time, in their exhibition work and public profile, know how to cut the finest figure, artistically and politically, so that they appear, all at once, overtly revolutionary, politically informed, and even self-critical, contritely beating their breasts for working in such a corrupt system.[28] The simple fact is that once a certain moral conviction becomes practically part of the job

27   Here the word "overlook" suggests a pun: the successful curators first "look over" the issue and see it all clearly, then, for the sake of their own interests, "overlook" it – pay it no regard. Those who are truly successful, after all, cannot help but notice this duality and see it clearly; otherwise, in the course of their work, they would not be able to ensure the "socially conscious" critical discourse needed for success.

28   Richard Flood, for example, notes that, in the curator's career, "every exhibition calls for a different response; some need entrepreneurship, while others require Franciscan modesty" ("Questions Re: Internships", *MJ – Manifesta Journal* (Ljubljana and Amsterdam), no. 4, autumn/winter 2004, pp. 90–91). Statements like this tell us that, for the curator, things such as modesty, independence, integrity, leftist conviction, and entrepreneurship are not part of some general human stance, the characteristic trend in the entirety of a person's work, views, and existence, but rather something the curator can put on or take off (himself or something else) as needed. I say "put on as needed" because clearly this is not about some internal battle that gives him attacks of ethical scruples, humility, or moral hangovers that might keep him from doing his job; rather, this has all become merely something the curator uses, quite rationally and deliberately, whenever the project demands it of him.

description, it can very soon turn into nothing more than a personal career strategy – an entirely pragmatic choice that ensures success in the profession, and not a matter of genuine commitment.

Interview
with
Charles Esche

First published as "Charles Esche", *Život umjetnosti*
[*The Art Life*] (Zagreb), vol. 37, no. 69, 2003, pp. 58–75.

 Beti Žerovc

Charles Esche, born in 1962, is a very successful British curator. From the end of 1992 to 1997, he was the director of the Tramway contemporary art space in Glasgow, Scotland, where he established an international reputation for both himself and the venue. After a short period of independent work, he became the director of the Rooseum Center for Contemporary Art in Malmö, Sweden, and since 2004 he has been the director of the renowned Van Abbemuseum in the Dutch city of Eindhoven. Of the large exhibitions he has curated, three of the most important were the 2002 Gwangju Biennial, which he co-curated with Hou Hanru; the 2005 Istanbul Biennial, co-curated with Vasif Kortun; and the 2014 São Paulo Biennial, which he again co-curated, this time with Galit Eilat, Nuria Enguita Mayo, Pablo Lafuente, and Oren Sagiv. He is also a famous debater and lecturer on both contemporary art and curating, and has written and edited, or co-edited, many books and catalogues. In addition, he is the co-editor of the publishing house and journal *Afterall*, a project he founded together with Mark Lewis.

In terms of his basic work principle, Esche is in a way typical of the curators who achieved fame in the 1990s. He developed a very distinctive politically committed curatorial position, which at the same time was the kind that could make him extremely popular with potential employers. In this perspective, developing a distinct personal "brand" has the advantage that, with a candidate so clearly positioned, the employer knows exactly what sort of production he will get in the art institution if he appoints him as its curator or director, and so is happy to hire him. Essentially, through such an appointment the employer is explicitly defining the institution's programme without being accused of manipulations or imposing his own interests, since the work the curator then performs is understood as a matter of the curator's own personal convictions and poetics. Since Esche gets hired quite a lot, and all over the world at that, it is fair to take his curatorial stance as "exemplary" of how people in the past two decades have had to position themselves if they wanted to succeed as curators.

Esche's views are also extremely popular within his profession. This is not surprising, as he considerably ennobles the curator's role and ascribes all sorts of attractive capabilities to the profession. He extols the medium of the contemporary art exhibition as a powerful, extraordinary instrument, one that, among other things, can be used to address the ills of the modern world and combat the forces of capitalism. My conversation with Charles Esche, therefore, was intended first and foremost as a reflection on this sort of "romanticism" and a consideration of whether the curator might not be a diligent collaborator in the reproduction of the existing social conditions.

The conversation was recorded in September 2002. It was later included as the last chapter in Esche's collection of essays, *Modest Proposals* (edited by Serkan Özkaya), which appeared in conjunction with his curation of the Istanbul Biennial.

The notion of the curator, as we understand it today, is something that is relatively new: 20, maybe 30 years old. To whom do you feel closer: to the traditional curator in a museum, to the private dealer, or to the critic? In my opinion, the curator somehow developed or took something from all of these positions.

> Yeah, I think so. There is also the historical meaning of curator, which is related not only to art. For instance, in Scottish law, a curator is actually a person who looks after a child when his parents are no longer alive. They have responsibility for the care of a child, which could be quite interesting in relation to the artist–curator exchange. Curator in its real meaning is also somebody who cares for a collection. So, curators have existed since the 18th century, probably since the beginning of the cabinet of curiosities. There's a long history of that kind of curator, and then there's the new meaning of curator as exhibition maker, *Ausstellungsmacher* or whatever, which comes in around 20 years ago. The latter is really a completely different concept to which the same word has been attached; there is very little relationship between this notion of caring for a collection or a child or whatever and the contemporary meaning of curator. So you could say we should actually find another word, because I am not sure that historical connection is very useful.

  What I can say is that I became involved in curating because I got interested in art but was not trained and did not think of myself as an artist. I fell into curating because that was what you could do in order to be involved with art and

   Beti Žerovc

not be an artist. So in some ways, I don't think very much about what the word means and I often don't use it about myself because I could also be called a writer and officially I'm an editor, director, and research fellow to my various employers. I actually rarely have the title curator, but of course I'm always called it. In terms of my actual work: sometimes I'm more a facilitator of an artist's project; sometimes I feel I'm working in parallel with an artist, where we are discussing the project from the start and I can see a real exchange of ideas; sometimes I make exhibitions, and recently I've been most concerned with developing the idea of the art institution itself – rather than just its exhibition programme.

Often, as a curator you feel like you have to back away from any kind of creative involvement, but I think we should admit to a real creativity implicit in this new term of curator. Probably the reason we back away from it is because of the legacy of the historical use of curator that pre-existed our activities. Now we're actually involved in production and the creation of contexts and opportunities, all of which have a creative element. And speaking personally, I'm most interested in art in the sense of a tool – a tool with which to imagine the world otherwise. I'm not so interested in aesthetic values for themselves, and I'm certainly not interested in art for art's sake. It's more about how art engages and changes conditions around it, how it operates on the imagination. So the limitations of my understanding of the possibilities of the curator are dictated by that personal and political agenda.

You were talking about the beginnings of your curatorial work as if you emerged from some point of nothing; that you just liked art and so on. But are there any people that you could call forerunners or are there special events, which inspired you?

> Yes, there are such people, but they're mostly artists. Well, I mean the reason I got into art was an artist called Stephen Willats, who was working on what we could now call social projects from the 1960s onwards. In terms of forerunners, I think I have to be quite personal and say the reason I got interested in art was through my disillusionment with politics. In my twenties, early twenties at least, I was a member of the British Labour Party and very active on what was then called the left. And gradually, particularly with the experi-

ence of the big miners' strike in 1984-85, I became extremely disillusioned with the possibilities of politics – its possibility to affect people's imagination, to affect changes in thinking and acting, to rethink globalisation, injustice, emancipation, almost anything beyond the hope for the revolution or everyday management. It seemed to me that the options were being closed down (particularly in Britain, because at that time my thoughts were still based very much on some kind of national understanding). I saw in art, through somebody like Stephen Willats, a way of dealing with some of the questions I felt I wanted to ask in the political sphere, but couldn't. And so my journey was from trying to change the world through politics to becoming interested in art.

But why couldn't you pose those questions in the political sphere?

> Because things on the left seemed already set in ideological stone and nobody was even considering ideology's relation to observable realities. Nobody was prepared, for instance, to question whether Marxism was correct, whether Trotsky was correct or not – you either accepted it or you were out. Nobody was prepared to use politics – and this is still absolutely true now – in an imaginative or speculative way. I'll tell you an example: in 1980–81 we were very involved in trying to support Solidarność in some way, even though many were troubled to be opposing a "socialist" government. Then in 1984 when the miners' strike was on, we went down to the docks in Hull, which is a port in eastern England, and tried to stop the ships that were bringing in the Polish coal dug up by the same miners who three years before had been occupying the mines to defend Solidarność. Yet, no one would seriously discuss the irony of our protest or the relationship between what we were doing in 1981 and 1984. In the end, it seemed we were fighting anybody who opposed our British working-class self-interests, and I couldn't see a future in that position at all, because the idea of the self-interests of a nation and class just didn't mean anything anymore. Nobody would discuss the possibility of a thoughtful response to globalisation, to the complexity of community and what it might mean, even to re-imagine a new International, nothing. It seemed everything global, economic or even aesthetically challenging was evil, it was that simplistic and defeat-

ist. The left was freaked out by the end of a coherent class structure and was clinging to its wreckage. Everybody around was just stuck in defensive mode, trying to protect the rights that had been won in the 1950s and 1960s but that no longer meant so much. There was no mechanism to imagine how global relationships could be renegotiated, or how Reaganism-Thatcherism could be turned against itself by changing our vision of the world. No, the future was fixed, we were in eternal opposition until the "revolution" and we were almost happy in our defeatism and lack of responsibility to effect any real change.

So, there was (and is) no imaginative speculation available in politics. And that's the only salvation that we have, actually, to think the world differently. We have to start from the ground and try to build up some different ideas of how we might want to organise ourselves as a society. Otherwise, we only have the one, free-market, democratic, capitalist model. And for me, it seems art could be the terrain where that can happen today. Since the 1980s, I have been even more sure it's not going to happen in traditional party politics, and other areas – philosophy, science, economics – are often so carefully specialised, they stop themselves from making effective statements. But this is another story ...

Please, continue with it.

> For me, art has possibility. "Possibility" is a very important word for me, because I think that's what we have to grasp, to create possibility. Ernst Bloch said there are interests in the world that try to deny possibility – so, "possibility" is a very political term. Possibility to change, possibility to imagine, possibility to speculate, possibility to think things otherwise, these are very important. Now, if we see art as a generalism, a field that can draw in various specialisms, bring them together, perhaps misunderstand or misuse them but create something else out of the combination that speaks to a common interest, then I think the position of art is unique in its possible effect on questions of commonality or community and a real tool to be used to think in that way. And that's what excites me about it. Of course, there are other aspects in this terrain of art that I have little interest in, which have to do with commercialism or to do with the gallery structure or to do with the way that art affirms the status quo or relates to

fashion. That's fine, I don't like them and I don't dislike them, they don't interest me. The real possibility for art is to be a speculative terrain, to imagine the world differently and to draw on other disciplines, whether it's philosophy, physics or football, to talk about our conditions and how they could be revised.

Taking all this into account, what exactly would be the task of the curator?

> The task of the curator is to cultivate that terrain of possibility, to look after it, to build institutions on it or structures on it in which such a speculation can happen. To develop an enclosure if you like, where some of these things can happen, within capitalism of course but a little bit defended from its destructive, mocking forces.

I read something where you were explaining that the curator is an expert on art and that he has real knowledge of art. I'm really interested in what that knowledge would be?

> Look, on one level, it's a simple knowledge of different practices that are going on around the world. I mean, curators are paid and expected to know what is going on at a particular moment and place. So their knowledge base and understanding of current activities should be much wider than somebody who doesn't spend all that time in the art field.

If you have somebody who has greater knowledge, does that mean that he or she would be a better curator?

> I see what you mean ... No, because it's about applying that knowledge. And how you apply that knowledge comes from the specific position that you articulate as a curator. So the curator has a specific position and specific interest. I've tried to point towards that in my own journey from politics to art. If you ask another curator, then you'll have another position and so on. I would hope.

So how can a curator be valuated at all or at best?

> Against each other and also in relationship to terms I would use, like "possibility", like notions taken from Jacques Derrida and Pierre Klossowski of hospitality, of generalism, perhaps even of fluidity. If a curator wants to do an exhibition, the judgement offered might be: Does it create possibility for that moment, for the place and for the artists? Does it work for an audience in a way that is hospitable, that encourages some kind of engagement? Does it function in relationship

to a social situation that is constantly changing, or is it fixed? Does it address broad social questions or only art's own issues? Those are the kinds of criteria you might bring to an exhibition that a curator makes. I mean there are all sorts of ways that you can judge, but those would be the criteria that I would want to use.

Does that mean that you see a curator as an independent author?

> I mean it more as a mediator or a facilitator than an author. Of course, you have your own idea; I don't think we should deny the fact that a curator has a position, but your position is to choose, select those artists or projects that you find compelling, interesting, that satisfy the criteria you have and then to facilitate them and mediate them to an audience. That's why the judgements have to be about the context as much as about the actual content.

You have often talked about your friendship with artists, the fact that you work very closely with them, how important that is ...

> Yes, it's important, vital.

But that probably affects your choice, your selection to a great degree?

> Totally, totally, I wouldn't deny it for a moment. But why do you want some objective criteria outside of myself? I mean, if you invite me as a curator to do a project, I bring the people I know, believe in, love and trust. It's based on previous experiences, so the circle does grow constantly, but I'm not independent from those people and I don't think I should be nervous about that at all. I have my own position. Like, if you want a building like Rem Koolhaas, you ask for Rem Koolhaas, if you want a building like Frank O. Gehry, you ask Gehry. Because, you know, they have positions.

Yes. But you can still ask Koolhaas why is he doing a particular building, why is he doing it in such a way, etc. – in the same way as I'm asking you those things. So for you, in a way, friendship and artistic quality coincide?

> Not always. Because it depends: because you discover situations by research, by travelling, by meeting people, by looking at work you're drawn to. You're drawn to it for those criteria I've already mentioned, as well as for reasons of surprise, innovation, things you can't predict in advance. I see

something and go "Wow! That's really great." Probably it's connected to particular social, political or economic questions that I'm interested in and I can see the artist is really investigating those in a way that I had never thought about. Then my job is to get to know them, my job is not to say: "Wow, that's great, let's take that work." I might do that, of course, but in saying it I also want to get to know who I'm dealing with. So, the friendship, the politics of that friendship come out of the work that I see and the work that interests me. In that sense, friendship is not a blind emotional reaction but grounded in my interests.

But do you see any problematic sides in this way of seeing things? For example, Viktor Misiano also has some special, and in a way very similar ideas on friendship as you do. But since he is the strongest, and if we exaggerate a bit, the "only" curator who is really working outside Russia and in the West that means ...

> ... you have to be friends with Viktor in order to get out.

How can we solve this?

> I think it may be slightly different in Western Europe because there's more pluralism; there are other people that you can work with. The weakness of it is when there are only very few people who are actually making these kinds of judgements. What we need are more people making these kinds of judgements and more transparency or honesty in how it works.

Let's say I'm a good artist from Slovenia whom you are interested in but who is now making you nervous because I'm posing these questions. What would that mean? That I don't fit in your exhibition? If I don't get along with you, does that then somehow affect the quality of my work with you?

> I find this interesting because it's making me think. So I'm quite enjoying it and it's more likely I'll want to see your work. But then, I'm not sure it really matters. My experiences working in marginal places like Glasgow and Malmö is that the situation in such places (also like Ljubljana) only really functions if it starts to sustain itself by developing a supportive local community, a critical mass of quite modest institutions and a self-confidence. That's the energy that somebody coming from the outside could see and get turned on by. So things are in your control as well, rather than only waiting for

                    Beti Žerovc

the blessing of the international curators. In Gwangju, we tried to reflect this by inviting 26 small groups and artist-run spaces to represent themselves.

You work in a museum. I read somewhere that you explained, before you started, that you would try to move the ordinary existing exhibition program into something more diverse, that it would have a more productive role. How far along are you with that?

> The first thing that I did was basically to divide what has traditionally been a showroom for art into different functions. We used the three floors differently and upstairs we made two studios that are semi-private/semi-public. The artists who are there won't necessarily ever show in an exhibition, but the invitation is for them to be present around the building. Meeting our visitors.

Upstairs we also set up a project room, which is a kind of a really boring idea and we did it because we couldn't think of anything else. Now we're running a course with the Art Academy in Malmö with eight students, four artists and four who define themselves as something else, curators or critics or even with a background in sociology. On the middle floor is the main exhibition hall, where we try to use the language of the exhibition as interestingly and effectively as possible. However, in April, we will use it as a film studio and open it only occasionally to the public. Our technical team will be used to build the sets or build the constructions that are necessary for the film. Then downstairs we're playing with the idea of an archive, so we have on one hand a Rooseum archive, where people can see what we have showed in the past, and a future archive, where we ask all the artists we work with to give us a list of 10 books, CDs or videos that are in some way inspirational, influential or important to them. It builds up as a very eclectic, strange library in which you can get to know the artists whom we're working with in different ways because you can see, maybe, where some of their ideas start from or some of their points of departure for their work, whether it's classical books like the *Empire* by Antonio Negri and Michael Hardt or a *Mad Max* film. And then we have a micro cinema/discussion space where we have a video program, club nights and talks. So basically, from the whole thing being a showroom, we now have four or five different kinds of spaces for different kinds of activity. Those spaces themselves are always open to question. So, for instance, the exhibition space becomes a film studio, the project room wasn't really good, so we closed it down.

I think that, in a way, now there is a trend of doing things like that, in a multifunctional, "laboratory" way. Is there a successful museum or gallery working in this way that you could mention?

> Hmmm …

Because, you know, I've been to some places with such an inclination lately – like Palais de Tokyo – and I did not find them very inspiring.

> I really hope that we're not like Palais de Tokyo. Not that I want to be critical, but I think it's very different working in a small town with a relatively small audience and doing something in Paris. You have to take the context into account, because if you don't, then you miss half the reason for doing the things that we're doing.

Sometimes such places, where they're trying to be very open, they are at the same time extremely closed, because they are maybe too concentrated on those few people they work with. And when you come to such a place, it's like …

> You feel thrown out of it. I understand that. I do believe in what I'm doing, but of course I'm self-critical. I don't want to defend Rooseum automatically because the question is fair enough. Again, I'm going to answer you through rhetorical language of defining terms, though I think our projects like Superflex are real examples of this. One term, which I used before, is hospitality, which I'm very interested in trying to embed into the institution. At least in Derrida's terms, hospitality is saying "Yes" essentially. It's saying "Yes" to the other, to the visitor, to the unexpected guest, alive or dead, vegetable or mineral, divine or human. Derrida says it's about trying to say "Yes", trying to learn, disciplining yourself to say "Yes" to the demands that come. Now, I think that hospitality is, on one level, a very pragmatic aspect of welcoming. So if you were to come to the Rooseum, I hope what would happen is that you would feel welcome in a way that perhaps you might have not been in other places … In other words, somebody would come and actually talk to you. On another level, hospitality means being responsive to your concerns, chan-

ging to accommodate the needs of the guest to the point of giving up ownership or authorship. Now how that works out in practice is under construction, but we have a programme called Open Forum that invites people from Malmö to propose and carry out their own projects. It's slow but it is beginning to work.

But Palais de Tokyo also promises that somebody will be there for you with whom you will be able to talk if you want to talk, etc.

> But nothing really happens.

Why is this?

> Well, if you've got that number of people coming in, it's maybe difficult to deal with it on such a level.

But that means that we are faced with a model that is, because it is trying to be one thing, turning into the exact opposite?

> Yes, I'm really sympathetic to you here and I'm thinking about these problems. But the attempts are genuine ones. I mean, we might fail – this I totally understand, and we have to learn and be self-critical, but I think the attempt to be hospitable is one that's worthwhile. The attempt to try, as Palais de Tokyo is doing, to create an institution that has a different sense of the time that you might engage as a visitor, a different sense of the way that you might work with the artists, a different sense of the possibilities of meeting – I think none of that is wrong. Perhaps the delivery should be criticised, but the fundamental approach is basically right. So, I wouldn't really want to criticise Palais de Tokyo, but I do think, in a strange way we have an advantage being provincial. Because we can have a more intimate relation with our audience, we're not a tourist city.

Before you entered the institution you seemed very proud of the fact that you were an independent curator, and you talked about that on numerous occasions. I would like to know: Why did you return to the institution?

> I made a very deliberate decision to return to the institution because I did not want to be an independent curator anymore. And what you might have read was absolutely true then, but I don't think I have to be always consistent. I think time passes and I learn more how to achieve things.

What were the main reasons for returning to the institution?

> Very precisely: as an independent curator working in an institution, you have very little possibility of changing the fundamental structures through which that institution is run. To a certain extent, you are a decoration on top of them. You're invited to do your thing, whether it's the Gwangju Biennial or it's the Tate, you're invited to do the thing for which you are identified as being interesting and then you go away and the institution is left completely unmoved. What I became interested in is not who to invite, not "this artist or that artist", but rather how that invitation is made, in what way do you have a conversation and create a possibility for an artist or a visitor. And that was impossible to do as an independent curator because you were only moving from one site to another and taking a crowd of artists with you (with this issue of friendship, I would agree), but you couldn't actually go very much further – all you could do is take them to another place. Now I didn't do it so much, but I did it enough to realise that it's not my main interest. And actually, I think with Rooseum my main interest is becoming structural, the "how" you invite, what the nature of the invitation is rather than the fact of the invitation.

When I spoke to Pierre Restany, he said that he sees a curator as a master of compromises.

> I understand that, because you're dealing with the whole series of pragmatics. Coming from the political position that I had before, and basically still have, makes me wary of compromise, but, as I said, there is no comfortable outside position anymore. You have to get your hands dirty to achieve anything you want to do, and that means compromise.

Do you see yourself as a master of compromises?

> Not a master, I see myself as forced into compromises.

Is that different?

> Yeah. I feel myself more as a victim of them, or them as an inevitable evil.

In contemporary theory, people like Christopher Lash, Robert Kurz, Slavoj Žižek, speak about our period as of a period of "self-inscenated criticism", which is not true criticism but more an appearance, a stance to be seen by

**others in. Do you think curators often use this appearance
of being critical, and if so, why?**

> Well, let me think about this because it's complicated. If there
> is no externally validated position from which to make critical
> judgements (socialist analysis or whatever), then criticism is
> staged to some degree. And the art world is often self-valid-
> ating, with collectors sitting on institutional boards, institu-
> tions supporting galleries and underwriting artists' projects
> that then have to succeed, etc. But the question is: Does the
> loss of external criteria make the activity invalid? Can we still
> think by using self-staged criticism, or does it just affirm the
> status quo? My answer is that it does not only affirm, but also
> opens up new lines of thought that might produce the break-
> through to another way of imagining the world. That goes
> back to our start, in a way.

**How do you see your position in the relationship with col-
lectors and the commercialism that you mentioned, and
how do you see in them your politics of friendship, which
could be problematic in a similar way?**

> I agree with that. But you know, first, I don't feel very en-
> gaged with collectors myself. I think there is a social demo-
> cratic position of working in an institution with public money,
> where we have to find justification for why you receive that
> money. It is certainly not in order to flatter board members'
> collections or support the value of an artist. The justification
> of that public money will be whether we create a real, active
> discourse, a speculative territory for artists internationally
> and people living locally to test out some ideas about them-
> selves and our society. Now, I'm not ashamed to have a close
> friendship with some of those people at all – in fact, I think
> it is necessary. I mean, the alternative would be to have a
> completely objective, scientific curator who has no relation-
> ships with anybody, is completely dissocialised and relates
> only to the objects. Now that is to some extent the old model
> of the curator, but I think that's more problematic than not
> acknowledging a social exchange that affects your opinions.
> However, the work should still be the primary element that
> facilitates that social exchange that leads to the friendship. I
> think the objective scientific view that you're looking for just
> doesn't exist. If you want the curator to be outside the capit-
> alist structure and collection, to be outside relationships with

artists, to be outside relationships with the institution ... that's somehow taking a godlike overview. I think that's really mistaken. What I'm talking about is being in the mess of social, political and economic pragmatism and still trying to take a position and create the place for art to contribute to social change and emancipation.

So you're placing a great deal of importance on the difference between the involvement in the private and public sector, the difference between private and public financing.

> Yeah, I really want to defend some of those things; for instance, I want to defend the difference between consumerism and civil society. I want to defend the difference between public money and private money. I think that's really important. Otherwise, we abandon ourselves to the worst parts of the American model, without their culture of individual responsibility.

But at the same time, as you are defending this model, you are involved in the private, commercial art sector. Not long ago, you were one of the British selectors for ARCO in Madrid.

> I mean ... ARCO was something that I would not want to theorise about too much.

But if you have such a strong political stand, don't you think you have to be consistent? Otherwise we come exactly to self-inscenated criticism?

> Well ... OK, this is a really good question. The reason I did ARCO was because it seemed to be an opportunity to create a possibility for a certain number of artists who otherwise wouldn't have their opportunity. The reason that I said "Yes" to it was because it allowed me to invite certain people, whom I admired because of their work, through the mechanism of the gallery system. So what we did was not to invite the classical commercial galleries but many different kinds of artist-run spaces that hadn't always been at the art fairs before. I think that was worthwhile. Anyway, the gallery sector is not bad in itself – it depends on how and what it does – it's possible for gallerists to have an ethical position. I just find most of what they do uninteresting.

Yes, but before you said to me: Look at the context. What's the "special" context here, why should you do it?

> OK, ARCO is, in terms of its context, different from other art fairs. It was set up immediately post-Franco, as the first cultural phenomenon that introduced post-modernism and pluralism to Spain. As such it occupies a special place in Spanish culture, and it has always had a very strong educational element. In contrast to Basel or Berlin, a huge range of people attend it, and they come to look, not only to buy. So it does have a different local role than other art fairs. I also saw the possibility of trying to recognise the energy of the artist-run and non-commercial, non-government funded spaces that existed in London, Glasgow and elsewhere. So there were specific reasons why I did it.

On numerous occasions you discussed how art should have a special place, a defended place in the capitalist system, and how the curator's role exists to provide that. "Providing art" for art fairs seems to me going exactly the opposite way. So, that's why ARCO caught my eye.

> Maybe you're right, but ... look, that "special place" is within capitalism anyway, so we have to work from the same territory as the market anyway. The point is to use the structures against themselves to some extent, not dumb opposition like we had on the left in the 1980s.

But, you know, almost every art fair lately has a special thematic exhibition, a special guest, "national" representation, is inviting young galleries, etc. Also Basel and Berlin.

> Not to the same extent as we did. No, really not.

Do you think that being appointed to positions such as the curator of the Gwangju Biennial could be seen as an award for being a loyal and diligent worker within the system? Usually you were very critical towards the system and getting those positions means: I'm really very much in the system.

> Yeah ... Because I don't think there's an outside of the system position. And I've said that and written about it many times. You know, we're all at the same table. So, I'm not unhappy about working within the system at all and I don't think that I've ever had a position outside the system – I have always been involved in it, even in the smallest initiatives in Tramway. What we were doing in Glasgow was trying to a large extent to be noticed by the system. We were also critical of the

system, and not only because we were ignored; but it was reformist rather than revolutionary in its approach. And I think
that's probably the only position that you can adopt as a curator – a kind of reformist one, rather than a revolutionary one.
Because revolution is problematic at the moment – though we
need to keep thinking about it.

And a reformist position is not problematic?

> Of course a reformist position is problematic as well. There's
no unproblematic position in this mess, but I think reform-
ism or, let's say working within the system but also trying to
use the tools that it provides, to offer or create different possibilities, is for me one that I'm happy with. I don't feel compromised so much by that because I don't see a productive
alternative. But your reward thing is probably quite true – that
we are rewarded for good behaviour.

     Beti Žerovc

Beautiful Freedom

First published as "Die Idee der 'schönen' Freiheit: wie KünstlerInnen und KuratorInnen der dominanten Ideologie zuarbeiten", *Springerin* (Vienna), vol. 15, no. 1, winter 2009, pp. 18–22.

 Beti Žerovc

The following is an abridged version of the text "Kurator kot organizator diskurza likovnega področja" ["The Curator as the Organiser of the Discourse in the Art Field"].[1] Here, I begin by summarising certain key ideas from the text in three points; the concluding section is presented in its entirety.

1. The curator of contemporary art, as he works on various levels, develops a discourse that is not confined narrowly to art production alone but is rather expressly directed toward organising the contemporary visual art field as a whole. Because the curator possesses an extraordinary arsenal of opportunities and channels for distributing his messages and, most importantly, because he does not merely prepare exhibitions but also creates the context in which we interpret and receive them, he is not only the principal organiser of the things that happen in the contemporary art field, but he is also their chief interpreter. The curator is the one who describes for us "the way things are", and the voices of curators, blending into a whole, are what crucially define the contemporary understanding of art, as well as our understanding of the meaning and role of art in contemporary society. Consequently, their voices also produce the meaning the art field and its work have in the outside world.

2. Among other things, the curator has also assumed the task of explaining how and why his exhibitions and other activities happen and how the people involved in them are related to each other. To this end, the curator must take all the different and contradictory interests and positions that thus accumulate and put them into coherent stories. Because the reality of the exchanges that take place behind the events must necessarily remain hidden, he cannot simply tell the actual stories but must be very careful in his discourse to select what to underscore and what to leave unsaid. Curator's words must result in the maintenance of a status quo in which the conditions of his work are presented in a way that allows his business to proceed smoothly without serious slowdowns. The curator therefore avoids placing his work within any clear and precise production framework but as a rule explains it outside this framework and so inevitably idealises it.

1   From my doctoral dissertation *Umetnost kuratorjev: Vloga kuratorjev za sodobno umetnost* [*The Art of Curators: The Role of Curators of Contemporary Art*], University of Ljubljana, Ljubljana, 2007.

3. If we sometimes wonder about the "existence" and status of art – not unlike the way we wonder about the existence of God – it is the curator who most loudly tries to convince us that art does in fact "exist" and is of the utmost relevance in the present age. It would appear that, just as there are no unbelieving priests, there are no unbelieving curators. In today's secularised European society, the curator and his "cult" seem highly successful; the curator is able to create a hyper-intense interest in contemporary art, which as a consequence also significantly increases the scope of his work and the number of those who are "called" to serve in his ranks. Of course, art does not revolve around some meticulously defined doctrine but rather allows hundreds of variations, where everyone can to some degree interpret art in their own way. Thus, a myriad of very different and even contradictory discourses are constantly being created and coexisting in the art field. Although we might expect otherwise, the conflicts between these different "sects" in art do little damage to "art as a whole". Quite the opposite in fact: the endless debates and quarrels about what the right approach to art is, what even is art, and so on, sustain and even strengthen our faith in art. A kind of permanent side effect of all this problematizing and criticising of art – when we say that something is not "genuine art", or "art of the highest quality", or "the most avant-garde art", etc., since that is the art we ourselves usually advocate – is the affirmation that "art exists", that "art is real".[2] In other words, as long as we remain in the art field, we continue to play the game, and, in fact, the more vocal, more radical, and more subversive we are, the more the "mutual bank of art" profits from our love and intense feelings toward art. This is true in particular because there has always existed in art the gratifying possibility that dissident avant-garde discourses, which were once, sometimes for decades, implacably opposed to the discourse of "MoMA, Tate, and the like", would eventually be accepted by the institutions, which would no longer be their mortal enemy but, in a way, their most logical extension, complementing them "quite naturally" with the beauty of astronomical prices and museum retrospectives. The art field's "lower" strata – a kind of dense forest of everything that can today be considered art, where a thousand and one intermeshing reasons exist for

2　Pierre Bourdieu, *The Rules of Art: Genesis and Structure of the Literary Field*, Polity Press, Cambridge, UK, 1996, pp. 166–169.

working this way or that, from anarchism to necrophilia – are, therefore, by no means autonomous but rather a necessary, active, and compatible part of this story.

Free Choice and Noble Intentions

Because capitalism is today even stronger than it was a few decades ago and covers nearly the entire world, and because the capitalist system as a whole swears allegiance to the concept of freedom and the possibility of an individual's free choice, we might say that freedom is today the key idea or concept that art must ideologically support. Nothing essential has changed, therefore, since the time of the first very clear analyses of such unavoidable utilitarianism in art (e.g. by Carol Duncan), no matter how different things might seem to us. Today, just as before, the artist must be shown as absolutely free in order for us to believe that we live in a free society. This is also necessary if we are to accept in the right way the things offered to us by exhibitions and permanent collections. Our understanding of art leads us to expect that artworks will show us a picture of the society in which they originated: to put it simply, if the artist works to order or on command, the picture will be distorted, but if he works freely, the picture will be correct. Consequently, for the ideological construction supported by art to be convincing, art needs to be portrayed as originating in conditions of total freedom.

Given that the curator is directly employed by those whom this ideology serves, it follows that his primary task and central mission are to maintain the idea of freedom in art as the key concept to which all others are subordinate, while at the same time promoting this idea as the actual situation in which contemporary art is produced. He shows himself to be distinctly successful in this task, helped considerably, we can assume, by his uncomplicated and contradiction-free conception of the issue. To put it very simply, artistic freedom is presented in the curator's discourse almost as a fact beyond discussion, as a vital condition for art, which, although perhaps not given to us directly, we quite naturally strive to attain – if, that is, we are truly "of God", if we are truly a democratic, socially just, mature society. This "state of blessedness" the curator presents as a kind of apex, difficult to reach but undoubtedly attainable, even as he successfully makes himself an utterly indispensable part of the story. By so adroitly offering himself as the one who, despite the power matrix around him, is able in his work to establish and organise a kind of protected zone of freedom for the artist, the curator convinces us to see freedom where, in fact, total dependence reigns and to believe that he himself is central to ensuring this freedom. Indeed, the peculiar belief that an artist is undoubtedly more free if he works in dependence on a curator than if he were dependent on a dealer or directly on his client seems to be universally accepted today.

No matter what the curator's position is, when it comes to portraying the idea of total artistic freedom, the pluralistic "lower strata" of the art system, where supposedly "anything goes", is essential to him. This realm is more than just a bottomless magic bag where he can always find new material; the curator must constantly turn to it if only because he can always use it as an illustration, as if to say, "See that? Everything is permissible and everyone does whatever they feel like doing." If freedom becomes so obviously more rarefied the higher we go in the art system, like air at high altitudes, the lower strata can, if interpreted properly, provide the appearance of freedom's authentic pulsation and deliver the most diverse demonstrations of its vital signs. Scandal and shock, for example – which regularly result from encounters between free art and "the uninitiated masses" and which can garner the kind of media attention art rarely enjoys – are therefore usually interpreted as the logical consequence of the clash between the free world of art and the "cave life" of ordinary reality.[3] A second useful feature of art's lower strata is that, because today there really are all sorts of things swimming around there in a more or less happy coexistence of constant conflict, the curator can always, with no real trouble or tiresome discussion of norms, "filter out" from these strata whatever he wants or needs

3   Such clashes often occur just as an art practice is passing from what we might call the "lower strata" to the "canonical realm", where vocal expressions of outrage arise when the art leaves the world of its primary supporters and fans (which the media has little interest in) and enters the world of prestigious art venues and high prices. There it may be "noticed" by some local politician or church dignitary, whose fury, as a rule, merely confirms the triumphant concept of artistic freedom, since only rarely does anyone today actually remove artworks in response to such outbursts.

    Beti Žerovc

at a particular moment and lift it up into the region of the greatest exposure and visibility.

Keeping all this in mind, if we look at what today receives the maximum visibility offered by the art system, we find it is all quite uniform. Although at first glance these works seem to be extremely varied in form and content, their "basic message" always somehow points in the same direction; so we quickly come to the conclusion that, basically, these free artists are all doing pretty much the same thing. What these works have in common is very soon apparent: no matter what the artist creates, he must always act as a kind of eternal altruist who inevitably has some noble intention behind whatever he does. Whether he makes Thai soup, criticises the banks, slaughters a calf, teaches poor children, or lacerates his entire body in a performance, he does it with the intention of improving and educating the audience and the general society. The artist we encounter at the most highly rated contemporary art exhibitions, then, appears to us primarily as someone who, in conditions of total freedom, does not, for example, put his own personal interests or pleasure before everything else but instead freely chooses to pursue some socially constructive or critical endeavour, or at least does something that could, at least in some respect, be interpreted as such.

Because it is hard to believe in the ethical superiority of artists and their curators where their actions derive solely from a devotion to ideals and some primary inner urge to help people in need, their work seems to be, to some extent at least, the product of simple calculation: the public, and those who commission art, must be offered such a critical/constructive form (within the bounds of present-day common sense, of course) since it will be more effective and better received than, say, the renunciation of political content in artworks. Just as non-figural abstraction was clearly the right approach in post-war times, so today, when we are so very aware politically, sociologically, psychologically, anthropologically, etc., and place a high value on critiques of every sort, the best approach is clearly one of direct politicising, criticising, and moralising. Not only is such work closer to us, but by practicing it the artist also demonstrates his absolute freedom – since "everyone knows", for instance, that it is only good, democratic systems that have a high tolerance for criticism and alternative views while evil, totalitarian systems do not. Because we do not see this form of work as something cultivated and commissioned, it confirms for us literally, by its very nature, that it originated in conditions of total freedom, since it is exactly the sort of work that, in our idealistic imagination, would appear in a free environment. When we also see how nobly and devotedly everyone supports the artist in his expression of criticism, we cannot help believing in this free environment, and in all the other beautiful aspects of this mature society, which is able to voluntarily subject itself to such self-reflection and the castigation of its faults. In this idealistic tale, where art in some combination with the social sciences will change the world, everything is so wonderfully complementary that we no longer think about the ideological aspect of such work, or anything like it – or if we do, then it is simply to reflect that this path is the right path toward the transcendence of ideology.

But if we shift our perspective slightly from the one the curator regularly arranges for us, we find, on the contrary, that the artist appears as a kind of ideal collaborator in constructing the underpinning ideology of capitalism – and this precisely when he produces such responsible and socially constitutive work in conditions of total freedom (which supposedly reigns now in art, even according to common belief). Today's artist truly is quite different from his severely criticised counterpart of a few decades ago; and while this change may be understood as an adaptation to criticism, it can also be seen as a further development: today, for the current needs of capitalism, the artist demonstrates not merely the state of total freedom in his society, but also the fact that this freedom is "morally good". Capitalism needs this because, if there was once a time when the very word "freedom" caused everyone's heart to leap, that time is long gone. Today, in fact, freedom appears more and more frequently in some very problematic combinations – in support of the absolute protection of private property, the unlimited movement of capital, etc. – and its limits are often defined by the individual's economic capacity. Consequently, freedom's face is losing its beauty. It can even be quite terrifying: today, the freedom of the owners of capital can often signify fear, anxiety, and a very real lack of freedom for those who are dependent on them, most often their workers. Because our society does not consider it a crime to lay off hundreds or even thousands of workers for the sake of a few owners' profit but instead does all it can to protect this kind of freedom, for many people today, such freedom is nothing less than the greatest nightmare of our time.

    Beti Žerovc

But because the concept of freedom is still absolutely essential to capitalism and because the freedom of the capitalists must not cause alarm (otherwise we might stop being peaceful and devoted collaborators in capitalism), they must make sure that freedom preserves as much of its exalted reputation as possible and that the beautiful idea of freedom's always-beneficial touch remains intact. And here the contemporary artists of today seem to be of real service to the capitalists, who could hardly find a better or more admirable illustration of the fact that freedom can only do people good and they will not abuse it.[4] Or perhaps it would be more accurate to say that it is their employee, the contemporary art curator, the manager and organiser of this "beautiful state of affairs", who truly serves them well, since we all too easily forget that exhibitions and biennials, art magazines and catalogues – all these celebrations of great social responsibility, these supranational platforms for critically bemoaning the problems of the world, where we consume and pay homage to this "good freedom" *en masse* – all these things are in fact the curator's children.

A Servant of the Dominant Ideology

That this "concerned" form of art does not necessarily spring exclusively from real-life social needs can be seen among other things in the fact that it may be developing not so much in relation to these social needs as in relation to an earlier art practice (as is usual in the history of art), and especially to a discredited aspect of that practice. Thus it seems that art is currently moralising and offering all kinds of political and social guidance partly in relation to an art that had renounced all connection with the political, or had seen its political potential hidden in its aesthetic aspect, until it became all too apparent that by doing so it had only made itself an even more effective servant of the

---

4 The art field's response to violations and deviations from this image can be extremely harsh. Peter Handke, for example, got a taste of the total non-freedom of "the freedom of the artist and artistic freedom" when he suffered real persecution after expressing support for Serbian president Slobodan Milošević and his regime.

dominant ideology. The idea of this art was that it could use defamiliarisation, total absorption in the painting, the state of grace it conferred, and the like, not to move the intellect to, say, perceive injustices directly, but to move the spirit and so bring about social change indirectly. But this idea eventually proved ineffective; for, all too obviously, the time never arrived when, to put it a bit sarcastically, Barnett Newman's paintings were finally understood correctly, that is, understood in a way that would have led to the downfall of capitalism and totalitarianism. It seems an ironic twist of fate that these artists' overheated political statements – belied by what time has shown to be the completely opposite effect of their art – have metamorphosed from the most resounding slogans of an age into the clearest possible illustrations of mistakes, illusions, and misunderstandings about the capabilities of art.

But instead of taking these lessons seriously and confronting the fact that Western art simply cannot fulfil such promises and that artistic freedom is itself a myth, at least in the present system, we have today merely changed the melody a little, or at most turned the record over. We want desperately to believe there is greater political potential in the work of Hans Haacke, Tim Rollins, and the group Superflex than there was in Newman or Pollock, even though today we see quite clearly that, ultimately, they all end up in the same museums, on the same walls, and can be sold by the same gallerist, even, broadly speaking, for the same price – one beyond the reach of ordinary mortals.

The Exhibition as a Work of Art and the Curator as Its Author

First published as "Razstava kot umetniško delo in kurator kot njen avtor" ["The Exhibition as a Work of Art and the Curator as Its Author"], *Maska* (Ljubljana), vol. 25, no. 127–130 and *Amfiteater* (Ljubljana), vol. 2, no. 2, 2010, pp. 87–134.

 Beti Žerovc

The Exhibition of Contemporary Art – A Distinctive Event

The art exhibition, which once tended to be a fairly nondescript vehicle or frame for displaying artworks – one that was only minimally "authored" by the person who made it, whether dealer or art custodian – has moved in a direction where it can now be, increasingly, also an independent display item in itself, a specific authored whole that tells its own story. As such, it can have very distinctive features. If we consider, for example, large curatorial group exhibitions, they are no longer some neutral vehicle for presenting various individual artworks or art projects but instead are ambitiously conceived total projects in which the artworks, too, or even primarily, are simply pieces of a bigger picture, the particles of a broader iconographic programme that, if it is especially successful, will then be repeated (in new adaptations, of course). The exhibition can thus be assembled on the basis of a very distinctive concept, which, simply by being repeatable, "joins together what was once apart" more effectively and more durably than we imagine.[1]

A second level in the development of the exhibition of contemporary art, which we can link in an active relation to the curatorship of the past few decades, has to do with its intensification as an event. Here, of course, we are hardly saying that the exhibition was not an event before the arrival of the contemporary curator. There is not the slightest doubt that it has always been an event and that being an event is, quite literally, in its very nature. It is clear, however, that this aspect of the exhibition is today greatly increased, in a way following the principle that the bigger and more ambitious an exhibition is, the more it tends toward this, and the more its structure is focused in this direction. It is

---

1 In his analysis of the big curatorial exhibitions of the 1970s and 1980s, Jean-Marc Poinsot makes it clear that such selections always propose some new order and possess a normative value, so that they become, in a way, programmes for reproduction (Jean-Marc Poinsot, "Large Exhibitions: A Sketch of a Typology," in *Thinking about Exhibitions*, Reesa Greenberg, Bruce W. Ferguson, and Sandy Nairne (eds.), Routledge, London and New York, 1996, p. 40).

just such an exhibition – where the curator succeeds in turning it into an event that is as highly acclaimed and distinctive as possible – that we currently consider the most ideal form of contemporary exhibition-making, for it can bring the greatest benefits to everyone involved. It is an excellent means for both mobilising the media and attracting viewers. As such, it can most easily establish the most extensive economic ties, while at the same time managing to inscribe itself in art history, which is increasingly structured precisely around distinctive events of this sort. Such an exhibition has a positive impact on the art market and on the careers of the curators and exhibited artists. Because the exhibition's intensified "eventness" is very difficult to define, we will not seek to formulate any definition in our discussion of it, but rather will try to describe it as illustratively as we can.

From what was once a relatively static event where the thing that "happened" to the viewer was mainly the artworks, the exhibition has become a chain of actual events, which "happen" not only within the exhibition itself – with interactive works, performances, cabarets, actions, whole interiors, video and audio recordings, etc. – but also in an entire palette of events accompanying the exhibition: symposia, lectures, presentations, "club nights", etc. But this vogue for creating something that is constantly happening, which will involve the viewer as much as possible, has become so strong that no longer is it only individual exhibitions that are focused in this direction, but also entire art institutions. How else to describe such an institution as, for instance, the Palais de Tokyo in Paris, which from its inception has literally been a kind of promise of a permanent happening where we can enjoy a genuine experience of living art that at the same time offers us a cordial welcome? In both the exhibition venue and the exhibition, then, the difference between past and present is, literally, physical, tangible and audible. If, for example, the art exhibition was once "silent", today it is usually loud, filled with sounds and noises, each obtruding on the other. If at an exhibition – after the opening as its central and often sole "event" – the "physical exhibition" itself once reigned until it closed, then today the exhibition venue keeps enticing us to visit, again and again, throughout the run of the show.

Still another level where the exhibition intensively "happens" is in the media, where it unfolds as the most conspicuous media event possible. In the modern life of the exhibition, media

     Beti Žerovc

reporting plays an extremely important role, since it is through the media that the exhibition transmits its message most widely. For active art viewers, meanwhile, media reports serve, among other things, to constantly stimulate expectations and remind them about the exhibition, which it delivers to them by a different route.

We can conclude this outline of the exhibition's eventness with the artistic level: eventness is intensified also by the creation of a direct link between the curatorial exhibition and art events from the past, in which the curatorial exhibition today acts in a way as an entirely logical extension of their tradition. Although this connection might seem entirely innocent, it is not at all, for it basically defines a context for understanding the curatorial exhibition. It redirects our "reading" from the individual artworks to the whole entity and sets the wavelength of our "reading" of these entities to the kind of perception we otherwise direct toward art.

In his relation to such an "exhibition-entity", the curator is the direct designer and author, and his intent determines what it essentially is. He is linked to the media level in a way that today is somehow entirely automatic; in the physical exhibition itself, where of course he collaborates with the artist, he acts as a director of the viewer's experience. In a production so designed, he moves closer to the viewer's position in particular, for in contrast to the cold and inaccessible attitude of the representatives of the older modernist doctrine, he clearly does not regard the viewer as some sort of superfluous "third person", whose only role in the story is to admire the artworks in silence; instead he takes seriously even the viewer's extra-artistic needs and desires. (He accepts the fact that viewers may go to exhibitions not so much to admire the art as to spend their leisure time, enhance their own "image", etc.).

By organising, interpreting, and publicising exhibitions in the right way, the curator actively helps viewers to experience the most appealing kind of events, to feel that something "cool" is happening and that their involvement/relationship with such events makes them more "initiated", to gain greater self-confidence in their cultural knowledge, and so on.

An Ambivalent Authorship

Although the situation described above could not be more obvious or unmistakable on first inspection, it is also clear that for some reason the art world would rather not see it highlighted in such terms. Very concrete depictions of actual circumstances can still arouse a certain discomfort, a nervousness, even among art professionals, especially when it comes to the clear concretisation of the curator's authorship. At the same time, however, we should note that this authorship is not yet uniformly defined even as to the level on which to seek it. Although all sorts of things are ascribed to the curator in this regard, this happens more or less abstractly, on a general level, while in discussions about concrete productions the acknowledgement of his authorship is rarely in proportion to his actual input. We may or may not talk about what the curator "made us feel" or helped us recognise, or the pleasure we received from his event, or how he involved us in his story; rather than analyse the curator's work or input in a specific exhibition, we can always redirect our speech, writing, or art criticism into a discussion about the artists and their works. Also, since we do not yet have any generally accepted reception theories about the way viewers experience these whole entities and what they take away from them – or rather, the theories we do have are not sufficiently applicable or, mainly, are not applied[2]

2 In this regard, there are a number of theories – such as those that view the exhibition as a *Gesamtkunstwerk* or a collective ritual, or that discuss the experience of exhibitions in terms of *"Verstehen im Gehen"* ("understanding as you go"), etc. – all of which clearly presuppose that, in relation to the viewer, the exhibition works as a whole entity and, as such, has extraordinary potential for creating for viewers specific pictures, messages, and perspectives on the world, as well as artistic pleasure. Here the collective-ritual theory of the exhibition, in particular, emphasises the fact that the viewer does not necessarily establish any direct contact at all with the works themselves (which means that the possibility of their influence on him is also not as self-evident as we usually presume). Especially in the case of the big exhibitions, the very awareness of participating in them itself presents an obstacle to the reception of the artworks, and, much more than the work of art, the visitor himself as participant becomes the object of perception (John Miller, "The Show You Love To Hate: A Psychology of the Mega-exhibition", in *Thinking about Exhibitions*, pp. 269–274. See n. 1; Harald Kimpel, *documenta: Mythos und Wirklichkeit*, DuMont, Cologne, 1997, pp. 228–230). According to the "under-

 Beti Žerovc

- we in fact persist in the extraordinary situation where a considerable portion of such exhibitions/events and their effect is left open and unexamined.

Given the extent of the influence of the curator and his production, this is of course an unusual situation, and if we are interested in exhibition-making and curating, it must not be ignored. Quite the contrary, we should probably treat it very seriously, for it appears to be a structural feature of curatorial undertakings, one that essentially defines their impact. This is all the more true because there seem to be concrete reasons for this situation, which are not only about the art community's unwillingness to accept changes that transfer artistic competences from the artist to the curator or even about the curator's own possible opposition to such processes for the good of the artist.

The persistence of such an undefined situation appears to be conditioned, in essence, by the fact that any concretisation of authorship in an exhibition would also lead to the concretisation of the connection between the author and the one who commissions the exhibition, and this would hardly be welcomed. The successful performance of a full spectrum of duties on behalf of those who fund exhibitions – the delivery of direct material profits[3], the constant favourable exchange of financial capital for high-quality symbolic capital, the maintaining of hegemony – requires at the same time that the very fact that these duties are being performed remains as invisible as possible, or that it is suitably idealised. The exhibition must be as far removed from its actual economic and production realities as possible, and the consumer must in no way think about the fact that, say, Erste Bank commissioned this "for him" from some famous curator, or that he is reflecting on anarchism because this is what Generali insurance company and the local chamber of commerce have decided. In order for the consumer to effectively internalise the notions that the society producing this work is solid and well intentioned, that the people in this society are actively engaged in

standing as you go" theory, viewers perceive the exhibition as a leisure time, non-compulsory, aimless activity, where they can stroll idly among the artworks, stopping only if anything happens to catch their particular attention (ibid., pp. 361–371).

3   I discuss elsewhere how the processes treated here are connected with the art market. Let me note only that the market and institutional platforms for contemporary art are not mutually exclusive; rather, they generally support each other to great mutual benefit.

social and global issues (and that art is the perfect field for this), and of course that Erste Bank and Generali are actually "cool" companies, exhibitions must "happen" to him for entirely different reasons.

It turns out, then, that we must consider the curator's authorship or non-authorship in the exhibition (at least to some degree together with the way others in the art field analyse the relationship between him and the exhibition) in connection with the production reality, and must accept that this factor fundamentally determines how curatorial authorship is established. Since the authorship of an exhibition can be established only in line with this factor, it is not possible, at least for now, for the curator to enjoy undivided, whole, 100 per cent authorship; he can move toward its greater concretisation mainly in directions that support the adapted view on contemporary art exhibitions we have described and that do not threaten any positive effect that benefits the funders. For this reason, presumably, we observe the curator developing in two directions. The two adapted forms of establishing his authorship – forms that can exist side by side and even support each other to mutual advantage – are, therefore: 1) the open authorial position, where, to put it simply, the curator defines himself as author (or not, depending on the specific conditions of the moment); and 2) the adoption of the position or stance of the artist, where the curator substantially constructs his identity in a way that approaches that of an artist.

For a more tangible idea of what I mean by these two forms, let us first examine a few of their capabilities for maintaining the status quo and existing relationships as, for all intents and purposes, unquestionable. Open authorship is, in all sorts of ways, an excellent mechanism for eliminating criticism, avoiding conflict, etc. – it will appear several times in this chapter in more concrete form, but we have already described its efficacy in keeping out of sight connections one would rather not reveal. At the same time, it serves as an always-useful base from which the curator can satisfy people on all sides of art without getting involved in the dramatic clashes between them or their contradictory interests. Because his position is not clearly defined, the curator can, for the financial backer, be primarily a conscientious and fully dedicated organiser of cultural offerings and a shrewd scout on the trail of the most important artworks, while, for the artist, he is a sensitive and understanding comrade-at-arms in

     Beti Žerovc

the fight for artistic autonomy or a more egalitarian society. At the same time, he can also be the one who makes sure that the backer and the artist – should they be incompatible – never have to meet. The curator passes with ease from the role of art expert to that of fellow artist and back again (and these two don't have to meet either!). And so on. This openness (if properly maintained, of course) is, so to speak, an invincible weapon, for it provides opportunities for constantly switching and staggering all sorts of things, always offering the curator the chance to shift problematic concepts to the background and bring positive ones forward.

The same can be said of the curator's adoption of the artist's position, which not only is the usual, accepted and, therefore, least questioned position for making statements in art (statements by producers, for instance, do not interest us and, what is more, we are inclined to be suspicious of them), but it also has many other positive aspects that help the curator maintain the status quo. The most concrete of these is, perhaps, the fact that, because of this shift to the artist-position, the exhibition acquires that additional veneer of authenticity, guilelessness, and even inevitability that we associate with anything "artistic". Instead of viewing the exhibition as a rational product created to serve the interests of the people involved, we have the impression that it simply had to happen as it did. At the same time, the artist-position is undoubtedly ideal for the curator himself, for it conveniently absolves him of not only professional and intellectual responsibility but social responsibility as well. After all, once things start originating from inner necessity and irrational impulses, he no longer needs to provide rational justifications. The main thing, however, is that this transition to and reliance on the artist-position and idea of "the exhibition as nature" are the easiest means he has for freeing himself from duties and tasks that derive from the positions of art custodian/expert and artist's helper – i.e. the way others in the art world largely see (and want to see) him – and moving on to telling his own stories. In order for him to speak independently, he must suitably "conceptualise" himself, and from the beginnings of curatorship to the present day, this process has only intensified. Here we should note in particular that the curator also to a large degree appropriates whatever mythology about the artist is currently "in effect".

It may be that the model of the curator's authorship, as outlined so far, is difficult to understand, but there seems to be no easy path in this case. For a fuller picture of the curator, we certainly need more research into his authorship (as well as, basically, the "legal status" of the other players in the art world, and their hierarchy and distribution of functions). Such research is also important for understanding other issues of particular interest – for example, how an exhibition conveys its meaning, message, beliefs, and so on, and ultimately, what basic purposes it serves. To get a clearer picture of what this specifically designed authorship is like and where it leads, given an event with such high potential, we will here try to answer the following questions: How does the curator find balance between the artist-position and open authorship? How, and in what ways, does he shift into art and conceptualise himself as an artist? How does he then coordinate his role with that of the artist? How does he maintain the image of the artist's autonomy and freedom while at the same time making the exhibition be exactly what he wants it to be? Why is his coercion so little seen, if seen at all? And, moving toward an answer, how does he avoid his authorship being concretised in the area of selecting, prescribing, and loudly demonstrating his power over the artist, even as he ensures that such concretisation takes place more meaningfully on other levels, for example, by elevating the status of the curatorial medium and reshaping art history in suitable ways? How does he thus manage to both preserve his open authorship and keep the artist in (seemingly, at least) such a high position that the artist is reconciled to his non-autonomous status while at the same time always being a suitable alter ego for the curator?

The Artistic Status
of the Curator

To put it more simply, there is a basic tendency on the part of the curator to move increasingly and as much as possible into art itself: his concepts are more tendentious than those of artists; his selections are allowed ever greater freedom from demands for objective criteria;[4] and the ethics he presents as his own is

4   The curator has radically distanced himself from such categories as nationality, school, style, etc., which, until recently, served as basic principles, as

    Beti Žerovc

at least as "storybook" in nature as that of artists, if not more so. Wherever he is unable to move safely into art – for instance, because he encounters conflict, criticism, unpleasant confrontations, or public complaints about his working for the interests of his commissioners, his exploitation of artists, etc. – he turns from his usual orientation onto a parallel road and brings in the artist, who is always available to him for this purpose, as his replacement on the main road. Because the authorship of exhibitions is not firmly defined, the curator can if need be easily step aside, at such moments most often becoming the art expert or even the traditional unobtrusive art custodian, as he pushes the "artisthood" of his subordinates into the foreground. At the same time, the concepts of his own artisthood and open authorship are somehow unproblematically combined, and the same person who a moment before was organising freedom and was guided in his ideas and activities solely by a moral vision of social change or a personal obsession with identifying and presenting a well-chosen selection of contemporary psychoses, or in some other way was conceiving exhibitions in line with his own subjective intention, now suddenly becomes nothing but a humble servant of art, the artist's personal secretary, without any tangible investment in the exhibition or the viewer's experience. For such cases, there is the always useful explanation that, after all, he can only exhibit what the artist makes, since that's the only way to do it.

This move is, truly, always available to the curator and at his full disposal, for the "old" principle of viewing, where we are focused on the artworks and not on the exhibition, is still understood in art as our "natural perspective". In such moments, the idea that we look at artworks more than at the exhibition itself is generally the best possible solution, for, in keeping with the established mythology, we are looking at the work of a person with unimpeachable status, a work made in the total artistic autonomy so fortunately provided by the contemporary art system.[5]

More concretely, however, such a "switch" is so ideal because it allows the curator to continually parasitize the artist's

it were, for positioning and combining artworks in contemporary art exhibition making. Today, the formal qualities of artworks only rarely become an object of study or "combining principle", and it seems that artworks are grouped primarily on the basis of their content, inasmuch as they are exhibited together if their content or message fits a certain curatorial concept.

5   See the essay "Beautiful Freedom", pp. 166-174.

status and thus organise a suitable basis for the kind of position he usually occupies. In both instances, the epistemological and ethical superiority we today usually ascribe to the artist becomes the foundation and starting point for the curator's message as well. Meanwhile, the status of artist not only ideally serves the needs of his message, it also fits ideally into the mechanisms of constant staggering and switching I have described. Concepts about the artist are suitably intangible and, above all, mutually interchangeable, while at the same time, his status remains solid and unquestionable, for it has been constructed – along with the mythology that delineates and fills it – over centuries.

To better understand what we are talking about, let us first summarise the key features of the artist's status that are explicitly supported, emphasised and applied by the curator – and which he applies to himself as well – particularly in the context of the politicisation of art, a topic with which the curator is often closely associated.

Clearly, the curator is well served by the standard contemporary belief that art approaches things unconventionally, without bias, impartially and, above all, without being motivated by self-interest, that it is a field with a great sense of social responsibility, and that moral values in this field are higher than elsewhere and capitalism is not the master – at least not completely. At the same time, the artist is equipped with a kind of supernatural intuition, so that, for example, he sees through the misleading and distorted perspective on the world that consumerist society "organises" for us. The artist has access to better, sounder and more enduring solutions to problems than those offered by others in society. When the artist sees something problematic, he wants to correct it, to improve the situation, for he is a person of exceptional integrity; he opposes political and economic elites, speaks on behalf of the disenfranchised, and so on. This image is supplemented and interlaced with yet other myths, especially older ones, which portray the artist as adventurous, ingenious, passionate, caring little for material goods, freedom-loving by nature, etc. A particularly fortunate aspect of this mythological diagram is that all these fine intentions and qualities, we feel, are truly realised by the artist today, for somehow we believe that – in this age of corporate culture, no less – he has achieved his greatest autonomy in history to date.

          Beti Žerovc

Two key features of this artistic personality (and therefore, of course, the curatorial personality) are, first, that the artist cannot help but speak the truth from his heart in every situation and is incapable of strategic love, and second, that he is the ultimate moral being, who is fundamentally inclined to (correctly) perceive injustice and try (correctly) to set it right.[6] The basic lesson from all this is that art must address society and its problems, for if we paid more attention to what the artist tells us and looked at art the right way, the world would be a better place.[7]

Here we are not especially concerned with how this mythology developed; what is important is that it is widely accepted and that, by including himself in it directly, the curator acquires a status and image that perfectly serve his needs. The tasks he performs acquire the status of duties; his exhibitions are guaranteed a powerful impact; and because his work is guided by artistic intuition and a high ethical imperative, his messages are shielded from scepticism.

How the curator designs these messages and "fills" even the mythology itself to suit his needs, without any of it being distressingly visible, we will now examine through an analysis of his relationship with the artist.

6   Myths are not drawn from history, and in the mythology of art, too, they appear and die out, become widespread or fall into decline. The profiles of art and the artist, as I have outlined them, are thus compilations of both very old and very young myths. For example, the idea that the artist says what he thinks and speaks from the heart is a very old myth, whereas the "leftist" features in art only started developing more intensively from the mid-19th century onward. Art mythology also appears to be only slightly connected with changes in style. For example, the myth about the artist's moral and epistemological superiority, which was developed to a high level by modernism in the mid-20th century, remains in effect today, despite the fact that art production has changed significantly since then.

7   When it comes to the acceptance of myths, it does not matter whether we believe them; what matters is that we behave in accordance with them, that we act as if we believe them. An extreme example of the potency of such a view of art could be seen in the 1970s, in certain Western countries, in the hiring of artists in the public sector – at different ministries, municipal offices, etc. – in the hope that, because of their special abilities, they would contribute to better and longer-lasting solutions to social problems (Grant H. Kessler, *Conversation Pieces: Community and Communication in Modern Art*, University of California Press, Berkeley, CA, and Los Angeles, 2004, pp. 61–63).

The Artist–Curator Relationship

If the visual artist today wishes to exhibit his work in the most prominent art institutions, or even to make a living from art, the choice of whether to work in tandem with the curator and within the network of the curator's projects and exhibitions has long been resolved. What is more, since things of no interest to the curator remain little seen while things he supports only really become "high art" once he supports them, the artist allows the curator to do things that may be in total opposition to his worldview and the ideas he advocates, and does so with a silent resignation that can only be the result of a constant fervent expectation that invitations to ever bigger and more important exhibitions will finally come his way. All in all, it is clear that from the artist's perspective there is at present no serious alternative to the hierarchy the curator is establishing in art. Since, in relation to the artist, the curator is, as it were, an absolute master even over the most prestigious contemporary art institutions (or is the closest thing there is to one), he also in a way has absolute sovereignty over the dreams and lives of artists: through him leads the road to survival; through him leads the road to fame.

The artist–curator relationship is captured most typically in the exhibition itself, for the exhibition seems a kind of key contemporary mechanism for pointing art production as a whole in a certain direction. It is through the exhibition that the curator today most literally dictates to the artist what and how much he should do, for the simple reason that the artist often makes projects literally to the curator's order and on topics the curator sets, if he is lucky enough to be invited to participate in an exhibition that also funds the execution of the projects.[8] What ultimately ensures that the artist makes these works entirely to the curator's wishes is nothing other than the mechanism of inclusion and exclusion, which the exhibition places in the hands of the curator:

---

8   For a comparative model that helps us understand how the exhibition "enslaves" the artwork through its content, how its intention defines the artwork, I recommend Barthes's analysis of the operation of mythic structures (Roland Barthes, *Mythologies*, Vintage and Random House, London, 2000, pp. 111–137).

any artist who is not wholly to his taste, or proves obstinate even, the curator can simply stop inviting to future exhibitions.

In such a configuration, the artist's success – which also brings sales, commissions, often the sheer possibility of making his works, etc. – is measured by whether he appears in exhibitions and in what sort of exhibitions he appears. It is entirely clear, therefore, that the artist will try in whatever way he can to comply with the curator's demands and expectations. The curator's invitations, or lack thereof, are key signposts in the artist's work and career; in such an inescapable predicament, the artist only rarely complains or criticises or even – and this is very important – objects to the curator's interpretations, whatever they might be and however much he might disagree with them.[9] If at first it seems a little hard to believe that the artist does not rebel against such relationships, the more we analyse this system of working, the more it becomes clear that rebellion is virtually impossible – or completely pointless, as it would bring no results. Since no objective criteria for good art exist in the art field, and since, for instance, we cannot count how many people have been made happy or enlightened by art but can very easily count which artists have appeared in exhibitions – in other words, since artists who rebel by refusing to participate in curatorial projects simply disappear into the crowd of nameless non-successes – this problematic aspect of the system is hermetically sealed against all possible criticism. Meanwhile, the successful artists, who of course are enthusiastic participants in the system, become the crowning proof that everything is working perfectly, even though such artists have no logical reason to rebel since, for one

---

9   Because such an exhibition-centred principle of working has been present, and in continual expansion, for decades in contemporary art, the artist, too, has fully adapted to it, even in the way he lives. When an invitation arrives, he simply "packs his wares" and heads off to wherever in the world the exhibition might be. And he does this, if need be, several times a month, 12 months a year, since when it comes to "high-quality exhibiting" – that is, exhibiting in the most important and highest-ranked exhibitions – it turns out that "more is more". In many cases, too, the artist lives, literally, in two or even more parts of the world. Basically, the more successful he is, the more he lives in a kind of special parallel world, as the rhythm of constant exhibiting and participating in all possible projects and events demands that he be always on the move. The artist, it seems, often suffers from certain "travelling salesman" problems, such as alienation from his own environment and travel fatigue. Clearly, however, he prefers these to the dread that the curator's invitations might start dwindling or even disappear altogether.

thing, they are successful, and for another, if they did they would simply stop being successful.

The fact that what exhibitions present as contemporary art has largely been orchestrated and even directly commissioned is successfully covered up again and again, on various levels, by an effective mythologisation. The "vassal" relationships I have described are seldom mentioned, and with every exhibition there is, as a rule, further mythologisation about how those at the very bottom of the hierarchy are, of all the participants, the freest.

Emphasising and celebrating freedom, however, are also effective ways to conceal a specific aspect of our reality: namely, while formal censorship is practically non-existent in the Western world and only rarely is anything forbidden, it becomes all the more crucial what gets seen and how, what is placed in our gaze and presented as important. In the art field, then, while it may be true that an enormous and extremely diverse production is being made freely, what we end up "seeing" is only, or mostly, something that has passed through the hands of the curator (the filter), who occupies his position precisely because he selects/ emphasises and marginalises/disregards art production in the "right" way.

Curating as Creating

By analysing the curator's and, especially, the artist's relationships to the exhibition, we have also defined the relationship between curator and artist. Now our analysis will try to show how the curator, in his connection with the exhibition, elevates his own creative and artistic status and cultivates the charisma of an author of an artistic event.

To continue with the situation outlined in the previous section, the fact that the exhibition does not merely exhibit artworks but also helps to legitimise them is of extraordinary importance in shaping the curator's status. More concretely, because the exhibition is understood and presented as something that, quite naturally, detects new trends, determines the most important art activity at the moment, etc., it can define in the most tangible terms what contemporary art in fact is. Indeed, because we have no clear criteria for what art is or even for how something becomes art (and this, of course, we would like to know), it is today the exhibition with its concrete answer in the form of a selection of exhibited items, that most clearly tells us what has the status of a work of art.

Understandably, the status of the exhibition is greatly elevated by such a development, while its basic tasks shift from merely presenting artworks to more complex functions. If today the most tangible proof that something is art is the fact that this "something" appears in an exhibition – in other words, if the exhibition acquires a truly active role in the creation of art – then the act of selecting works is itself constituted as an act of creation, or at least co-creation.[10] The curator's status, then, increases monumentally not only in the sense that he becomes a "master"[11] with actual powers of consecration, but also in the sense of his potential as a creator.

Again, this increase in status is facilitated by the fact that it happens in silence, without frequent objection. People who write about art, whether as journalists or experts, seem reluctant to take this "mechanism" seriously when they discuss actual exhibitions; there is, certainly, too little emphasis placed on the fact that what is in the exhibition becomes a new touchstone, the most important art of the moment, precisely through its connection with the exhibition – if this is how the exhibition presents it. It makes perfect sense that this would not be underscored by those who "operate" this mechanism, for it would hardly be in their interest to reduce their own status or threaten their "supernatural power". On this level, too, is another reason why creating

10   Boris Groys, who also discusses the exhibition as a legitimising mechanism that today determines what is art, examines this aspect more thoroughly in connection with selection as an artistic process that has been well established for the past 100 years or so. He also reflects on the exhibition's connection with the art installation, for in their selection and placement of objects in a three-dimensional space, the exhibition and the installation are essentially bound to similar principles (Boris Groys, "Multiple Authorship", in *The Manifesta Decade: Debates on Contemporary Art Exhibitions and Biennials in Post-Wall Europe*, Barbara Vanderlinden and Elena Filipovic (eds.), MIT Press, Cambridge, Mass., 2005, pp. 93–95).

11   "If one demands signs, he who performs them in abundance becomes a master for him who demands them. If one questions philosophically, he who can reply becomes a master for the perplexed subject" (Alain Badiou, *Saint Paul: The Foundation of Universalism*, Stanford University Press, Stanford, CA, 2003, p. 59). The quotation is taken out of context, but it describes the existing situation very well in only a few words.

the idea of "the exhibition as nature" is so effective in supporting the curator and the expansion of his power: for the less such a mechanism is exposed, the more capable it is of magic.

The bigger and more important an exhibition is and the more ambitious its promises are, the greater is its power in this regard. In his analysis of documenta, Harald Kimpel wrote about the effect such an exhibition has:

> This, then, is the Midas effect of documenta: the touch by the institution constitutes that "ontological difference" ... which then causes us to treat an "ordinary thing" as an artwork. Like a catalyst, documenta changes the "modality" of material objects. In the touch of the mediating body there occurs an ennobling process from ordinary to artistically perceived production; that which is touched by the documenta myth opens to the aesthetic consciousness.[12]

The curator's transition to artist happens not only in the sense that the act of selection becomes, quite obviously and "naturally", an act of creation, but also in that the curator, through his events, not only links himself with "ordinary" art exhibitions but he also tries as much as possible to approximate the ground-breaking exhibitions and events created by artists. While his creativity, on the one hand, thus derives from an understanding of selection as creation, on the other, it is justified by its direct link to artistic production, from which it also borrows such features as openness, experimentalism, improvisation, intuition, and so on. Such a conceptualisation, then, effectively supports the understanding of the exhibition as a natural and creative process, while the curator also gains the right to have his exhibitions accepted as independent aesthetic statements.

The fact that the curator undoubtedly wants to see and present himself in this image is clearly supported by the "proper" construction of art history mentioned earlier, in which curatorship and curatorial exhibitions are positioned as near as possible to art; meanwhile, the curator presents his work as an entirely direct continuation of the alternative, oppositional artist-organised exhibitions and avant-garde art events of the past. At the same time, the curator situates himself in this tradition also

12   Harald Kimpel, *documenta,* p. 232 (see n. 2).

through his discourse, where he not only announces change – that is, champions the same position claimed by the avant-garde movements – but also adopts the promises of the avant-garde and alternative exhibition-makers, particularly by saying that his projects will be an open space where people can think outside the box, have authentic experiences, distance themselves from existing cultural norms and ideological paradigms, etc.

To better understand the "nature" of this transition, we will first look briefly at the art event as it used to be "when it still was in the domain of artists."

The Artistic Event

After the initial formation in the 19th century of the solo exhibition as a media event through which the artist could effectively address the art public and clearly set forth his position, a broader understanding of this form's great potential developed among artists at the start of the 20th century. It was then that such events – which were more and more "authored" and adapted to the individual needs of the art maker – quickly became the favourite vehicle and tactic of conceptually sophisticated and highly motivated groups and individuals. The principle of acting through well-publicised exhibitions and similar events soon proved to be highly rewarding as well, for it ensured the artists and their work rapid success and a visible position in the art world. If the event was well planned and properly structured, there were immediate results – in particular, artists acquired the much-desired and very appealing charisma of being a great avant-gardist.

These, of course, were not the only attractive features of the event; indeed, it took hold so widely because it offered an entire spectrum of interesting new effects and creative possibilities. In the view of Stephen C. Foster, who edited the book *"Event" Arts and Art Events*, an exhaustive collection of essays on the topic:

The "artistic event" made a live, active response to live "social events", and served as an alternative to the presentation of ideas through a conventional art and literature that had clearly been rendered impotent by the abuses of a dysfunctional and failing society.[13]

In short, the event, on the one hand, appealed to artists as a new form that allowed them to work outside the established norms – for instance, to combine dance, poetry, theatre, visual art and other forms of creativity – while, on the other, its value was greatly increased by the fact that it seemed to operate effectively on both the artistic and political levels.

Examining this second aspect first, we can say that the event as a medium corresponded very well to the strong political ambitions of the early avant-garde movements, for it seemed much better suited to such aims than the more traditional media.[14] Avant-garde artists liked the event because it gave them a chance to make powerful, shocking statements, which almost always elicited heated responses; from this we can gather that they also at once began to see the event as a suitable means for re-interrogating the social functions of art, for addressing the most pressing topics of the day, for raising political questions, and so on. On its most exalted levels, the event was even seen as an effective mechanism for transforming consciousness and bringing about social change; thus it also had a positive effect on the artistic self-esteem of the avant-gardists, for in the art event they possessed a much-desired tool for exerting a positive influence on society.[15]

Because this principle of working was new and, therefore, still unexamined and unexplained, it was all the easier to ascribe such tremendous potential to it. And indeed, it is the preservation of this context that makes the art event so appealing today; every new generation, it seems, can associate it with notions of artistic and political progressivism and features such as directness, genuineness, allusiveness, openness, unconventionality, experimentalism, spontaneity, improvisation, etc. If we seem to find it harder to object to the art event than we do to more con-

13   Stephen C. Foster, "Event Structures and Art Situations," in *"Event" Arts and Art Events*, Stephen C. Foster (ed.), U.M.I. Research Press, Ann Arbour and London, 1988, p. 4.

14   Ibid.

15   The distinctive event is, in its very basis, ideally poised to be connected with change, for in our usual view of history, we understand important events as vehicles of change. History is "created" through important events, which seem to offer the most meaningful point of reference for explaining how and why something changed (ibid., pp. xiii, 6–7).

          Beti Žerovc

ventional artistic forms, this may simply be because the event is not necessarily concentrated around a physical object, which is what criticism usually focuses on because of its clear and unambiguous connections with the market and private property.[16]

The Auratic Event

The features we connect with the event (we have listed some of them) are also associated with its artistic and aesthetic sides. Indeed, the event seems able to offer us a very special, compelling and valuable experience precisely because of its unconventionality, openness, experimentalism, etc. - and because it seems vital and unmediated, something that cannot be fully planned.

Michael Erlhoff's assessment of the event on the artistic level is of particular interest for our discussion. Erlhoff examined the possibility that the event was one of the ways art responded to the loss of its earlier auratic presence, a loss that in the late 19th century threw the art world into a state of deep and lasting crisis concerning art's importance, meaning and possibility of justification, and so also its self-evident status and self-confidence. Because art seemed to be less and less meaningful, because more and more there seemed to be something wrong with it, art, if it did not want to be merely trivial representation, had to change, had to offer something new. And it was the event - which Erlhoff defines in the broadest possible sense - that proved to be an effective new answer to old questions. It proved to be well suited to the deep conservative desire for aura, or something similar, which all the avant-garde movements, one after the other, wanted in some way to retrieve.[17] In the process, artists, perhaps

16 For example, the event is even ascribed the function of purification. In the tradition of Dada and Fluxus, the event serves as a suitable medium for purifying all sorts of things, whether physical objects or non-material structures such as language. I suspect that such powerful defences against criticism derive also from the fact that the event does not really belong to any of the traditional art forms. It is neither literature nor theatre nor even visual art. While critics who write about events might on one occasion assess their poetic aspect and on another their visual art aspect, the event as event always remains somewhere outside all this. In this regard, the event benefits from being permanently in a kind of non-binding category, for given its insufficient elucidation, its powers more easily remain unquestioned.

17 Here I am merely summarising, in a very condensed and simplified way,

quite instinctively, abandoned their focus on the art object as primary and concentrated directly on confronting the public with art. This, indeed, is one of the central themes in the event: the event allows the public to be right where art "happens". With the event, it seemed that the viewer was again experiencing something genuine, true and powerful and was even getting a kind of direct look at the inner workings of art. What is more, not only was the viewer offered the chance to be an eyewitness to creation and genius, but he practically became a co-participant in creation, which meant that he, too, and not just the performer/designer of the event, was guaranteed "true" access to the auratic moment.

The curator, it seems, tries to align his production as closely as possible with just such a principle of perception and effect. This suits him because he has no concrete object of his own that could unobjectionably be declared art – but, with this "calibration" of the exhibition as art event, neither is any "auratic object" needed, for the performer/designer of the event acquires his aura through the event itself. His events become myths, as Erlhoff says,[18] but the curator himself is also clearly invested with an aura, which he not only bestows on his own exhibitions but through which he also effectively consecrates the objects he presents.

By posing his exhibitions as art events, then, the curator gains quite a lot. He consolidates his right to make aesthetic and political statements, while at the same time he reinforces his power of consecration, for, clearly, the aura he thus receives is easily joined with the "aura" that comes from his position as the "master" of the exhibition as the legitimising mechanism that determines what is art. In such a "consecrated" event, too, the collaboration between the curator and the artist more easily appears as something quite natural – we are less curious about how the artist ended up in the show – and they both achieve a high degree of charisma as well. Their "switchability" and the openness of authorship are preserved.

Erlhoff's more thorough discussion (Michael Erlhoff, "Eventually Events: Some Unjudged Sentences", in *"Event" Arts and Art Events*, pp. 283–287. See n. 13).

18   Ibid., p. 285.

The Exhibition as Artwork, the Curator as Artist: A Comparison with Theatre

First published as "Razstava kot umetniško delo, kurator kot umetnik: primerjava z gledališkim področjem" / "The Exhibition as Artwork, the Curator as Artist: A Comparison with Theatre", *Maska* (Ljubljana), vol. 25, no. 133–134, autumn 2010, pp. 78–93.

 Beti Žerovc

In the present discussion, I will attempt to explore parallels between, on the one hand, curatorship and contemporary art exhibitions[1] and, on the other, certain phenomena in the field of theatre that appear related. To that end, I will first begin with a more general introduction, as this will help to locate our topic more concretely within the overall structure of contemporary visual art.

The Contemporary Art System's Structural Focus on the Event

One of the crucial changes that happened in contemporary visual art in the 20th century was the formation of an immense new economy based on money allocated specifically for contemporary art by public funds and private capital; this new economy operates alongside and together with the traditional economy of contemporary art where the people involved, and their respective activities, have mostly relied on income from the marketplace. In the new, young economy, there quickly emerged a broad and multi-branched platform of the most diverse institutions, which not only exhibit, house, and support contemporary art, but also directly commission and produce it. In recent decades, these usually public or non-profit private institutions have been the most vocal and most active agents in the contemporary art field, which is, in terms of the history of the field, something

---

1   When in this discussion I speak about the "exhibition", I am mainly thinking of the large group exhibition in contemporary art, and in particular, the thematic invitational exhibition, in which the curator is able to realise his authorial approach most explicitly.

   For earlier similar discussions that attempt to "take the measure" of the curator, including by comparing his role with related artist roles from other artistic fields, see, for instance, Nathalie Heinich and Michael Pollak, "From Museum Curator to Exhibition Auteur: Inventing a Singular Position", *Thinking about Exhibitions*, Reesa Greenberg, Bruce W. Ferguson, and Sandy Nairne (eds.), Routledge, London and New York, 1996; and Søren Grammel, *Ausstellungsautorschaft: Die Konstruktion der auktorialen Position des Kurators bei Harald Szeemann. Eine Mikroanalyse*, Revolver, Frankfurt am Main, 2005.

quite new, as is also the vital dependence of artists on these institutions, even for their livelihoods. Among other things, these changes and the artist's dependence are linked to the fact that today these institutions are clearly developing in the direction of ensuring a vast supply of constant events in which the physical exhibiting of art is merely part of a greater whole and is itself "packaged" and mediated by all sorts of other events. In this young economy, events are the primary focus, forms, and even objects of exchange; as crucial pillars in an institution's finances, they have become increasingly complex, strategically planned, and carefully stage-managed. Events can occur in the most diverse connections, while the exhibition, with its extraordinary potential for intensifying the eventive aspect on various levels, has become a privileged form in this production. As a rule, the exhibition tries to become, as much as possible, a celebrated and distinguished event in itself, which, in fact, is often done by interconnecting the physical installation with a whole array of related events.

Given such overabundance, the collision of interests among the people who are needed to bring all these events to fruition – funders, organisers, artists, other performers, and so on – is extraordinary, as is, too, the fascination we observe on the part of the public.[2] I should also stress that this structure is encouraged and supported by the media, which are, indeed, a permanent co-participant and, therefore, no less a key player in the system. The media are also among the factors that ensure the intense standardisation of events, in which even the "craziest" ones are first announced, then are carried out in front of an audience, and finally, if lucky, culminate in media reaction (where the rule tends to be "the more, the better").[3]

2   The fact that there are so many art professionals that we make up an audience unto ourselves ensures a decent turnout for specialised events. Research shows, however, that "lay" viewers, too, want to do much more than merely stand and meditate in front of artworks. As key reasons for visiting a museum, people cite the opportunity for socialising and "actively participating in something". See Maren Ziese, *Kuratoren und Besucher: Modelle kuratorisher Praxis in Kunstausstellungen*, transcript Verlag, Bielefeld, 2010, pp. 21–22.

3   As part of this process, art institutions – in addition to their primary tasks of housing and exhibiting works of art – are increasingly becoming the producers of events in which their role *vis-à-vis* exhibitions and their authors is similar to that of institutional theatres. The art institution is usually led by an artistic director, but he is first and foremost a manager, or has a managerial

Because the system is large and very competitive – there is, after all, an enormous amount of money involved as well as many opportunities for work, development, and experimentation – events and their creators go through an intense process of differentiation. In this process, we see, among things, that the art exhibition is developing in the direction of an extremely subjectivised means of expression and, at the same time, that such exhibitions and their curators are able to enjoy extraordinary visibility and attention and reap high awards. This trend is supported, too, by circumstances outside the field, such as, for instance, the general rise in precarious labour. Clearly, this puts further pressure on curators to establish a profile for themselves through their production so as to be more visible on the labour market; not only does this foster carefully stage-managed events, it also indirectly stimulates the diversity and testing of new ideas, pushing events to, and beyond, the limits.

A Comparison of the Theatre Performance and the Art Exhibition, and of the Director and the Curator

The History of the Evolution of the Theatre Director as Comparative Material for the Evolution of the Curator

If we consider the contemporary art system as I have presented it, a comparison with the field of theatre makes sense, since by definition theatre is centred on an artistic event and its treatment.

> figure right next to him. He also has a team of employees, who are turning more and more from a body of art experts into a bureaucratic and organisational apparatus. At the same time, the use of visiting curators is becoming a standard practice. Certain similarities can also be observed between curators and the artistic directors of theatres, and especially of theatre festivals, but this is a topic for a different discussion.

Such a comparison, indeed, seems inevitable when we consider the question of whether the art exhibition might itself be art and the curator an artist (and not merely some undefined "author"), for the person in the theatre whose position toward the theatre performance is similar to that of the curator toward the art exhibition is someone we already consider to be a creative artist. To make my argument as clear as possible, I will use theatre as a kind of contrastive medium in my analysis, focusing on three aspects that, together and separately, seem especially suggestive: the similarities between the theatre performance and the art exhibition, the similarities between the work processes and expressive possibilities of the curator and the theatre director, and – to begin with, briefly and in a very general way – the similarities in the historical development of these two roles. Indeed, it was not so very long ago – in the 19th and 20th centuries – that the theatre director went through his potentially similar transformation from a non-artistic to an artistic figure.[4]

A look at the evolution of the theatre director's vocation is especially useful for our investigation since, like the curator, he obtained his status as an artist by setting himself up in the leading role of an already existing "old" medium with a long tradition in which a fairly large number of established artistic figures were already involved – and in the process, the entire structure of the authorship of the participants was somewhat altered. From a non-established position as the one who organised "stage traffic" and mediated between the playwright and the actors, the director managed to win an artistic position for himself, which, indeed, has proved to be the leading position in relation to what is inevitably a group work, i.e. the theatre performance. It is true, of course, that even before this happened, the theatre performance itself was considered an artistic medium, but it was no more the director's medium than was, until recently, the art exhibition the curator's medium.

Here it is worth pointing out certain circumstances and chains of events in the process that can also tell us something about the rapid rise of curatorship. The period in which the role of the theatre director became more widely established as an ac-

4   For a more detailed history of the profession, and one that goes further back in time, see the entry "Staging" in Patrice Pavis, *Dictionary of the Theatre: Terms, Concepts, and Analysis*, University of Toronto Press, Toronto, 1998.

       Beti Žerovc

cepted artistic position with an expanded range of activities and authorities (from the late 19th to the mid-20th century) was an auspicious time for theatre, when the field was undergoing an extremely rapid and robust institutional expansion on the physical level, while at the same time the complexity and demands of the theatre performance were becoming significantly more intense. There had previously been a much greater standardisation in the means of expression, with a largely conventional enunciation of dialogue and generic painted sets and lighting, but this was increasingly being replaced by a specific expressive approach in which every aspect of the performance had to be developed each time from scratch. In such altered circumstances, it suddenly became necessary to have a person who was able to master the complete whole, someone who from then on would hold all the strings. And it is no surprise that this person quickly accumulated power. It soon became clear that not only did having a director make it easier to produce a play, but also that the director's events had a greater impact; they were more ambitious, more profiled, and full of attractive innovations that aroused general attention and provoked discussion in the press. Because of such positive results and benefits for the entire production, the director's *raison d'être* solidified very quickly and we can more easily understand why actors and playwrights – that is, the people who had the most to lose with the rise of the director – had the least problems accepting his role. Since they were directly dependent on the play getting a good response, and were the ones most familiar with the actual state of affairs, they were naturally the first to agree to work with the director and did not see his interventions only as an encroachment on their artistic liberty and integrity.

Reviewing history, we can also see that, when the theatre director tried very intensely to establish his ideas and authority, he encountered in his evolution many of the same kind of obstacles and difficulties on the institutional level as the curator does. For instance, he felt "compelled" to distance himself from the established institutions and operate as much as possible as an independent production unit, either alone or with his own group. Many of the same criticisms that today are aimed at curators were once aimed at overly aggressive theatre directors. It is only today that the consensus view is positive about the rise of the director and the medium's autonomisation in his hands, but there was a time in the Western world when the notion of a theatre without the solid basis of a script and clear story line seemed as implausible and nonsensical as did, until recently, the notion of exhibitions without artworks or with works that are specially commissioned for them.

But interestingly, if we take the evolution of the theatre performance and the director as a projection for the future of visual art, it might actually reassure "curatorial sceptics". While it seems obvious that the autonomisation of the medium (the theatre performance) necessarily increased the importance of the creators (the directors), and vice versa, the autonomisation of the director has meant greater autonomisation of the performance – at the same time, it is also obvious that this in no way means the end of previously established roles and practices, nor the end of "classic" repertory theatre. Old and new have found ways to coexist.

Comparing the Theatre Performance and the Art Exhibition

In contrast to earlier institutional exhibitions of contemporary art, where the standardised events were the opening and the occasional guided tour and where the specifically conceived installation and concept of the exhibition were never themselves in the forefront, today the art exhibition can be a distinctly independent entity and authored event, carefully calculated in all aspects to achieve maximum impact with the viewer (and with the media) – all of which brings it very close to resembling the theatre performance. Of course, I am not saying at all that the two are identical, but only that the curated group exhibition, and especially the thematic exhibition, can be very similar to the theatre performance as a composite stage-managed event in which the mediation of certain ideas, narratives, experiences, or messages is carried out through careful dramaturgical guidance of the viewer's attention. Inevitably, such a structure opens itself up to dramaturgy, theatricality, and multimediality, in the accretion of (theatre-like) levels of expression that have to be directed and executed in a coordinated way in order to successfully create an

 Beti Žerovc

integrated whole.⁵ To put it somewhat differently, we could say that the art exhibition today is more like a theatre performance than it is like itself a few decades ago, when there were only a few established criteria for selecting and, simultaneously, structuring the installation – such as chronology, nationality, or school – which supplemented decisions such as "how much space should go between the artworks when we hang them."⁶

A development on a different level, and one that reinforces the similarity between the theatre performance and the art exhibition, is the very real process of homogenising the means and strategies of expression, which were once field-specific but today are available to both directors and curators. If we are to grasp this point, we must not view the theatre performance in the traditional way but rather in the sense of what recent theatre, and in particular, the contemporary postdramatic theatre, is presenting, while we must take the art exhibition seriously as an increasingly autonomous and flexible medium and not merely a "dead vehicle" for presenting the works of artists. If we adopt such a view, we will see that both media have long ago overflowed their venues and no longer happen solely on the stage or on walls and pedestals; their permanent autonomisation has already completely obliterated the boundaries of what goes where and what happens where. In the process, each of these creative spheres borrows techniques, expressive means, and strategies from the other very freely – but here we should remember that the person in the art field who does the borrowing is not only the artist but also the curator, or rather, the two often do it in tandem, with the curator "casting" and "producing" a specific type of artist. The fact that, for instance, performance art, actions, and similar phenomena do not just happen by themselves but primarily occur in the context of exhibitions changes not only visual art

---

5   The written plans for the exhibition are often in the form of a document, similar to a scenario, which in English-speaking countries is, perhaps not coincidentally, called a "script".

6   This last statement is, of course, a generalisation, but we can say that in this area, too, the exceptions prove the rule. I should mention also that, historically, the curator's authorial exhibition should be first compared to similar ambitious exhibition projects by artists, but I will not address these here, as I am limiting my discussion to a comparison with theatre. Before the 1960s, institutional art custodians made only very rare appearances in the history of innovative exhibition making.

explicitly but also the medium of the exhibition, which now becomes something "live" that is viewed collectively.

Similarly, in the theatre performance – which long ago ceased to be necessarily a single, unified "object" that can be encompassed by the viewer's gaze – "opposite" strategies and techniques can be applied. Among other things, a theatre performance can work "like a gallery", as a total installation, or instead of being received collectively it can seek "one-on-one" contact with the viewer, or it can unfold through different spaces, similar to the way the art viewer moves through a gallery.

We could list many more borrowings between the two fields, on various levels of production, increasing to the point of total interchangeability between the exhibition and the theatre performance. When the exhibition, which no longer requires any emphasis on pre-existing artworks, or even on artworks at all, strays from its traditional relationships with artworks – just as the postdramatic theatre of the 20th century strayed from the prescribed text of the playwright – it often moves into a postdramatic-like organisation of the viewer's experience. Here I am thinking of such exhibitions as *Repetition Island* (Centre Georges Pompidou, 2010) or *Hypnotic Show* (various locations), by the curator Raimundas Malasauskas, the stage-managed "narrating fortress" at Manifesta in the Tyrol in 2008, or the exhibition *Shopping*, which among other things explicitly guided and "walked" the viewer through the shopping streets of Vienna (Generali Foundation, 2001).[7]

Of course, it is only in extreme cases that we get the total merging and interchangeability of the theatre performance and the art exhibition, but the consequences of these processes can be felt on a general basis as well.[8] Thus, a general characteristic of

7   In *Repetition Island*, the same day-long programme of activities was repeated at the exhibition site every day for a week. At the Tyrolean Manifesta, an abandoned fortress became a space that was entirely "directed" by the curators. Among other things, as visitors moved through the fortress, they heard recorded narratives that various cultural figures had written at the curators' request.

8   We can observe remarkable similarities in the work processes and methods between the invitational thematic exhibition and what is known as "devised theatre", which, because of their common principle of inviting participants to work together on a selected theme, have both developed processual methods of production that are clearly related. (Perhaps the right term for such art shows would be "devised exhibitions"?) At the same time, both have created similar forms of a largely collective authorship that shifts back and

both fields is the awareness that methods are no longer field-specific, that it is fully expected and accepted that the art curator or theatre director can use any means whatsoever to address us, while it is primarily the artistic venue that serves as an identifying frame to demarcate artistic perception from ordinary perception.

Given all of the above, it is not surprising that the definitions offered by a number of theatre theorists about what is happening in today's theatre remind us of the feelings we experience in our reception of and relationship to art exhibitions. Hans-Thies Lehmann, for example, says:

> Theatre means the collectively spent and used up lifetime in the collectively breathed air of that space in which the performing *and* the spectating take place. The emission and reception of signs and signals take place simultaneously. The theatre performance turns the behaviour on stage and in the auditorium into a *joint text*, a "text" even if there is no spoken dialogue on stage or between actors and audience.[9]

He goes on to say that it is the theatre situation itself that "forms a whole made up of evident and hidden communicative processes."[10]

Comparing the Director's and Curator's Work Processes and Means of Expression

My thinking on this topic was particularly prompted when I noticed an unusual phenomenon: theatre directors in Slovenia were not only often serving as curators of art exhibitions and related

forth between the collaboration of all participants together and the centralised control maintained by the director or curator. Here, broader changes stand out visibly in the area of authorship in visual art, in which not only is the curator becoming an author, but a collective authorship of various types of artists, and others as well, is also being established alongside the exhibition.

9   Hans-Thies Lehmann, *Postdramatic Theatre*, Routledge, Abingdon and New York, 2006, p. 17.

10   Ibid.

projects, but they were even staging exhibitions as theatre performances, that is, as their own explicitly artistic production. So I decided to find out why theatre directors were interested in a medium that did not (yet) have the accepted status of an artistic medium in the visual art field. A number of directors and choreographers took part in my research, but here I will mention only the four for whom, we might say, this phenomenon appears most explicitly: Janez Janša (the former Emil Hrvatin), Barbara Novaković, Mare Bulc, and Bojan Jablanovec.[11] There is not a great deal of material, nor could there be given the circumstances of Slovenia, so I am not at all claiming this as a significant pattern. But it does offer very suggestive material that can help us consider the question of the exhibition as an art form and the curator as an artist. Clearly, something that curators and visual art experts prefer to see as material for scholarly treatment or as a tool and aid in their work can also be seen as a means of expression that offers great potential for developing one's own personal style and narrative.

With everyone I interviewed, the first thing that very quickly became clear with regard to the differences between the theatre performance and the art exhibition was that, when curating and "staging" art exhibitions, the directors did not see themselves as doing "non-artistic" work as "non-artists" – that was simply not how they felt the situation. They saw themselves as doing the same thing they always did, only with somewhat different means: they experienced the whole process as doing their usual artistic work. Their attitude was that there are no "wrong" media: the important thing was to find the right medium for the best expression of their ideas. At the same time, they did not have any sense or understanding of the curator as a lower-ranked, or weaker, author or artist, although they had heard about the curator's undefined position and the critical discourse on this topic in the visual art field. There were also a few explicit references about this in their production; one of the directors (Mare Bulc) even devoted a project specifically to reflecting on the curator's powerful position as an author and its similarity to that of the theatre director.

11   In my research, among other things, I conducted personal interviews, and some of the theatre directors, including the four I mention, also contributed their own written views on this phenomenon or participated in short written interviews.

 Beti Žerovc

My two main direct questions – What makes the curator's work artistic? and: Do they see any clear differences whatsoever between the exhibition and the theatre performance on the artistic level? – did not elicit any immediate, definitive answers. The directors focused on analysing and comparing the work processes in the two media and came up with a very interesting and suggestive way to do this: they analysed and schematised their own work process when directing theatre and then applied this scheme to curating and exhibitions and tried to find the differences between them. What was revealed was a clear similarity between directing and curating: to achieve the final result, curating requires doing most of the same tasks that the director does for the theatre performance. Even directors with the dual experience of both curating exhibitions and directing exhibitions could not find any substantial differences in the tasks they saw as essential once the basic concept was established: selecting the people you want to work with, delegating work and authority, constantly guiding everyone involved, and successfully coordinating all the parts and participants to produce an integrated whole. Differences became more evident only on the level of the specific characteristics and expressive possibilities of the medium, and the directors often cited these aspects, in fact, as their primary reason for deciding to work in the exhibition format.

These directors' dissection of their work processes, for which they usually used the concrete examples of their own productions, revealed the broad and remarkable palette of expressive levels and means that are available to the curator for conveying his messages and ideas and that allow him to take a distinctly personal and creative approach in doing so, even when he bases the content on some narrow art-historical question. At the same time, these expressive possibilities allow the curator, no less than the theatre director, to create his own personal poetics and style, for he can implement extremely personal (and therefore also very characteristic) choices and decisions on the most diverse levels in the execution of his production, and he can do so through a wide variety of methods. These numerous methods he can use entirely at will; as a rule, they all offer him extensive possibilities for intensification and nuance.[12]

12 For comparison: "The 'style' or rather the palette of stylistic traits of post-
    dramatic theatre demonstrates the following characteristic traits: parataxis,
    simultaneity, play with the density of signs, musicalization, visual dramat-

Apart from choosing the basic idea of the exhibition, the directors cited primarily the incorporation of the works and poetics of the chosen artists as a powerful narratological, expressive, and stylistic element in their work on an exhibition – or in the work of curators in general. Here the story of the exhibition could be further intensified and nuanced through the number of works from individual artists, their size, serial nature, the closeness or disparity of their dates of origin, and the like, as well as characteristic ways in which the works were installed, grouped, and juxtaposed, their correlations and dialogues. It was very clear to the directors that the curator himself also essentially defines these works through the context of the whole installation; in doing so, he can set himself in the foreground or background, be pedagogue or agitator, use a minimalistic or classical style, and so on – most often in accord with his typical approach. To this end, he has available numerous physical tools that allow him to actively enter the installation in a physical way as well. He can, for instance, add various inscriptions and comments, use lighting or colour in the exhibition architecture, add sounds and noise – or do none of these things. I should mention that the theatre directors obviously found it very attractive to work with "non-living material",[13] not only because this allowed them to be very precise but mainly because such work happens without the kind of stressful mediation that can often happen where a director has trouble finding the right actor and directing him in the right way so he realises the director's vision.[14]

The directors also experienced the selection and organisation of the space of the event as powerful dramaturgical elements. They described staging the viewer's journey through the install-

urgy, physicality, irruption of the real, situation/event. (In this phenomenology of postdramatic signs I will only marginally discuss language, voice and text….)", Hans-Thies Lehmann, *Postdramatic Theatre*, p. 86 (see n. 9).

13 The directors were also of course interested in the art object in terms of its sale potential and in the way it tangibly places the artist in history.

14 Some of the directors were also very enthusiastic about their direct work with visual artists. They noted that visual artists did not work from instructions as actors do but rather behaved with self-assurance and as the director's equals, while at the same time they also worked very well as a collective. Thus, the production developed as a collaboration among equals, with an entirely different erotics and productivity. This last observation again speaks to the fact that, while the visual art field has perhaps not yet moved into collective work on a cognitive and nominal level, many visual artists (together with curators) have been working in this manner for a long time.

ation as a serious directorial challenge that, based on what they have seen in exhibitions, is often handled too casually and with little imagination.[15]

Primarily, however, the directors liked the exhibition's extraordinary possibilities for conveying a story or message, for it can mix together very different kinds of media in legitimate and accepted ways. Thus, the "non-living material", which in itself is quite varied and has a specific aura, can be combined with live presence, ranging from performers to lecturers, from parties at night to all-day symposia, and so on. An enormous amount of material can be contained in a single art exhibition (more than in a theatre performance), and this can be presented much more asynchronically than in a play, in parallel lines or worlds, which may be connected very loosely and, above all, differently from theatre direction.[16] The directors were generally thrilled by the wide range of possibilities for organising the viewer's time, a task that is, as it were, doubled in the art exhibition, for alongside the organisation of the time spent in the installation itself, there is also the organisation of time (far more extensive than in the theatre performance) for everything else connected with the event as a whole. Here the curator has, as a rule, a month or two to work with – the whole duration of the exhibition – and he can place the different events, dispersed over time, either within the installation itself or outside of it.[17]

15   Similarly, they described the choice of venue for the installation and events as an extremely important determining factor: it makes a critical difference whether something takes place in an established art institution, the curator's own kitchen, an old factory, or a remote abandoned fortress, since the venues in themselves can make a very strong impression on us. Given the ambivalent nature of some of the projects we discussed – these "theatre performances/ art exhibitions" – the directors often described their dilemma in deciding whether a theatre or a gallery was the most suitable place for these shows.

16   Theatre, it seems, still requires directors to intensely synthesise the material; the condensation and linearisation of time are "imposed" on them to a much greater degree.

17   In contemporary curatorial practice, we do not talk enough about the structuring of the viewer's time; in my research, however, this proved to be a very important topic. Consider the significance of the time structure in the project *Via MSU Zagreb*, by Bojan Jablanovec and the group Via Negativa, which revolves around the fact that performances happen simultaneously in various parts of the exhibition venue and the viewer cannot see all of them (Museum of Contemporary Art, Zagreb, 2010), or the emphatic time structure of *Repetition Island*, in which the same events are repeated every day for a week (see n. 7).

To top it all off, as part of this complete whole, the curator also interprets and explains his product in public – and this is even expected of him – literally imposing his understanding on the viewer through catalogues or guided tours, or even through poetry, collections of political texts, labels on cigarette boxes, and all kinds of other things. It was obvious that this aspect of the curator's work was of exceptional interest to the directors; but at the same time, they found it difficult, first, to clearly define what this was, and then to bring it into their formatting of the exhibition. In our conversations, we often found ourselves returning to the idea that the specificity of the curator's expression lies precisely in the fact that, along with the event itself, he also establishes a context for interpreting it, that along with the presented content he also projects a certain relationship toward it, creates an opinion about it, or an opinion that is associated with it.

To judge from my interviews with the theatre directors, the art exhibition can without question be a very complex artistic medium, one that offers expressive means and possibilities that are nothing short of extraordinary. In the discussion above, of course, I have hardly come close to listing all of these; my main desire was to illustrate the specific principle of working with the exhibition, and the similarities and differences between art curating and theatre directing. Also worth mentioning, at times, I had the impression that these directors, when curating, felt as if they were in a shop where there's "everything you could ever want", as if the medium allowed them to do even more than they could imagine.

Turning from the views of theatre directors to the curator's home territory, we in fact see that curators who characteristically and more explicitly emphasise their own subjective choices and narratives are felt to be more artistic by the audience for contemporary art. It would appear that, despite any vocal deprecations, we enthusiastically honour this kind of behaviour, and the development of a personal style, in the curator just as much as in the artist. The curator receives a large turnout for his exhibitions and a great deal of media attention, while institutions reward him by appointing him to curate prestigious events. We need only remember how much attention was given the declaratively artistic Jan Hoet, or the huge stylistic vogue of the "political commissariat" of curators that dominated the art world in the 1990s.

          Beti Žerovc

Just as with artists, we are drawn to curators' conceptual and formal innovations; it seems we accept as most artistic those curators who recognisably change their medium and the established practice of doing things. In such cases, auratisation is at its peak and the names of these curators are oftentimes today no less famous than artists' names.[18]

A Few Words About the Differences

Listing the curator's potential expressive means also led me to certain noticeable differences between the theatre director and the curator; similarly, there began to appear certain reasons that keep the curator from crossing over, on the declarative level, to the status of artist.

Although, like the theatre performance, the curator's medium has a certain characteristic and, especially, limited spatial and temporal range, and is a temporary constellation that later breaks into separate parts, it is nevertheless different, and all these things are in a way less true or only partly true for exhibitions.[19] During the exhibition's physical existence, it is not (like the theatre performance) merely a more or less unified whole that the viewer can consume in two hours; rather, it is stretched out over a long period of time, and in this broad expanse of time

18 Are we really all that mistaken when we respond to the question "Who is the most famous living Swiss artist now that Szeemann has died?" by saying, "Hans Ulrich Obrist"? The truth is that curators have to know how to present their innovations effectively. In the process, certain aspects sometimes appear that remind us of artistic innovations: self-referentiality and reflecting on the medium itself, the transfer of artists' exhibition practices into curatorship (which we often see with Obrist), etc.

19 Compare Beatrice von Bismarck, "Haltloses Ausstellen: Politiken des künstlerischen Kuratierens", in *The Artist as …*, Matthias Michalka (ed.), Museum Moderner Kunst Stiftung Ludwig, Vienna, 2006, pp. 38–39. One thing that makes the exhibition very different from the theatre performance is the catalogue, which, compared to the theatre programme, is much more successful at keeping the exhibition alive after it has closed. Through it, the exhibited works remain, in a way, together for all time, and it can serve as a permanent template, a guide for potential reproductions, which can be distributed all over the world. Thus the catalogue is the exhibition's "functional tail" by which it maintains contact with historicisation and the marketplace.

viewers can "load up their plates" in various ways. The exhibition usually has different offerings for different viewers: "lay" viewers will choose only the installation and guided tour, and maybe the creative workshop for the kids; performance aficionados won't bother looking seriously at the installation at all but instead will come in the evenings, when the performers they fancy are scheduled; while art professionals might do everything, including the symposium.

The complexity of the medium is further increased by the fact that not only are the component parts of the exhibition extremely varied, they have entirely different natures: some things are art, others are not. The viewer is expected to switch entirely automatically from the perception of art to real life or scholarly discourse, and back again. While the reception of such events is not yet fully researched, most of what has been discovered on the topic tends toward the conclusion that the event as a whole drifts into the realm of art perception.

Although in our discussion we, too, have not resolved the ontological status of the art exhibition, a comparison with the theatre performance helps us, I think, to be more aware of certain aspects of the medium that are too little noticed; more importantly, it helps us move forward in our thinking about exhibitions from dealing only with the installations themselves. If we truly wish to understand what it is we do when we make an art exhibition, we have no choice but to begin discussing the exhibition medium as comprehensively as possible and to think seriously about how the production of art today, through its extraordinary power to homogenise multiplicities ("to make one out of many"), produces the event.

Similarly, the comparison with the theatre director should also help us see the large degree of very subjective and artistic content in the curator's work. However: despite the great similarities between the two fields, the comparison does not come out even – primarily, it seems, because the art system itself, despite its desire for grandiose events, also wants to retain the curator (at least nominally) in the position of an expert, for thus it can most easily capitalise on his production and messages. Unlike the theatre director, the curator has set himself up in a medium that also has explicitly functional, non-artistic tasks inscribed on its template; for instance, even if he is confessing his innermost personal pain and saying so aloud, the current general structure

     Beti Žerovc

and understanding of the curator's position ensure that he is at the same time making some pronouncement about what good art is and, above all, that his opinions are taken as "objective", as expert views on the present society and its culture. It is the curators themselves who are often responsible for this kind of "packaging", for the art system's highest rewards go to the schizophrenic stances they assume in stage-managing grandiose events, even as they enthusiastically proclaim these events to be "objective" in content and selection. And then when curators say they are guided in this objectivity by a moral imperative, or by the logic of "the objective through the subjective", rarely does anyone ask what this actually means.

Interview with Walter Benjamin

First published as "My Dear, This Is Not What It Seems To Be: An Interview with Walter Benjamin" / "Meine Liebe, das ist nicht das, was es zu sein scheint: Ein Interview mit Walter Benjamin", in *What Is Modern Art? (Group Show)*, Inke Arns and Walter Benjamin (eds.), exh. cat., Künstlerhaus Bethanien, Berlin, 2006, pp. 28-34, 69-76.

 Beti Žerovc

An artist whose insistence on anonymity allows him to assume different identities for his projects was of particular interest for my research because for decades he has been dealing intensively with the constructed nature of the story of modern art and its supreme achievements, a story that is usually taken for granted. The mediated nature of art, the construction of the canon and narrative of art, the roles different people play in this connection, and similar issues are things his work constantly reflects, plays with, sets in new relations, and removes from established contexts. In an unusual game of charades, disguises, mystifications, copying, switching identities, and so on – where we can always sense both a kind of idealising and criticalness toward what he addresses – he develops his characteristic and alluring recreations of important past art events, venues, and artworks, which while following historical facts, do so in entirely idiosyncratic ways.

Thoughts about the constructedness of art and art history served as the main starting point of our conversation, inasmuch as the contemporary art curator is crucially involved in these processes – his positioning makes his potential in this direction greater than that of any previous art figure. Our conversation provides further insight into a question touched on in preceding chapters, namely: how is it that the curator is not only the principal organiser of the things that happen in the contemporary art field but is also their main interpreter, equipped with an extraordinary arsenal of ways to communicate and establish meaning? The story Walter Benjamin tells draws us almost seductively into reflections on the curator's ability to delineate and establish how a certain art is perceived, and paints for us – quite calmly and without hesitation, and thus with great effect – a vivid picture of famous historical examples of the political use of contemporary art.

A second, and for me very important, aspect of this interview is the fact that Benjamin was one of the few people I interviewed who was willing to seriously discuss the analogies between institutional and ecclesiastical art. It is, of course, well known that art institutions incorporate an enormous body of religious and ritualistic objects. But it is rarer to encounter consideration of the long-term effects of this situation, and people generally avoid questions about whether other aspects and elements of religious practice also find their way into art institutions.

The interview was recorded in June 2005 in Ljubljana, where the artist stopped on his way back from the Venice Biennial to his hometown of Belgrade (although most of the time he lives in New York). As an interesting point about my interviewee's identity, I should note that before the interview he himself did not yet know who he would be and the "Walter Benjamin" identity emerged only during our conversation.

———————————

In recent years, the artworks shown at the most important biennials (Biennial of Sydney, Whitney Biennial, Venice Biennial) have included re-creations of important artistic events of the past. I'm wondering why people re-create events in this way at all and why they opt to stage this or that event in particular. But of course, I'm also wondering why I am speaking to "Walter Benjamin".

> Obviously, the name I took for this conversation refers to the well-known early 20th century philosopher; but it also refers to the same Walter Benjamin who gave a lecture in Ljubljana in 1986 entitled "Mondrian '63–'96", a lecture that was about Mondrian's paintings dated between 1963 and 1996. It is the same Benjamin whose statement "Copies are memories" served as a motto for the *Americans 64* exhibit at the Arsenale in Venice this year. I not only had a chance to see most of the works and exhibits we are going to talk about, but also I learned a lot by seeking to understand them, trying to explain them to myself. I assume we are talking about (authorless) projects like the *International Exhibition of Modern Art* (dated 2013), the Salon de Fleurus in New York (established in 1992), the small-scale Museum of Modern Art (dated 1936 and attributed to Alfred Barr, Jr.), the Museum of American Art that recently opened in Berlin and, finally, the Museum of American Art's *Americans 64* collection only just shown at the Arsenale. The theme of this last exhibit is American representation at the Venice Biennial 1964.

Yes, these are the projects I meant. Why re-create specifically these projects?

> As you have already said, the themes of these works are clearly some events that are important for the Art Historical narrative. For example, Gertrude Stein's salon in Paris

     Beti Žerovc

and the Museum of Modern Art in New York could be understood as American interpretations of European modern art. It seems that it was Gertrude Stein's salon where certain works by Cézanne, Matisse and Picasso were exhibited for the first time (1905). Alfred Barr Jr. was only three years old back then. From today's perspective, Gertrude Stein appears as a proto-curator, while her salon looks like a precursor of the Museum of Modern Art. Until recently, MoMA's permanent exhibit started with Cézanne, from whom the story then splits into Fauvism (Matisse) on the one hand and Cubism (Picasso) on the other.

Conversely, the theme of the Museum of American Art in Berlin is all about the "invasion" of post-war Europe by American art. The museum's collection is built around four travelling exhibitions curated by Dorothy Miller in the 1950s. It is about the European reception of American modernism and the gradual expansion of American art, which was in a way officially recognised by the awarding of the Grand Prize to Rauschenberg at the Venice Biennial of 1964. I would say that, *de facto*, these events shaped the narrative of 20th century modern art, especially Barr's concept of the Museum of Modern Art, as conceived at the 1936 exhibition *Cubism and Abstract Art*. Seemingly, it is still not entirely clear that here Alfred Barr was not acting as a chronologist, recording events as they unfolded before his eyes, but as someone who retroactively constructs (or invents) a narrative. It is this particular narrative of modern art that subsequently became dominant. Barr didn't only manage to historicise the first three decades of 20th century art at this show, but later assembled and arranged MoMA's permanent exhibit according to this scheme as well, so that the exhibition *Cubism and Abstract Art* served as the blueprint for MoMA for many years to come.

Of course, all of this makes for an interesting story. But then again, it is no more than a story. An artwork that takes that story as its subject matter, however, is something completely different. It is a material (physical) reflection (interpretation) of that story. In fact, this work contains its own context, its own narrative, so that you don't need additional clues if you know modern Art History. You don't even need to know who the authors of these works are. It is questionable if the notion of the "author" is even applicable.

There is a good chance that these works are not going to be seen as art at all. The fact that they are shown within an art context today does not imply that they could only be seen as works of art. This is why it is important that, for the time being, both the Museum of American Art in Berlin and the Salon de Fleurus in New York are located in private spaces. They attempt to gain modest visibility without seeking total incorporation into the art world, meaning that their reading doesn't only take place with the context of art.

But do they really want to resist incorporation into the art world? What I mean is that they don't seem to be trying very hard; they were included in the last two Venice Biennials, and were also present at the Whitney Biennial and the Biennial of Sydney some years ago, etc.

> They are definitely shown in the art context, but what other venues are there today for such works/ideas? As I said, the fact they are shown in the art context doesn't mean that they are works of art. A group of visitors at the Arsenale talking in front of the Museum of American Art exhibit used the word *Meta-Kunst* [*meta-art*]. This might be an appropriate term. If Art History as a narrative becomes the internal subject matter of a work (becoming its inner narrative), if it is contained within that work, then this immediately opens a possibility for a position "outside" of Art History. This would, in fact, be a meta-position in relation to Art History.

I don't have a problem with the fact that these works could also be seen as something else one day. That could be true. But for now, the situation is that these works are, in fact, accepted by the art system; they are understood, written about, exhibited, and have a price as artworks and not as something else.

> Yes, of course. They are definitely perceived as more or less interesting works of art. But there could be another explanation. When, for example, Copernicus wrote his treatise on the movements of celestial bodies, it was not a scientific but a theological paper, because back then there was no science, no scientific infrastructure, no scientific language. Basically, there was only one dominant platform (ideology) with a developed physical and conceptual infrastructure, namely, Christianity. It took several centuries to fully develop another position (platform), which we call science today.

Today, similarly, Art History is the dominant narrative, and there is no other platform or infrastructure from which you could "read" these works in any other way. This is the limitation of the time we live in. It is why I think these works are only seen as art today. Not because they are inherently artworks. The very fact that those visitors could see it as *Meta-Kunst* [*meta-art*], shows that, even today, some people don't see it as *Kunst* [*art*].

It may well be that Art is a concept that only has meaning within Art History. It has no meaning, or might have a different meaning, outside of Art History. The way, let's say, that the notion of God has a different meaning for a believer and a non-believer. Take, for example, the notion of "African art". It was just recently (in the last 100 years) incorporated into the Art Historical narrative, almost as an appendix, along with several other non-Western traditions. This could be understood as some kind of "positive colonialism", where the "other" is treated "equally but on our own terms." Here, Art History has appropriated the production of ("ritual") objects (masks, sculptures) from Africa and given them the name of art. But within those societies where these objects were produced, they had and perhaps still have another meaning and purpose that has nothing to do with the concept of art, which is a Western invention. I think these objects are works of art only in the art books and art museums, but they are also something else when they are used as "decoration" or in "rituals" within the societies that produce them.

However, we should be aware that history didn't only colonise the "others". First of all, it colonised the past of the very society within which it was conceived and articulated. This is why there is a similarity between "African art" and "Christian art". Within Art History, objects (paintings, sculptures, frescos, icons, etc.) that were produced as illustrations or reflections of the Christian narrative are named as art, while, within the Christian universe, these are sacred, religious objects, objects of worship. A Christian painting is primarily a religious object. When you apply the term art to it, you have already moved to another discourse, another narrative.

If you have a painting representing the Madonna and Child in a church and you are a believer, you will immediately know what you're looking at. The Madonna and that

Child are both real characters for you, since these are the main characters in your story, the Christian story. If we now establish another story, like Art History, materialised in the form of the Museum, and we move this painting to the Museum, then "the Madonna" and "the Child" are no longer this new story's leading characters. Now Raphael the artist and his painting *Madonna and Child* are important as (unique and original) protagonists. This is how you actually change the meaning of the same object by changing the narrative in which it plays a role. A painting that is a religious object in the Christian story becomes an object of art in Art History. Raphael, who doesn't exist in the Christian story at all, appears as an important character in Art History. We see how the same painting means one thing for those who believe in the Christian story and something else for those who believe in Art History. Within the Christian universe, there is only one narrative that is both inside and outside of the painting. This painting is practically submerged in its own narrative and there is only one possible reading of it within that universe. But when we see the same painting exhibited in the Museum, we face two parallel narratives. One is its theme, its internal (Christian) story and another is its external story, namely, Art History and its meta-narrative. If the Church is a materialised "position", then the Museum is a materialised "meta-position" in relation to it.

There is another point that is also important. Not all objects that are called works of art today have the same nature. We should distinguish between at least two main groups. One group includes objects manufactured *before* the Museum and Art History were established. Though these objects were produced beforehand, they were retroactively selected to illustrate this new narrative and "promoted" to the status of artworks in the process, regardless of their previous meaning and function. Another group consists of objects produced *after* the Museum and Art History were established. Perhaps those objects conceived inside the "field" of Art History and the Museum are the only *real* works of art. They were produced exclusively to *be* works of art, to be included in the Museum and in Art History. Somehow, this group of works coincides with what we call modern art in a broader sense (indicating roughly the last two centuries).

Also, we should distinguish those works of 20th century modern art produced before the 1936 exhibition *Cubism and Abstract Art*, which became a blueprint for the MoMA display, from those works produced afterwards under MoMA's influence. Modern art before 1936 was made and interpreted within the context of a 19th century narrative based on "national schools". Many of the same works and movements were included in Alfred Barr's "international movements" narrative. This inevitably changed their interpretation. Thus, the production and interpretation of modern (abstract) art after World War II, which took place under the influence of MoMA, appeared to be the continuation of its (i.e. Barr's) narrative.

Today, we should start thinking about how to define a position (platform) that represents a meta-position in relation to Art History and thus a meta-meta-position in relation to the Christian narrative. In other words, the question is how to move beyond Art History, how to establish another platform from which we could see Art History from the outside. The point is not to forget Art History and its Museums but rather to place them into a new context.

This is why those works that have Art History as their subject might help us in establishing this meta-position. Based on copies, these authorless works contain the narrative of Art History as something "buried" within the work itself, together with the notions of the Artist and Artwork as unique entities. We can see that the subject matter or internal narrative of such works *is* Art History. But it is still unclear what the meta-narrative for this work could be. Basically, it has yet to be established. On this meta-level, it will, of course, still be possible to use notions like art, artist, work of art, art history, but they'll have quite a different meaning, and will probably not be that important. In other words, they will not be the meta-position's formative notions.

So, the fact that these works are shown within the art context and that they came out of the art context does not mean that this is the only way they can be read. Furthermore, I do not think that this is the proper way to read them. I am more and more convinced that they are, in fact, not works of art.

So, in an exhibition like the last Venice Biennial, everything around the exhibit *Americans 64* was art and …

> Absolutely. Out of everything shown at the Arsenale, I think only the exhibit *Americans 64* was not a Work of Art. That also explains why the notion of an artist (author) was not necessary. It does not belong to that story. I don't know whether the visitors are going to see it as an artwork or not, but the fact that it is shown within the art context doesn't necessarily mean that it is an artwork at all. It is, in a way, the opposite situation of the one established by Duchamp's ready-made, which is still dominant today: "anything shown within the art context is a Work of Art." Here we have something that is shown in the art context, and that is even *about* art, but most probably is not a Work of Art.

But claiming a special status for these works just doesn't seem to be enough, especially if everything else concerning them is done "by the book". Also, precisely this stubborn claim of a special position somehow seems typical of the existing narrative of art history. You know, one of the fundamental sociological rules says, don't just pay attention to what people say about what they do, but first check what they do in reality. Since you were very much involved when these projects were prepared and exhibited, you must have had plenty of chances to observe both the people who participated in them as well as the visitors who looked at them. So, based on your observations, what do these projects "do" to these people? Do they become suspicious and critical, or do they enjoy them as nostalgic "theme parks"?

> I assume that people involved in these projects take on roles such as "doorman", "technical assistant", "volunteer", etc., because unlike an "artist" or a "curator," these are non-creative roles. Also, as I said before, the notion of the "artist" belongs to the Art Historical narrative itself, while the "curator" and the "art historian" are storytellers (narrators) of a kind. Art historians usually tell the story through texts, while curators tell it through exhibitions. (Alfred Barr, for example, was both).
>
> As for the visitors, different people react differently. It is like reading a text that has different layers of reading. For some visitors, these projects are probably "nostalgic theme parks", and this reading is absolutely legitimate. Some people

    Beti Žerovc

just go through these exhibits without thinking about what they're looking at as if they were walking through a familiar landscape, since most of these images are well-known icons. But then, some get confused when they realise what they're looking at is not what they see. Once, when I was standing near the entrance of the *Armory Show* exhibit in Venice (2003), I noticed an elderly gentleman with his wife both standing at the entrance looking at the entire show in front of them. Then, at one point, he turned to his wife and said: "My dear, this is not what it seems to be." And I said to myself: Exactly, all this is not what it seems to be.

So, you think the people who make these projects want the visitors to get confused? Does this disorientation already provide a means of reaching another level, a meta-level?

> Confusion is sometimes the first step towards learning or re-learning. In the Museum of American Art in Berlin, for example, you have two rooms. In one room, there are paintings of the pages of the catalogues of four American exhibitions that were exported to Europe in the 1950s. In the same room is also a Museum of Modern Art, 2 x 2 m in size. Many think it's a kind of a model, but it is in fact the real Museum of Modern Art, in a way more so than the one in New York. Another room looks like a living room from the 1950s with large paintings/copies of Kline, Rothko, Pollock, Gottlieb, and Newman. Those who know something about Art History and these particular exhibitions will recognise that these paintings are all from the catalogue of *The New American Painting*. This was a landmark exhibition of abstract expressionism that took place in 1958 in many European cities. Here, they're decorating the walls of a living room. When you enter the room, you find yourself in a very familiar environment. Jazz music playing from a record player helps people to relax. But at some point, the visitors start to understand that what they're looking at is not Kline, or Gottlieb, or Motherwell. But what is it? I don't know. I have no answer to what these paintings mean. If you start to analyse them as paintings, you're definitely wrong. But still, these are real, physical paintings. And this confusion, so to speak, gives you goose bumps. If a painting looks like a Kline, with heavy black brush strokes on a white canvas, like abstract painting par excellence, what is that painting in fact? What is the copy of Kline? Is that an abstract

painting? It's not and it is. So, suddenly, from the territory of certainty you enter the territory of uncertainty, and a familiar landscape is not familiar anymore.

The notion of the modern is somehow associated with the notion of frontier. Modern means looking outward. It is about pushing the boundaries, turning the unknown into the known in the process. You have as something you call the "known" a place where you feel good and safe. And then you have as the "unknown" some kind of dark and dangerous place on the other side of the border. The entire era of modernism could be understood as a process of pushing the boundaries and broadening the territory of brightness by turning this unknown into the known. Some examples of this are the new laws of science, new discoveries, numerous expeditions in every part of the globe, through the jungles of Africa, to the North Pole, to the top of Mount Everest, diving with Cousteau down to the deepest waters of the ocean, traveling to the Moon, to Mars, expeditions into the human body and mind, etc. Practically no stone has been left unturned.

Now, we are dealing with works that actually pursue the opposite approach. They turn the known into the unknown. There are no more boundaries, and danger is no longer beyond some distant frontier. The very place where you stand and feel safe begins to look a bit strange; we recognise it but it is not the same. Then the ground beneath us starts to shake, and all of this scares us. I think I can feel the entire world today becoming this "known/unknown" place. The thing that is "unknown" and "dangerous" is now our backyard, not some distant jungle; it is right here and not "over there" anymore.

But is it really so frightening? I would say the process of turning the known into the unknown has been an accepted art procedure for decades. Surrealism regularly used devices that turned something that looked familiar into something different or unknown. What is more puzzling to me is, where do (or will) those projects belong if they don't belong to art? Since you explained your view on the past so precisely, I'm sure you must have some insights about the future? Some idea what this new narrative, this new position/realm will be?

> You are right about the Surrealists, but only regarding the internal narratives of their work, which have more to do with

     Beti Žerovc

psychology than art. I think they didn't do much to address the very nature of the Work of Art and to try to move out of the Art Historical narrative. They were still producing Works of Art for the History of Art. The overarching narrative was left unchallenged, if not rhetorically, then as a consequence of their work.

Let me try to answer your question regarding these projects and why I think they do not belong to Art. If, let's say, apples belong to agriculture, then a painting of apples doesn't belong to "agriculture"; it belongs to something else, to some other place that we today call Art and Art History. And what is, in fact, Art History? It is just a story whose main characters are unique (original) entities: Artists and Artworks. If you have an Artwork, then by definition it belongs to Art History. Hence, a work whose subject matter is Art History itself could hardly belong to Art History. It most probably belongs to some other narrative that has not yet been established, that is in a meta-position in relation to Art History. Today we can only speculate about what this meta-position will be and what it will look like. It will definitely be outside of the historical narrative, but it will also incorporate this narrative as one of its building blocks. It is probably not going to be linear (chronological), but will have a web-like structure instead, consisting not of one but of several narratives existing simultaneously, even with some interchanging artefacts, characters and notions. Thus, it will not be based on the notions of the uniqueness of the individual identity or the originality of its artefacts. The same icons will be able to simultaneously play different roles in different narratives.

Also, we, whoever "we" may be, will be able to play different roles, simultaneously becoming characters in a number of different narratives.

Many artworks, especially in the last decades, look backwards to works and events from the past. So, we could say that many works are about art, that they have art as their subject.

> I agree. Those were works about other artworks (appropriation art, copies, quotations, etc.). Here, it's not only the artwork that is depicted as the subject matter, but is also the art narrative.

But the art narrative is not something that is completely separate from works of art.

> Actually, it is the art narrative that gives meaning to any object (artefact) it incorporates, supplying it with the legitimacy of a Work of Art. In fact, it is the narrative that is important, more than artefacts. It's like branding. Art History itself is a brand. It is also a way of branding products (artworks). And this is exactly the subject matter of all these works that we're talking about, the Salon, the Museum of Modern Art, and the Museum of American Art. For example, look at the Salon. It is a dark and dusty Victorian apartment whose walls are covered with sepia paintings. In the Salon, you can see, let's say, a copy of Picasso's *Woman with a Fan*. Then you have Gertrude Stein buying that painting and putting it among other paintings on the wall of her Paris salon. There you have Gertrude Stein looking at Picasso, looking at the woman. Than you have this place in New York called Salon de Fleurus that is looking at Gertrude Stein looking at Picasso looking at the woman. It doesn't look at Picasso directly. It looks at Picasso through the eyes of Gertrude Stein.

No matter how much you claim that these works are trying to belong to some new logic, I can also see that they fit into the present art system and its needs. The art market and the contemporary field of visual art as a whole have a very strong need for the ennobling of their practices and especially of the exhibition. For, let's say, almost two hundred years, they have been trying to lump together art and the exhibition, even though these are not at all the same thing. They don't have the same features, they don't have the same aims. By presenting those glorious moments of our history as enjoyable environments, the maker of these projects may be helping to ennoble this practice of the exhibition more than opening people's eyes to the structure and the construction of the past events they thematise. You can't really predict perception in contemporary art. Besides, these projects are done in such a way that they also provide a convenient romantic illusion of beautiful curatorial work, maybe of some really dedicated curatorial amateur. They are done in a kind of "low profile" manner, but very precisely and obviously with much care, by an anonymous author who doesn't work with originals

but makes all the work by himself, playing all kinds of roles from real life as in a game, etc. I can easily see why they are so appealing to curators.

> Well, I don't know about the psychological make-up of the people involved, but in spite of their anonymity, the projects they are involved in are neither humble nor modest. On the contrary, judging by the scope of their themes and by their positioning in relation to the art context, these are clearly very ambitious works. But I think that is not a matter of choice at all. I have no idea why they are so appealing to curators. Personally, I do not think that this is so obvious, but even if it is true, it could be because the curators are the subject matter of these works. We're talking about Gertrude Stein, Katherine Dreier/Marcel Duchamp, Alfred Barr, Dorothy Miller, Alan Solomon, etc. Not only the authors whose reflections are shown in these projects, but also the curators who put these authors and their works together are the central theme. It seems that the importance of the curator's position in organising and exhibiting art became more and more apparent as the 20th century progressed. First, this role was associated with art institutions. In museums, these were people like Barr and Dorothy Miller and, in galleries, people like Peggy Guggenheim, Betty Parsons, and Sidney Janis, who were art dealers at the same time. Perhaps it is interesting to mention that Dorothy Miller was named *editor* rather then *curator* of her series of exhibitions entitled *Americans*. In a way, the curatorial role in the museums could be understood as non-commercial (only to show, to create a spectacle, but not to sell – *exposition*), while in the galleries it was commercial (to display merchandise for sale – *exhibition*). The so-called "independent curator" is a more recent development, but we might see Marcel Duchamp as his distant precursor. Clearly, the concept of an independent curator as a single and long-term position or career that is fully conscious of its potential and power is basically associated with the European art scene, where someone like the late Harald Szeemann helped to shape it as it is defined today.

One of the artists who became aware of this development was Daniel Buren. Regarding Szeemann's curatorial work documenta 5 (1972), he correctly noticed that "increasingly the object of an exhibition is no longer the exhibition of works of art but the exhibition of the exhibition as a Work of Art". It is clear that the position of the curator is a meta-position in relation to the artist. As such, it could be quite uncomfortable for the artist's sense of "independence and freedom". We could say that the notions of "independent curator" and "independent artist" are two sides of the same coin. I expect that both will gradually diminish as the importance of the entire art scene together with museums, galleries, exhibitions, artworks, Art History, etc., either fades away or completely changes its meaning.

But for now, the fact is that curators are interested in ennobling the medium of the exhibition by any means possible. Can't we see the Salon de Fleurus as something that contributes to romantic, noble ideas about the exhibition, since the majority of the public presumably doesn't take it as a critical tool but as an enchanting, nostalgic experience about the past where you feel really good and special?

> Sure, and I'm glad. Things like the music from *West Side Story*, which was used at the *Americans 64* exhibit, are there to make people feel good. The thing is that the real change is not going to happen through shock and scandal anymore. It is going to take place unnoticed, getting under your skin while you are even not aware of it. Shock belongs to modernism. This is why, for example, "shock and awe" art from Britain is in my opinion anachronistic and totally uninteresting today. The real change is going to be subtle, almost unnoticed, and with some feeling of pleasure. But it's going to be a real, radical, and fundamental change.

So, you think that these projects will make this change.

> Absolutely. They *are* making the change. I believe this is where the change is taking place today. Gradually, it will become clear that Art History and Art itself are exhausted concepts. They're going to be abandoned, or perhaps will become little more than entertainment for some people who continue to believe in History, the way religion is entertainment for some people today.

But that's already how it is now. Art is just entertainment for some people.

> Sure. This is why Art as such is not relevant for me anymore.

So, wouldn't it be more fun and make more sense now to leave the art context altogether?

> You see, you have to have a place from where you start learning things. Sometimes, a certain narrative already gives you a platform from which you can start and from where you can make the "next move". Why abandon it completely then? When Art History was being established, it didn't forget the Christian narrative; it just recontextualised it. And these *meta-art* works are not forgetting the narrative of Art History. They might be one way of recontextualising it. So, what we have is a recontextualisation rather than a deconstruction of the historical narrative. While deconstructing is in some way closer to forgetting, recontextualising might come closer to remembering. Copies are memories.

Why Is It Important in the Art Field to Think about Art Events?

First published as "Zakaj na likovnem področju razmišljati o umetniških dogodkih?" / "Why Is It Important in the Art Field to Think About Art Events?", *Maska* (Ljubljana), vol. 27, no. 147–148, summer 2012, pp. 10–21.

　　　　Beti Žerovc

- Because today the art event[1] is a very pertinent medium of expression in this field.
- Because in the art field, which "by tradition and definition" is committed to static works, i.e. paintings and sculptures, the art event is, in fact, a paradox.
- Because, given this fact, the art event offers a good entry point for thinking about the changed structure and nature of the art field, which interest us.

In the first part of the present article, I will attempt to outline and briefly describe the sequence of major changes that have occurred in the art field since the early 20th century and especially in recent decades; in the second part, by analysing the art event and its specific embeddedness in the field, I will suggest a few points of departure for thinking about the potential workings and effects of this changed structure.

New! Institutions of Contemporary Art

In a world where institutions that treat and present contemporary art have become a permanent reality, it is hard to imagine that a little more than 100 years ago such institutions did not exist anywhere or that there were only a few at the most. Today, these institutions are of different kinds, most often exhibition spaces, while geographically, they can be found almost everywhere in

---

1   I am using the phrase *art event* here as a general term for the broad range of events organised for the public and carried out by artists in art institutions (actions, performances, gestures, happenings, interactive projects, etc.), as well as the same kinds of events that happen outside the art institution and occasionally even without any audience, though almost always with the aim of being included in the same artistic sphere.

   The essay's specific focus on such art events, as well as the deliberately provocative and pointed statements, that were meant to stimulate debate, and the unusual structure of its first half (the sections with exclamatory headings that encapsulate some of the book's key ideas), are due to its original function as the introduction to the symposium *The Event as a Privileged Medium in the Contemporary Art World* (Moderna galerija, Ljubljana, 4–5 November 2011) and later to the publication under the same name that appeared as a special issue of the journal *Maska*, no. 147–148, summer 2012, Ljubljana; available on the journal's website, http://www.maska.si). The symposium was one of the main components of the 29th Biennial of Graphic Arts in Ljubljana (titled *The Event*), which I curated in 2011.

the world, but most densely in regions that have some version of the neoliberal capitalist system and a fairly high standard of living. The institutions may be small and even have no physical structures, or they may be represented by gigantic and extremely expensive building complexes that are located on the most valuable sites in the countries and cities that build them and, in some cases, counted among the most famous architectural achievements of their time. To illustrate the extraordinary speed of this development, we need go no further than Slovenia. The first Slovene exhibition space dedicated to the art of its time was constructed and opened in 1908–09. Today, according to statistics from the Ministry of Culture's website, Culture.si, there are more than 130 exhibition spaces that present contemporary art, either exclusively or as part of a broader programme.[2]

In retrospect, it is clear that such an extraordinary institutional development cannot be explained solely by contemporary art itself or by the devotion of its active supporters; rather, this can only have happened because of the specific inclusion of art in a certain notion of culture and because of the importance this notion has acquired, beginning in the 19th century and growing and developing right up to the present. This development is also reflected structurally in the shift from an uncontrolled, patronage- or donor-based approach to culture to permanent organised forms and a cultural politics with clear purposes and goals and with the instruments, authorisations, and financial resources needed to carry them out.

As central, defining moments in this development, we should mention the nationalisation and state ownership of culture, the increasingly widespread understanding of culture as an effective instrument for achieving social progress and intellectual maturity, and also the many different ways culture has been drifting in the direction of a secular religion. Already in the 19th century, politics understood culture as, among other things, its (co-)per-

2   It was impossible to obtain any concrete published statistics about the number of exhibition venues in Slovenia devoted exclusively to contemporary art; the website's editor, Alenka Pirman, very kindly assisted me with this calculation. Published statistics are available for all exhibition venues in the art field as a whole. In the book *Kulturna politika v Sloveniji* [*Cultural Politics in Slovenia*], in the chapter on visual art, we find the statement: "There are more than 800 occasional exhibition venues and 254 permanent ones" (Vesna Čopič, Gregor Tomc, and Michael Wimmer (eds.), Faculty of Social Sciences, Ljubljana, 1997, p. 179).

former, in an ever more secularised society, of numerous tasks that had once been performed by religion. In this view, the cultural field was, in particular, supposed to prevent society from slipping into anomy, and it was expected to do this by maintaining the cohesion and shaping the collective values and representations of society.[3] We should add that, in the 20th century, culture established itself further as the key medium for the permanent organised outward representation of societies, becoming, in a sense, a fixed international currency for exchange on the global level (as a "gift that demands reciprocation"). Culture thus became established as a vast field in which there is constant and intensive representation taking place, both internally and externally; as to what one is or at least wishes to be (wishes to appear as), what one's central values are (or at least what one wishes them to be seen as), and further, who one is compatible with (or not), and so on.

Within these frameworks, art acquired an important place, probably, among other reasons, because it was prepared to be actively included in these processes and to align itself with the purposes and goals of cultural politics, whether public or private.

Returning to the subject of the contemporary art institution, its activity in the universe of culture is generally accepted and understood (even today) as being museological work or at least analogous to such work. Nevertheless, in contrast to other museum institutions, the curator of contemporary art does not (usually) retroactively discover, meticulously research, and then present certain existing materials or actual historical situations; on the contrary, the pure rationalistic scientific approach is, in fact, viewed as inappropriate and even cynical. The curator today behaves, above all, as someone who adores art – usually he does not exhibit what he does not like – and as someone who is committed to the realisation of positive social values. For this reason, love, faith, political conviction, feeling, etc., can all be given as

3   In this regard, France is a textbook example of a utilitarian understanding of culture, which may be why the processes that here are merely indicated have been elaborated most thoroughly by French theorists: Jean Caune, Olivier Donnat, Claude Mollard, and Alain Quemin are a few of the current writers on the subject. French theory has also discussed such connections as, for instance, between the establishment of ministries of culture as state institutions and the subsequent flourishing and growth of art institutions, including exhibition venues for contemporary art.

legitimate and appropriate primary motivations for his decisions in organising exhibitions.[4] Most importantly, what we might call the curator's "counter-museological" form of working has become entirely acceptable and standard: here it is the institution, through curators, that actually generates the art scene, its content and production, which is all, quite literally, commissioned, produced, and even paid for by the curator through the institution. Within the sphere of museums, then, the system of contemporary art institutions has the distinction of generating – to a large degree – the objects of its own museological activity.[5]

New! Curators of Contemporary Art

With this last paragraph, we have already lit upon the phenomenon of a special layer of workers who see to the operations of contemporary art institutions, which since the start of the 20th century, and especially in recent decades, have multiplied into incredible numbers from practically nothing. We will return to the curator and his activities later, but the main point I want to make now is that today, as a rule, a special layer of middlemen stands between contemporary art and the public – who usually consume their art institutionalised.

Change! Artists

The artist population experienced extraordinary growth in the 20th century, expanding uncontrollably especially in the past

4   The statement, "I adore *X* and that is why I am exhibiting him," seems reasonable, while a statement in the style of the traditional art custodian – "I wish to show what is currently happening in art, even if the material is not necessarily to my taste" – seems cynical. Thus, it seems, contemporary art curators work better if they are more subjective.

5   We are talking about a system of mutually connected institutions in which some may do more "producing" and others more "museological work", although most of them do both and, what is very important, they employ the same people. (For example, the work I produce over five years as the director of a Kunsthalle, I might then be able to work on museologically over the next five years when I become the director of a museum of contemporary art.)

   We should remember that other museum institutions are, of course, also changing, and that the art market is an active and essential factor in the art field.

two decades. A large part of the artist population has adapted to the new conditions I just described, and today live off the care of this institutional network, with a large segment of art being produced, quite literally, exclusively for institutions. In recent decades, then, the creation of a broad layer of contemporary art institutions has brought this growing population of artists a new way of earning a living, one in which a large part of them (and a portion of curators, too) scrape by on various grants, residencies, and, especially, *per diems* and honoraria for exhibitions, as well as institutional purchases. Here we should note that, in Europe at least, the institutionally recognised artist is also, as a rule, supported by the state, since extensive exhibiting is a key criterion for receiving state grants and subsidies. Today, then, it is even possible for artists to be completely absent from the "classic" art market and still live quite well; to a far greater degree, however, the system mainly generates harried individuals who live on the edge of survival, without any economic guarantees for income outside of their involvement in whatever projects they happen to be doing at the moment.

It is important to note also that, despite the fact that the contemporary art system has, in recent decades in particular, very clearly turned artists into a specific and extremely dependent precarious proletariat, the artist has preserved his mythologised image from the past – an image he successfully lends the entire field. The contemporary art system, then, continues to rely on the extremely powerful and appealing mythology of the artist as a free subject who "speaks from his heart" and who is epistemologically and ethically superior in his society; it also relies on the belief that contemporary art approaches things unconventionally, without prejudices, impartially, with a great sense of social responsibility, unmotivated by self-serving interests, and so on.

New / Change! Media of Expression

In the structure I have been describing, certain quite specific media of expression have also prospered; indeed, this structure is what provides the necessary conditions for "non-traditional" art media to flourish, media that are tied, in their execution, to the spaces and support of art institutions as producers. Here we should note that, within this structure, media that are able to cater successfully to the needs of the institutions – by attracting audiences, mobilising groups of people, etc. – are clearly favoured. The privileged medium of this structure, in fact, appears to be the exhibition, which is, above all, a curator's medium;[6] it is within this structure, too, that the art event, once an "alternative" practice, as we might call it, has become a globally recognised and popular general practice.

Despite the fact that all these changes are quite obvious, very little thought has been given to why this particular kind of institutionalised structure for contemporary art has developed (and is still developing today), why it is so enormous and has developed so rapidly, and what the relationships are between its various parts. For example, what is the relationship between a certain concrete art event and the concrete cultural politics that stands behind it? What is its relationship to the actual chain of group exhibitions and biennials or festivals in which it finds itself during its "life span"? In other words, how does the art event live and exist within the powerful current that is constantly being produced by the institutionalised structure we have described, and what in fact regulates its appearance in the structure? What does this constant presence of events mean, and should we be reflecting, in fact, on the specific ritualisation of the field? We might be led to this last notion also by the fact that this unusual replacement of static exhibits, sculptures, and pictures by a kind of odd set of rituals is happening in one of the sectors of culture, that is, in a field that expanded in society partly by taking on the work of religion.

In the section that follows, then, we will continue in this light, bringing together reflections on the art event as ritual, on some of its specific features, and on the manner of its inclusion in the

6   The medium of the contemporary art exhibition is undergoing a boom: the numerical growth of exhibitions is extraordinary; specialisations in exhibition making (curating, lighting, exhibition architecture, catalogue editing, etc.) have become standard; specific exhibition genres are emerging; etc. Also, there are an increasing number of discussions about the exhibition as a medium of expression. See the article, "The Exhibition as Artwork, the Curator as Artist: A Comparison with Theatre", pp. 198–215.

broader structure, all the while being particularly alert for possible comparisons with religious structures.[7]

Interestingly, the art event's attraction (for artists and the public, as well as for curators and institutions) relies to a large degree on aspects that have also been stressed as central to the kinds of rituals practiced by religious groups, as described in various theoretical literature. After several years of researching the phenomenon of the art event, I, too, can confirm that the event is still popular as a medium that has an extraordinary capacity for dealing with social norms effectively, in particular because of its great ability to mobilise and activate groups of people. This ability is significantly greater than in traditional sculpture and painting, which usually "speak" to people individually and do not encourage interactivity.

Less present, it seems, is any thinking about art events as rituals in which, at least potentially, participants can also experience unusual psychic states and a different awareness of themselves and their surroundings; meanwhile, a certain specific complex of values and "truths" is constantly being celebrated – among other things, our faith in art is being affirmed. And the reluctance to think seriously about such aspects occurs even though the extraordinary attraction of the art event lies, in essence, in its "mystical" ability to satisfy the art public's desire to experience something unusual and exceptional, including in the sense of having genuine contact with art, a kind of direct co-participation in art, the fulfilment of the tendency to seek an aura or something similar. Indeed, in the event, no matter what its subject matter is, the public's direct confrontation with art is a central and always-present theme: one of the essential aspects of the event is that it enables the public to be directly present when art "happens". What is more, because the public is often a co-participant in such creations, the feeling of having "true" access to the auratic moment can be even more potent. These aspects of the event were, it seems, well understood by the early avant-garde

---

7   I should note that the aspects I discuss in the following paragraphs can be seen as well in a wide spectrum of other branches of contemporary life, from sport, theatre, and science to mass shopping. Isolated comparisons seem wise if they contribute to greater insight into the phenomena we are discussing and to the perception of features that are otherwise difficult to see and define.

artists, and from their time to today we find numerous testimonies by the public and by the artists/performers about the way certain special emotions are experienced at events, even a specific kind of "performance high".[8]

I am not at all claiming that, in general, the public takes part in art events in a kind of special psychological *modus* – certainly not without more concrete research to back up such a claim; neither am I able to describe this *modus* in any specific detail. Nevertheless, I can note yet a further telling observation, namely, that in art events we tend to adopt a special regime in which our normal social status and obligations no longer carry weight; this is true even if we usually have our doubts about contemporary art and are critical toward it. In art events, it seems, the participants voluntarily, and quite generally, tend to form a homogeneous group, to respect the equality and anonymity of the participants, to obey the one who conducts the event, and to perform instructions, no matter how ridiculous or mystical they might be, doing things they would never do in their everyday lives. In ordinary life, for instance, we would not allow a stranger to kiss our wounds or wash our feet, nor would we tear apart a living room or take part in burnings. In the art event, however, we even allow ourselves to be yelled at, insulted, tormented, and tortured – or we ourselves do these things to other people.[9]

In this regard, then, the situation looks somewhat like this: art professionals and the art public know, generally, that without participation and staging there can be no art event, and we ac-

8   These emotions are generally described as positive ones. At the 29th Biennial of Graphic Arts (2011), which I curated, in the series *Conversations with Artists*, there was a great deal of discussion about the aspects of the art event and rituals that I mention. The artists spoke at length, happily and enthusiastically, about the special states of mind and the feelings produced by the event, but they did not wish to address the issue of whether and how the institution instrumentalises such states of mind.

9   It is a well-known fact in the art world – one that artists have known and even thematised ever since the Futurists – that at art events the public puts up resistance only in extreme cases. We discussed this topic in the biennial's *Conversations with Artists* series with regard to Siniša Labrović's performance *Punishment* (at the Miroslav Kraljević Gallery, Zagreb, 2007). In this performance, the artist, brutally and with all his might, beat himself with a whip every time a visitor left the performance space. When asked whether anybody tried to interrupt the performance or at least take the whip away from him, Labrović said, no, and noted that the performance dragged on and on, for more than two and a half hours.

           Beti Žerovc

cept this. We are less concerned, however, with the fact itself, that this staging (performativity) is, as in ritual, the very thing that most likely gives the event – whether we "believe" or not – its actual power of effect, and we give less thought to what its real-life short- and long-term effects might actually be. Or rather, in our thinking about the event, we soon drift into the art field's traditionalist patterns of thought, isolating the event from the structure and treating it as an autonomous work of art. We fail to see it as a perpetuated practice, a set of rituals that can, in a very regular way, follow us through our lives – and we do not think of it as being embedded in a wider structure. But if we take seriously the fact that ritualisation is not simply a reflection of the social structure but rather one of the forces that creates and processes the relationships within it, and which also plays a role in encouraging or hindering social changes, then such thinking seems essential. All the more because the art event today is not, as a rule, created on the street or in the context of a few rare alternative spaces, but rather, these events are performed in a totally organised, regular way within an institutionalised system of global dimensions, which I have described above.

Among other things, it is crucial to consider the way in which the art event is embedded in this structure; in this regard, it seems worthwhile to underscore two connected observations: the growing structural similarity between the institutional platform for contemporary art and the institutional platforms of different religions, and – a point we will consider first – the fact that the art field is processing more and more topics from the repertoire of the religious sphere.

From the perspective of its content, contemporary art, or rather, art institutions, today offer numerous means for processing the positive and negative emotions caused by living in society. This of course is not done in relation to any Christian or other kind of traditional religious dogma, but rather in connection with the belief in art as a higher good and the artist as someone who is epistemologically and ethically superior, as well as a belief in the transformative power of artist's works. Of all artistic media, the art event is the one medium that revolves around social norms in a truly abundant way; I would point out that, in doing so, art events also often process our negative or positive feelings toward these norms in a metaphorical language that is not unlike the one cultivated by religious ritual (a similar use of symbols, the "repetition" of Christological gestures and parts of the Christian liturgy, ritual burnings, etc.).[10]

From a structural perspective, however, what seems key is the fact that the global network of contemporary art institutions is managed by "experts" in contemporary art (by curators, not artists!). These are the ones who administer programmes and call together groups to participate in a variegated and constant series of events, which consist of a well-considered mix of "liturgical" art events and events of "exegesis", "catechesis", and "homiletics" (guided tours, lectures, round tables, etc.). One of the key similarities between the two spheres, then, is precisely the aspect that, as in religion – if religion operates by processing feelings in a metaphorical way – so in the art sphere, as well, supervision of "the holy" is assigned to a special authorised group of people (the experts: curators, publicists, etc.) who are qualified to lead "the faithful" (the public) and who use a certain corpus of metaphors and conceptual abstractions to do this. "The faithful", meanwhile, do not as a rule themselves interpret "the holy" but, rather, grab hold of these given metaphors and abstractions without processing them autonomously.[11]

To understand this situation, we must always also keep in mind the current position of the artist, who, although he may indeed be exceptionally emphasised in a declarative way in this system, is in fact actually a secondary figure who must, literally, remain in the precarious world of the social anti-structure and the social margins (there are exceptions, of course) because,

10   In my formulation of the ideas in this and the following paragraph, I have relied on Luisa Accati's book *Beauty and the Monster: Discursive and Figurative Representations of the Parental Couple from Giotto to Tiepolo* (European Press Academic Publishing, Florence, 2006; Slovene translation *Pošast in lepotica: Oče in mati v katoliški vzgoji čustev*, Studia Humanitatis, Ljubljana, 2001, pp. 115–215; originally published in Italian in 1998). Accati very precisely analyses the way Roman Catholic ritual and symbolism function and how even in the contemporary age we are not immune to models from the past, since in our modern emotional education they have not been replaced by new ones.

11   In the art field, indeed, the question is asked from time to time: "Do I perceive and understand at all independently the things I see when I go to an exhibition? Or do I accept them simply on the rationale that the curator has already looked at them, thought about them, 'consumed' them, and even enjoyed them, all on my behalf?" This may also be why we feel no need to view the entire video, read the entire catalogue, etc.

          Beti Žerovc

among other things, the art public believes that in such an environment and under such conditions is it more likely for subversive alternatives to arise, for new metaphors to be born, etc. But then, the art events that the institution "raises and presents" out of this extraordinary pool of possibilities are the institution's selection; in the process, they are not merely chosen with deliberation but rather strung together in an established flow and also always placed in a common framework. They are formatted in a uniform way (with the media announcement, the orderly arrival and departure of the public, security measures, documentation, etc.), and most importantly, they are also always interpreted by the institutions. In the institution, it seems, the event has an entirely predictable path. Each and every time, it attracts and creates a group of people in whom it attempts to arouse strong feelings and make an impact. Additionally, it also always has an explanatory part – the media announcement, the catalogue description, a lecture or conversation – that presents the rationale behind the event and "puts it where it belongs" in the art universe. In this process, the curator is the caretaker of the event, the one who assumes responsibility (even before the courts); he is its first interpreter and, indeed, the one who ascribes meaning to the ritual act; he explains what is incomprehensible and "prefigures", "transfigures", etc., what is comprehensible. And most importantly, he makes sure that everything happens in accord with the doctrine and mythology of the art field.

In no way do I wish my text to sound like some oversimplified equation between contemporary art and religion. Through this comparison and contrast, it seeks to reflect on aspects of the art field that are harder to recognise and define. First and foremost, it seeks to shift the focus of our gaze from individual events as autonomous entities to the practice as a whole in this field. And on this level, too, religion offers a practical comparison, as a kind of well-established and easily understood model of how to read, concurrently and connectedly, a structure and a practice as well as the individual parts of this practice. With religion, it would never occur to us to interpret the individual rituals as entirely separate and autonomous, without at the same time keeping in mind their place in the entire flow of religious practice.[12]

12   Perhaps it would be wise to turn more often to the experts on religious ritual

A widened perspective will, perhaps, allow us greater understanding of what is happening in the structure as a whole; we will also better understand the art event, for we will not be observing it always on the level of transcendence but on the level of celebration, and will, therefore, also be less disturbed by its "pseudo" nature. Currently, we are too much focused on that segment where the event tenses itself for something new, something different, some real-life impact, each and every time, and we take too little account of the fact that, even if nothing momentous happens, in this tension we participants are each time "bringing before the altar" our hope for something more, our faith in art and artistic freedom,[13] while at the same time coming to terms with difficult aspects of our existence in society. The charm of the art event, then, lies not merely in the fact that it touches us at the point where we are most "avant-garde". It is found much more in the fact that the art event guarantees a stable influx of something we do not notice or may even consider banal, though it is far from that: socialising, celebrating, being comforted, sustaining illusions about all sorts of possibilities, the cleansing of guilt – because in an unjust world, we live on the side of the unjust – the beauty of yielding to hope, and similar things that help make the world bearable.

for comparative material. After all, theoretical writings about the rituals of, for instance, the Christian church are, because of the church's two thousand years of experience with ritual, a genuine treasure trove of complex understanding about the way events operate in an institutionalised structure, the nature and effect of performative events, the combination of different kinds of events, the blending of several events into a bigger event, and so on. The ideas, for example, that the mass, other rituals, and the sacraments do not merely presuppose belief but also nourish, strengthen, and express it through words and actions; that rituals and sacraments operate through the logic of performativity, i.e. *ex opere operato* ("from the work itself the work is done"), and the like, are things that liturgical and homiletic textbooks present as irrefutable facts in their opening chapters. What seems to bother people in the art world is precisely the fact that the church has no doubt about the efficacy of these practices; it seems to be completely convinced that "you believe as you pray" (*lex orandi, lex credendi*) and that's just how it is.

13   On the exceptional importance of constantly celebrating and commemorating artistic freedom, and the long-term consequences of this, see the essay "Beautiful Freedom", pp. 166–174.

Afterword

Mary Anne Staniszewski

Some Notes on Curation, Translation, Institutionalisation, Politicalisation, and Transformation

Beti Žerovc has not only written a thoughtful, provocative, and insightful book, but an especially timely one given that it's subject - curating - has become of late an almost "universally" adaptable and applicable term. What had previously been an activity principally associated with the rarefied domains of aesthetics and museums has now infiltrated a diverse range of territories, from the mundane to the esoteric, morphing and multiplying at an exponential pace, serving as a strategy for "coping" with our networked and globalised world.

During the past decade, quite ordinary endeavours such as selecting food from a menu, shopping for clothes, and choosing music for an iPod have been deemed curatorial concerns.[1] Simultaneously, new and highly specialised domains of knowledge have been established, such as "biocuration", which involves the analysis of the biological "data avalanche" now that we are in the "petabyte era".[2] Some of the most hyperbolic manifestations are those created by corporate marketers who wax ecstatic on curating commerce as a means to tame the digital chaos, gain customers, and increase capital.[3] With the expansion of Internet networks, data, and mobile devices coupled with the DIY strategies of social media, this terminology and activity reached a crescendo in 2011 when journalists began "curating the revolution" by culling twitter feeds, cell phone videos, and reports from online posts during the proliferation of people's uprisings that

1   I have been researching this new type of curation in lectures and articles since 2011. For a more in-depth examination and references, see, for example, "Alternatives and Attitudes: Today and Yesterday", in *When Attitudes Become Form: Bern 1969/Venice 2013*, Germano Celant (ed.), Fondazione Prada, Milano, 2013, pp. 457–476; and the forthcoming "Curatoria Euphoria, Data Dystopia", in *Histoires d' expositions/Exhibition Histories*, Éditions Hermann, Paris, 2015, (French and English).

2   The September 4, 2008 issue of *Nature* featured articles related to "big data". For the quote, see "Editor's Summary", *Nature*, September 4, 2008, http://www.nature.com/nature/journal/v455/n7209/edsumm/e080904-01.html (accessed June 8, 2015). In Slovenia, this type of work can be referred to as "medical informatics", see for example, Slovenian Medical Informatics Association: "Slovenia", The European Federation for Medical Informatics (EFMI) http://www.efmi.org/index.php/about/efmi-countries/slovenia/pluginclass?plugin=cbgroupjive&action=groups&func=show&cat-=4&grp=32 (accessed June 2, 2015).

3   One of the most representative references is Steven Rosenbaum's *Curation Nation: How to Win in a World Where Consumers Are Creators*, McGraw-Hill, New York, 2011.

spanned from Egypt's Tahrir Square to New York's Wall Street.[4] The varied practices associated with curators, curation, and curating continues to diversify and disseminate, with an unprecedented visibility and currency. This book is therefore being published during a moment of what I call: "Curatoria Euphoria".[5]

In this book's essays, Žerovc is, of course, not investigating curating consumer goods, bioinfomatics, or the media during the so-called Arab Spring. She is, however, incisively examining a similar context out of which this phenomenon has emerged: the efflorescence and institutionalisation of curation and the advent of the contemporary art curator. Žerovc – a Slovene art historian, theorist, and curator whose areas of research are visual art and the art system since the mid-nineteenth century – chronicles, and critiques, two key concerns in this collection: the rise of the contemporary art curator and related curatorial conventions; and the exhibition as a creative medium, event, and ritual. She portrays the former in terms of a development configuring in the late 1960s and early 1970s with the appearance of a new type of curator and related art practices; and then a consolidation in the mid-1990s with the professionalisation of the field of contemporary art curating as realised in its concomitant publications, degree programs, organisations, conferences, and so on – to which this collection is a contribution. The latter is investigated as an augmentation of these earlier transformations, which has become a norm for the internationalist art world in the 2000s.

Throughout her work, Žerovc takes a "systemic" point of view that integrates the analysis of culture within extra-aesthetic societal spheres. This is seen in the essays included in this volume, as well as in her other research and writing dealing with Slovene art in the Central European context and with feminist issues, such as those related to her publications on 19th century painter Ivana Kobilca.[6] In this book devoted to the field of cur-

4 See as one example, and for the quotation, Phoebe Connolly, "Curating the Revolution: Building a Real-Time News Feed About Egypt", *The Atlantic*, February 10, 2011, http://www.theatlantic.com/technology/archive/2011/02/curating-the-revolution-building-a-real-time-news-feed-about-egypt/71041/ (accessed March 22, 2013).
5 See Mary Anne Staniszewski, "Curatorial Euphoria" (see n. 1).
6 See Beti Žerovc, *Rihard Jakopič – Artist and Strategist*, *cf.*, Ljubljana, 2002; "Ivana Kobilca: A career in the context of nineteenth-century women's painting," *Biuletyn historii sztuki* (Warsaw), vol. 76, no. 3, 2014, pp. 509–534; and "Ivana Kobilca and her painting for the Ljubljana Town Hall, Slovenia

     Mary Anne Staniszewski

ating and "institutional art", Žerovc raises questions about the character and limitations of the "exhibition-maker as artist" and the "exhibition as a work of art" (especially in relation to the thematic group show), asking whether the socio-political objectives for these projects actually manifest contradictory or even opposite effects, given the inescapable conditions of capitalism.

One of Žerovc's key concerns is what she describes as the "institutionalisation of art". This is seen, for example, in the way a curator works with a cultural organisation, such as a museum, a biennial, and so on, and goes beyond the traditional practice of exhibiting and preserving art to commissioning and collaboratively manufacturing creations that serve a matrix of financial, political, and social purposes and functions related to this sponsor. Projects such as these do not need to be admitted into the entity's "canon" or collection, for they are engendered by it. Žerovc draws parallels between this newer breed of production and patronage and those of the aristocracy and church in the pre-modern past. The role of the curator within this type of system is highlighted and questioned by Žerovc. In the more recent entries, she makes inquires regarding how the "exhibition as an event", ritual, and theatre-like creation serves these institutionalising processes.

Fundamental to this book are issues of interpretation and "translation": not only because these texts have been rendered from Slovene into English, but also due to the enhancement of understanding that is possible by contextualising Žerovc's point of view. In her interviews,[7] Žerovc stressed the fact that she is "from Slovenia, a country which gained independence in 1991 and is now a tiny part of the European Union, but which used to be a part of the much larger socialist Yugoslavia and before 1918 a part of the even larger Austro-Hungarian empire. This means that in my almost daily practice-routine as a researcher and a pedagogue I have to switch all the time between very different political systems and their dealings with art. I guess that makes me very aware of the role of different production systems." This

bows to Ljubljana, in the context of women's painting in the late nineteenth century", *Radovi Instituta za povijest umjetnost* (Zagreb), vol. 37, 2013, pp. 167–178.

7   The author had interviews with Žerovc in May and June of 2015 and the quotations and references to Žerovc's statements and discussions throughout the text are from these interviews.

internationalist and multi-regime framework is something Žerovc sees as "inspiring" her macro world view. But this perspective most likely has also contributed to her probing analysis. For having lived through Slovenia's transformation from a locally specific version of socialism to a market-based economy seems to have augmented Žerovc's capability to envision cultural realisations that are critical, or at least somewhat outside of, the strictures of a ubiquitous, all-encompassing capitalism. Significantly, Slovenia was undergoing these socio-economic-political changes when the consolidation of the curatorial profession was coming to the fore in the mid-to late 1990s, and so for Žerovc, the current affiliations between capitalism, so-called globalisation, and curation are especially visible and inextricably intertwined.

Translation and interpretation are not only featured on a macro-structural level in this book, but also on the micro-level of word choice: for this volume's foundational concept of "curator" is known in English as one word, and in Slovene – as is case for a number of other non-Anglo languages – as two: in its current use, *kurator* and *kuratorka*, being grammatically gendered, designates an exhibition-maker and also, more historically, was defined as administrator or trustee of a person or organisation, such as a school or library. The more traditional *kústos* or *kústosinja*, which has both masculine and feminine forms, is generally associated with a caretaker of a collection, but can also signify the former denotation as a creator of exhibits.[8] In English, "curator" has historically also had a number of meanings: in its modern aesthetic usage it can be synonymous with both *kústos/inja* and *kurator/ka*, that is, exhibition-maker and/or keeper of a gallery or museum.[9] The English word also has range of definitions, with the earliest being from the 14th century, that signify stew-

8   These definitions are based on my discussions with Žerovc, and references
     for traditional meanings of these terms, see, for example, Inštitut za slovenski jezik Frana Ramovša ZRC SAZU, *Slovar slovenskega knjižnega jezika*
     [Institute of Slovenian Ethnology, SRC, SASA, *Dictionary of the Slovenian
     Language*], "Kustos", http://bos.zrc-sazu.si/cgi/a03.exe?name=sskj_testa&expression=kustos&hs=1 and "Kurator", http://bos.zrc-sazu.si/cgi/a03.
     exe?name=sskj_testa&expression=kurator&hs=1 (accessed June 8, 2015).
9   See "curator, n.", *OED Online*, Oxford University Press, http://www.oed.
     com.libproxy.rpi.edu/view/Entry/45960?redirectedFrom=curator#eid
     (accessed June 8, 2015). This issue of terminologies is often discussed in
     the contemporary curatorial literature, see, for example, Paul O'Neil interviewed by Anne Fletcher, in *Curating Subjects*, Paul O'Neil (ed.), Open Editions and De Appel, London and Amsterdam, 2007, p. 12.

          Mary Anne Staniszewski

ardship of "souls", properties, universities, and persons and that can also have connotations of guardianship and legal protection. These latter descriptions may seem to be related to *kústos*, but actually match meanings of *kurator* as well. A somewhat simplified, but revealing way to compare these terminologies is to designate the more traditional meaning of custodian and keeper, as someone who "makes safe" precious objects or those who need care, whereas the more contemporary curator signifies "making sense" of artworks, cultures, concepts, and socio-political concerns. Žerovc wrote using both *kústos* and *kurator*, and in this English version, the language has been adapted and modified to best represent these two choices. These linguistic calibrations, however, have additional, less obvious, but revealing affiliations and are resonant of some of the core questions Žerovc poses in this book in regards to dualities and contradictions.

Žerovc introduces this volume with reflections on the 19th century proto-curatorial practices of the founder of the Catholic Rosicrucian Order of the Temple and the Grail, Joséphin Péladan, who used the exhibition as a creative medium, foreshadowing what comes to pass a hundred years later. But her key focus is individuals like Harald Szeemann, who is commonly regarded as the person, or one of the key people, who transformed the contemporary curator's role;[10] the artist Daniel Buren, who, early on as these changes were taking place, is known to have publically criticised some of these reconfigurations; and Charles Esche, whose work can be seen as an exemplar of this approach and who is a prominent proponent of the legacy of these practices in the present day. These interviews were created between 2002 and 2003, which is before the final versions of most of the essays were completed, and they can be viewed as primary documents and a substrate out of which many of Žerovc's formulations emerge. They serve, in a sense, as case studies for the more theoretical formulations Žerovc explores in the other essays. There are also key concepts or phrases introduced in these dialogues, such as Pierre Restany's characterisation of the curator as "the master of the compromise"[11] (variations of this phrase become a leitmotif

10   I would like to stress that Szeemann was an innovator, but his work was part of a matrix of innovative practices created by individuals and collectives that included artists, dealers, curators, critics, and museum directors, one noted example is Pontus Hultén.
11   See Beti Žerovc, "Interview with Pierre Restany", pp. 54–64.

throughout the book). Thus these different types of chapters that form this "collection" provide an interwoven arrangement of what could be considered a textual "curatorial project".

The revelations – and limitations – of language that are evident in the translation of the term "curator" is mirrored in the chapters' subjects, for all the voices of curatorial wisdom, expertise, and authority are "white" men, and, in this day of gender pluralities, the standard personal pronoun remains masculine. Although in the current globalised art world, diversity of all kinds does substantially exist in many positions of leadership and overall participation, these manly features of this book are representative of the fact that the "tippy-top" tiers in the various hierarchies of the mainstream art world, such as the premiere directorships of museums and international exhibitions, remain mostly male. Žerovc was aware of this sexual selection in terms of those interviewed, whereas the gender neutrality and diversity that has become common in English is, according to Žerovc, less standard in Slovene, and she notes both of these issues in her introduction.

In terms of the scope of this collection, the Szeemann interview is a seminal chapter because it provides a foundation for mapping the characteristics that mark what Žerovc describes as the "tectonic shifts" that took place regarding the role of the curator and curatorial practices in the late 1960s and early 1970s.[12] Szeemann's initiative at *When Attitudes Become Form*, as well as those of others who produced several almost simultaneously held international group shows, were, of course, representative of a reconfiguration of art conventions and practices that were "affiliates" of the extra-aesthetic transformations that had been taking place during the 1960s and early 1970s globally. These broad-based changes were initiated due to protests against and

12   The change that took place in the 1960s and 1970s, as well as the prehistory of this shift, was a focus of my book, *The Power of Display: A History of Exhibition Installations at the Museum of Modern Art*, The MIT Press, Cambridge, Mass., 1998. A great deal of work has been published on these changes in curatorial practices and exhibitions and related subjects since the mid-1990s. Given the brevity of this "Afterword", I will just cite two key early examples: Bruce Altshuler's *The Avant-garde in Exhibition: New Art in the 20th Century*, Harry N. Abrams, New York, 1994; and *Thinking about Exhibitions*, Reesa Greenberg, Bruce W. Ferguson, and Sandy Nairne (eds.), Routledge, London and New York, 1996, the latter of which Žerovc references in her writings.

    Mary Anne Staniszewski

critiques of imperialism and capitalism and the myriad movements for peace; racial, gender, and ethnic equalities; and worker and student's rights. It is within this social-political-cultural matrix that artists began producing new types of process-based, site-specific, and conceptual work that ranged from the aestheticised and formal to the more political and institutional. Simultaneously, individuals and collectives began to establish new kinds of organisational structures, what by the 1970s would be called "alternative spaces" – entities that were created, in part, to avoid some of the compromises Žerovc addresses in this collection.

Central to Žerovc's proposition is that among the changes in conventions that took hold in the late 1960s and early 1970s was a permeability among the activities of artists, curators, dealers, publishers, critics, and administrators during these years. The exhibition-maker began to perform almost any, and perhaps all, of these constituent responsibilities that insured the functioning of the art system. Žerovc's interview with Szeemann, completed just two years before his death, is noteworthy in that for most of his professional life he eschewed the designation of artist, and as it is commonly recycled in the literature, claimed to be an *Ausstellungsmacher*, an exhibition-maker.[13] But in the Žerovc interview, Szeemann admits that: "For a long time, I protested against being called an artist" ... and that now "I see myself functioning much more as an artist, without being an artist – one who has chosen the exhibition as his medium of expression",[14] an admis-

13 See Hans Ulrich Obrist, "Mind over matter: Interview with Harald Szeemann", *Artforum International*, November 11, 1996, http://go. galegroup.com.libproxy.rpi.edu/ps/i.do?id=GALE%7CA18963443&v=2. 1&u=nysl_ca_rpi&it=r&p=ITOF&sw=w&asid=303d823d392223fcc64bbf8f37 f7d301 (accessed June 8, 2015).

   For an example of Szeemann referring to himself as an exhibition-maker, see Urs and Rös Graf's 1970 interview, "Agency for Intellectual Guest Labour: Interview with Harald Szeemann, December 28, 1970 (first version)," included in *Harald Szeemann: Individual Methodology*, Florence Derieux (ed.), JRP Ringier, Zurich, Le Magasin, Grenoble, and Royal College of Art, London, 2008, p. 83. Thanks to Mariana Roquette Teixeira for assistance with bibliographic information on Szeemann. See also Teixeira's unpublished manuscript: "The Exhibition as Means of Personal Expression: Harald Szeemann's 'Grandfather: A Pioneer Like Us' (1974)," which is a version of her 2011 Masters Thesis, Universidade Nova de Lisboa, and see page 32 for this reference in particular.

14 For quotations, see Beti Žerovc, "Interview with Harald Szeemann", p. 88.

sion that serves the depiction that Žerovc presents throughout this collection.

What distinguishes Žerovc's perspective from most assessments of this curatorial history is her emphasis on the paradoxes linked to the power possessed by this "ambidextrous" curator-as-artist of today. In her first chapter and in the other theoretical essays, Žerovc portrays the contemporary art curator as an individual with "extraordinary influence in the art system",[15] but also a master of compromise whose exhibition projects cannot surpass or exceed the limitations of a global capitalist system. Locating a source of this authority, among other things, in this nexus of responsibilities, she systematically reviews how the curator has assumed many of the characteristics of the gallerist-dealer and art critic. Most significantly for her thesis is that now the curator "is deeply involved in the way money is distributed in the art system", in very direct, indirect, overt, and covert interactions with the market and the distribution of financial support and rewards. This economic dominion is evidenced in the involvement by some curators with the buying and selling of work (which can be both transparent and concealed), as well as the more general oversight of the attainment of grants, commissions, exhibition honoraria; support from the non-profit and academic sectors; and the more ambient career enhancements due to inclusion in exhibits and projects. These fiscal dynamics were certainly always present to a certain extent historically, but Žerovc emphasises the increased degree of this activity, which is crucial to the overall proposition of this book. The art critic, on the other hand, is presented as an especially diminished figure due to a number of changes in the cultural apparatus, one of which is the fact that their writing does not have the exhibitionistic extravaganzas that strengthen, publicise, and perpetuate the curator's productions. All of this, according to Žerovc's thesis, has magnified artists' dependencies on – and the power and patronage of – the curator.

Žerovc's most trenchant critique – which is broached in the first chapter, but is most elaborated in "The Curator and the Leftist Politicisation of Contemporary Art", and is also laced throughout this collection – is the question of the possibilities for

15   Beti Žerovc, "The Role of the Contemporary Art Curator: A Historical and
      Critical Analysis", p. 17.

                Mary Anne Staniszewski

a political, and specifically left or progressive, realisation in this curatorial and aesthetic realm and for a curator's participation to be anything other than an agent of the status quo. Žerovc argues that this "condition" has been integral to the initial formation of this cultural figure and locates this historically in the late 1960s and early 1970s. This narrative leads back directly to Szeemann and *When Attitudes Become Form*. As Žerovc relates, it has come to be known that the cigarette manufacturer, Philip Morris, actually initiated the exhibition with Szeemann.[16] Certainly businesses, companies, national entities, and all kinds of non-aesthetic interests had been, in a sense, co-creators or at the least highly prominent supporters of exhibitions throughout modernity and especially during the first 60 years or so of the 20th century. But what occurs in the late 1960s and early 1970s is a shift from exhibitions that made visible these affiliations (often governments or businesses that shared a kind of co-ownership and authorship) to shows of extra-aesthetically engaged conceptual, site-specific, process-based, and installation art that were more indirectly paid for by corporate sponsors. The latter situation, importantly and paradoxically, re-inscribes these external concerns within the "signature" of the artist's work, rendering the illusion that the institutional context is more ideologically neutral. It is with the famous *When Attitudes Become Form* show that this disavowal of socio-politico-economic aspects of exhibition-making was, ironically and "mythically", made manifest.

Žerovc pressed Szeemann in his interview about this "great compromise" of this great exhibition. But the great curator saw no conspiracy, nor complicitness. Rather, he seemed to sincerely stress that there are those who are "pure" curators, and as he had stated in other interviews, in the 1960s he had a very modest salary and very minimal budgets for projects. After a "successful" Christo and Jean-Claude project of wrapping the Kunsthalle Bern in 1968, Philip Morris offered him "money and total freedom" to create a show. Szeemann described this exper-

---

16　There is now a substantial literature on related issues. But given the analysis I am presenting here, I will, again, refer to my own research in regards to *The Power of Display*, which Žerovc mentions in her interview with Szeemann. To my knowledge, this was the first time the ideological implications of this shift from the business/industry and art collaborations of earlier in the 20th century to the corporate underwriting later in the century was investigated, and the Philip Morris *When Attitudes Become Form* situation was featured.

ience as "liberating".[17] It is paradoxes like this one that Žerovc considers to have set a precedent and have become inextricably intertwined with curatorial practices and the contemporary art system.

An earlier example of an affiliated political-aesthetic configuration is presented in Žerovc's examination of the prehistory of the contemporary art situation in Slovenia in her interview with Zoran Kržišnik, who was the primary founder of one of the first of these multinational group shows, the International Biennial of Graphic Arts, which was opened the same year as documenta, in Ljubljana in 1955. Kržišnik – whose interview was completed later than the others, in 2007 – affirmed her thesis that curators were interested in using these types of exhibitions not only for cultural, but also for strategic and ideological aims: "For me, it was the social aspect that was most important in this work. We set up the biennial in order to make our way into the world... [T]he biennial of graphic arts was actually a materialisation of what was being referred to as openness, which was then seen as non-alignment."[18] As Žerovc emphasised in our discussions, the biennial would never had been realised without Yugoslavian state support, and this exhibition could be considered a symbiotic aesthetic-political enterprise. This could be compared to the deployment of exhibitions for liberal democratic propaganda in the United States, as seen in the well-known promotion of abstract expressionism during the Cold War, but this was also visible in the extensive circulation internationally of the Museum of Modern Art's *The Family of Man*, which opened at MoMA the same year as the International Biennial of Graphic Arts in 1955.[19]

---

17   The "pure" quote is from Žerovc's interview with Szeemann, p. 86; the "money" and "liberating" quotes are from the Obrist interview, n.p. (see n. 13).
18   See Beti Žerovc, "Interview with Zoran Kržišnik", pp. 70–71.
19   Žerovc made explicit what she saw as parallels between the International Biennial of Graphic Arts, U.S. Abstract Expressionism, and the use of exhibitions for political and strategic issues in her interviews with the author. There has been extensive research done on the history of abstract expressionism, MoMA exhibitions, and the U.S. government and the following are two early examples in this literature: Eva Cockcroft, "Abstract Expression: Weapon of the Cold War," *Artforum*, vol. 15, no. 10, June 1974, pp. 39–41; and Serge Guilbaut, *How New York Stole the Idea of Modern Art: Abstract Expressionism, Freedom, and the Cold War*, University of Chicago Press, Chicago, 1983. These issues and the relationship of the United States Information Agency to the deployment of *The Family of Man* are examined in *The Power of Display*, particularly pp. 235–259 (see n. 12).

        Mary Anne Staniszewski

As Žerovc states in her introduction to the Kržišnik interview, these shows were intended to convey "the presence in a given society of such abstract values as freedom, modernity, democracy, openness, etc. Institutions of modern and contemporary art thus found themselves becoming a special kind of projector of propaganda and ideology, a role they have maintained ever since."[20]

In 2011, Žerovc was the curator of the International Biennial of Graphic Arts in Ljubljana, now titled according to the show's number in its history and according to a particular theme, which in this case was: *The Event: The 29th Biennial of Graphic Arts*. The focus on "event" was based on Žerovc's ongoing inquiry about the increasing manifestation of the exhibition as a participatory project, one that is ephemeral, ritualistic, and akin to theatre. Among the reasons Žerovc accepted this position was to enhance her research on these issues, and she believes the work on the biennial brought her "closer to certain aspects of … the institutionalisation process." The experience augmented her understanding of the questions she was addressing in her writing and she presented a version of the last essay in this collection, "Why Is It Important in the Art Field to Think about Art Events?", as the introduction to the biennial's symposium *The Event as a Privileged Medium in the Contemporary Art World*.[21] In this essay as well as others, such as "The Exhibition as a Work of Art and the Curator as Its Author" and "The Exhibition as Artwork, the Curator as Artist: A Comparison with Theatre", Žerovc investigates the transformation of the exhibition from what could be described as a primarily contemplative situation where a collection of objects are on display to a series of various interactive presentations staged within and outside an installation. Her comparison of a shift that took place in the history of theatre and directors to the changes in regards to contemporary exhibitions and curators serves as an illuminating elucidation of developments that have increasingly become standard practices in the art world since the late 1960s and early 1970s. Related to these areas of interroga-

20   See Beti Žerovc, "Interview with Zoran Kržišnik", p. 67.
21   The symposium *The Event as a Privileged Medium in the Contemporary Art World* was held at Moderna galerija, Ljubljana, 4–5 November 2011 and this text was later published with the same title in a special issue based on the symposium: "Why Is It Important in the Art Field to Think about Art Events?" *Maska* (Ljubljana), vol. 27, no. 147–148, summer 2012, http://www.maska.si/index.phpid=163&L=1&tx_ttnews[tt_news]=1109&cHash-=c6635894fa057e789dabbe1fa34c3ebb (accessed June 29, 2015).

tion is Žerovc's association of these exhibitions-as-events with religious rituals, which is linked to her attempt to counter treating these aesthetic productions as autonomous creations and to foster a more critical analysis that envisions these shows as elements of a social system.

In "The Curator and the Leftist Politicisation of Contemporary Art", Žerovc zeroes in on these systemic contradictions where she specifically asks "whether art may be used today ... for doing active political work and bringing about positive social change (justice, equality, and a better life for all)."[22] Although Žerovc concedes that there are differences among curators in terms of "commitment and radicalism", she sees throughout the field a unified belief that this type of work can contribute to progressive social change. Stating that there are those who go "so far as to present art as virtually the last remaining field not completely subject to the logic of global capitalism", this new breed of curator is presented as someone who envisions art as the source for "real possibilities for experimentation, the activation of society, and political action."[23]

The latter point of view is represented by Žerovc's interview with Charles Esche, who in his early 20s was a member of the British Labour Party and very involved with politics, but became disillusioned. Esche relates: "I saw in art ... a way of dealing with some of the questions I felt I wanted to ask in the political sphere, but couldn't. And so my journey was from trying to change the world through politics to becoming interested in art." In his search for more "imaginative speculation" on the "possibilities" for work for something other than the "one free-market, democratic, capitalist model", he ended up becoming one of the most well-known contemporary art curators, and is currently director of the Van Abbemuseum. In the interview, Esche affirms Žerovc's concerns, conceding that the art world is what he calls: "self-validating, with collectors sitting on institutional boards, institutions supporting galleries and underwriting artists' projects that then have to succeed, etc." But Esche nonetheless believes that these inbred "compromises" do not foreclose opportunities for "breakthroughs" and new ways of "imagining the world". Admitting that his approach is reformist rather than revolutionary, and

22 Beti Žerovc, "The Curator and the Leftist Politicisation of Contemporary Art," p. 125.
23 For quotations, see Beti Žerovc, ibid.

  Mary Anne Staniszewski

despite the problems of these social exchanges that come with this pragmatism, he believes a curator can "take a position and create the place for art to contribute to social change and emancipation."[24]

But Žerovc remains skeptical regarding the limitations of the contemporary art exhibition system. She relates how she witnessed an escalated version of institutionalisation in the 1990s as Central and Eastern European nations gained their independence or changed their political systems, and there was a great deal of "interest from the international art world ... money from the foundations ... regular visits of international curators presenting new models of dealing with art ... [This was] presented, among other things, as helping in the progressive development of those quickly changing and therefore fragile cultures and also as helping to affirm democracy in those countries, but soon it could be seen that this had a role in affirming liberal capitalism, too – a role which has not yet been fully analysed. We were not used to such attention and support, things were happening quickly and we could also say euphorically, which probably made us accept many things with too little critical reflection." This collection of essays gathered within this volume can be interpreted, in part, as Žerovc's counterpoint to this assimilation within the international system, and as an attempt to offer a catalyst for a more systemic analysis and reflection on these contradictory concerns. The book culminates with Žerovc's queries about the ritualistic function of contemporary art exhibitions, and this is evocatively expressed in her introduction: "There was once great discussion about how removing artworks from their original context and installing them in the museum meant their certain death. Today, it seems, we need to be thinking about different questions. Does the institution of visual art bring something to life ... what, in fact, are we summoning to life?"[25]

Reading these essays from a very different personal and relatively restricted geographic milieu, some of the questions Žerovc addresses can be considered from another perspective. In New York City, during many of the years Žerovc deals with in this book, leading curators did not necessarily prioritise a commitment to a politically and socially engaged art, nor had this been

24 The quotes in this paragraph are from "Interview with Charles Esche", pp. 161–162.
25 Beti Žerovc, "Introduction," p. 12.

publicly promoted among mainstream institutions as a solution for the problems of our time. This locally specific view can be seen in the "case study" of major Manhattan museums after September 11, 2001, where there was almost no programming dealing with anything but formalist and relatively innocuous explorations of art and culture coupled with one-person shows for artists who just happened to be "white" and male.[26] Among the offerings of this too narrow range of the vast spectrum of possibilities for contemporary art, there was no evidence, with few notable exceptions,[27] of the great transformations that were taking place in regards to the so-called Age of Terror or the fact that the U.S. was, by 2003, in wars with Afghanistan and Iraq. This is not to say that exhibitions must only deal with the most literally political subjects, but an absence of any register of such seismic cultural shifts is a denial of a different nature than the ones Žerovc confronts in her essays. Although there began to be more explorations of these kinds of realities since 2008, this stands as just one example of a condition that has often been the norm in the hyper-market-driven New York City.

I refer to the situation in the 2000s in New York City as one instance of a different type of micro-art-world-culture in order to raise questions regarding how to define the character and scope of "the political", "the social", "the economic", and so on.[28] In this way, this "Afterword" can serve as a supplement in which there is an expanded acknowledgement of some of the other parameters of effectiveness, criteria for assessment, and degrees of impact regarding what might be considered creative and progressive aesthetic realisations that might engender cultural, social, economic, and political transformation. One such different framework or query could be related to who is given ac-

---

26   This lack of engagement with any political or social concerns was an issue that I investigated and presented in a number of lectures and articles, such as, "Looking for Signs of Life", *Special Issue: The Modern Art Museum, Konsthistorisk tidskrift/Journal of Art History* (Stockholm), vol. 78, no. 4, 2009, pp. 193–203.

27   One of the notable exceptions was the 2005/06 Museum of Modern Art exhibition produced by MoMA Architecture and Design Department Curator Paola Antonelli and Curatorial Assistant Patricia Juncosa Vecchierini, *Safe: Design Takes on Risk.*

28   These questions could be explored as a dialogue with social or political theories, which is a common strategy for such examinations, and this can be a valid option, but is beyond the scope of this essay.

      Mary Anne Staniszewski

cess, invited to participate, and possess authority in arenas such as exhibitions: Does it matter that there were only three women among the artists invited to participate in *When Attitudes Become Form*? Does it mean anything that there was scarcely any work by women in the inaugural show of the newly renovated MoMA in 2004? Is it significant that most of the documenta directors have been European men? Did anything change when Catherine David became the first woman to hold this post in 1997, or when Okwui Enwezor, who is originally from Nigeria, had the position in 2002? Is it important that recent international biennials are more representative of the varied genders of humanity?

A number of these different criteria are subjects Žerovc has addressed in her other work, which has not been included in this collection, as seen in her publications on Ivana Kobilca and women painters of the 19th century.[29] These "Afterword" questions therefore are intended to augment Žerovc's assessments regarding the broad-based and systemic contradictions and challenges of contemporary art curating as outlined in this book's texts. Certainly much of my own research has been devoted to disinterring issues related to the origins and implications of such topics as corporate underwriting in the arts. But, additionally, I see possibilities for what might be vestigial – or at times even strong and vital – prospects for progressive aesthetic, creative, political, economic, and social realisations in the systemically compromised contexts portrayed in this volume. I also sustain a belief that there is an enhanced potential in other categories of productions and structures, like particular alternative spaces, or artists projects, or curated exhibitions. But I would like to stress that the specificity of all aspects of these entities is critical to their materialisation and assessment of their character.

The "problematic duality" that is so central to Žerovc's investigations and her concern for the uncritical "excitement" regarding assimilation within the mainstream art world, shares an illuminating filiation with the "curatorial euphoria" of recent years.[30] Žerovc's thesis is that the contemporary art curator – who has emerged as a powerful figure within the contemporary art world – produces theatre-like and ritualised events that are

---

29 See, for example, Beti Žerovc, "Ivana Kobilca," 2014, and "Ivana Kobilca," 2013 (see n. 6).

30 See Beti Žerovc, "The Curator and the Leftist Politicisation of Contemporary Art", pp. 124–146.

overtly promoted as catalysts for leftist politics and progressive social issues, but are actually, and more covertly, enterprises that maintain, stabilise, and preserve the status quo. There is, however, an additional dualism and paradox here: the curator in this context is not only operating as the exhibition-maker who conjures new cognitions and creations, and "makes sense" of culture, but is, in some significant ways, like the old-time caretaker of a collection who preserves. But it is not the precious objects that are safeguarded, rather it is the powers that be and business-as-usual system that are rendered secure.

Not unrelatedly, the recent varied and widespread ecstasy about curation can be seen as symptom of, and a salve for, an ever-increasing global crisis, what I refer to as "data dystopia".[31] Born of the post-9-11 international climate, the increased availability of digital technologies, and the expanded territories of Internet networks, this "new abnormal" is characterised by incalculable quantities of documentation, the loss of privacy, and the seemingly ubiquitous surveillance by governments, corporations, non-state actors, and anyone else who might be able to make a soft- or hardware breach. So much of our personal information and activities – from our emails to our genomes – are collected, tracked, hacked, and analysed in constantly circulating, morphing, expanding, and arcane algorithmic domains. So many of these new genres of curation are considered a means to tame the chaos, organise the avalanche, make sense of the petrabyte era – offering sanity, security, knowledge, healing, and profits. Although there are somewhat less anxiety-producing and potentially less invasive versions of curating, like choosing items from a restaurant menu, this newly proliferating phenomenon is generally manifesting as something akin to the traditional meaning of the word signifying managing, conserving, and making safe.

There are, of course, distinctions that can be made between these two types of curation, but a comparison does reveal some of the less visible workings of each: Žerovc posits that art world curatorial activity may be merely safeguarding the smooth workings of a capitalist system; similarly, these new varieties of curation – engendered within our dystopic present – are providing promises and strategies to preserve, protect, and control.

---

31   "Data dystopia" is related to my on-going research on this topic, see "Curatoria-Euphoria" (see n. 1).

     Mary Anne Staniszewski

Index

A

modernism / modernist, 37n, 39, 179, 187n, 219, 226, 230

Mondrian, Piet, 218

Money & Value – The Last Taboo (exhibition), 91

morality / moralism, 64, 145, 171–173, 185, 186–187, 215

Moreau, Gustave, 45

Motherwell, Robert, 225

multiculturalism, 136

Museum of Contemporary Art and Design, Manila, 121

Museum of Modern Art (Moderna galerija), Ljubljana, 67–69, 96

Museum of Modern Art (MoMA), New York, 72, 108, 113, 168, 219, 223, 228

Museum of Modern Art, Tokyo, 71, 72

Mušič, Zoran, 68–69

mysticism, 40, 41, 53

myth, 48, 56, 174, 186, 187n, 192, 196

N

Nabis, 40

Negri, Antonio, 157

network / networking, 9, 43, 47, 52, 110–123, 131n, 133–135, 188, 237, 242

New Realism, 55, 56

Newman, Barnett, 174, 225

non-alignment (political movement), 70–71

Novaković, Barbara, 208

O

Obrist, Hans Ulrich, 24, 88, 213n

obsession, 31, 82, 185

occultism, 40, 41–42

Oliva, Achille Bonito, 56–57

Ostrower, Francie, 115–116

P

Parsons, Betty, 229

Palais de Tokyo, Paris, 55, 158–159, 178

participation, 19n, 45, 50, 55, 87, 96, 102, 103, 127n, 143n, 180n, 189n,
    200n, 239, 240

patronage, 234

*Pay Attention Not to Leave Your Dreams, You Could Find Yourself in
    the Dreams of Others* (exhibition), 91

Péladan, Joséphin, 38–53

Péladan, Louis-Adrien, 40

S

IZA Editions

Beti Žerovc
When Attitudes Become the Norm
The Contemporary Curator and Institutional Art

Editor
Urška Jurman

Translators
Rawley Grau, David Limon, and Polona Petek

Proofreader
Eric Scott Dean

Design and layout by
Ivian Kan Mujezinović / Ee

Printed by
Fotoprospekt, d. o. o.

700 copies printed

Distribution
Anagram Books
contact@anagrambooks.com
www.anagrambooks.com

Les presses du réel
info@lespressesdureel.com
www.lespressesdureel.com

RAM Distribution
info@rampub.com
www.rampub.com

Perimeter Distribution
hello@perimeterdistribution.com
www.perimeterdistribution.com

First published: Ljubljana and Berlin, November 2015
First reprint: Ljubljana and Berlin, February 2018

Published by

Igor Zabel Association for Culture and Theory
Trg Prekomorskih brigad 1
SI-1000 Ljubljana
info@igorzabel.org
www.igorzabel.org

Archive Books
Müllerstraße 133
13349 Berlin
mail@archivebooks.org
www.archivebooks.org

With the support of
ERSTE Foundation

ISBN 978-3-943620-39-9

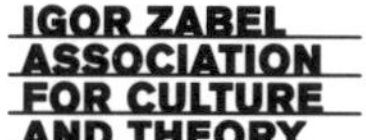

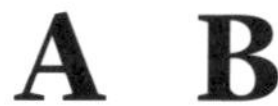

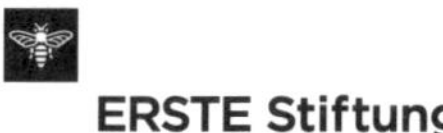

CIP - Kataložni zapis o publikaciji
Narodna in univerzitetna knjižnica, Ljubljana

7:069.01"20"

ŽEROVC, Beti
When attitudes become the norm : the contemporary curator and institutional art / Beti Žerovc ; [translators Rawley Grau, David Limon, and Polona Petek]. - 1st reprint. - Ljubljana : Igor Zabel Association for Culture and Theory ; Berlin : Archive Books, 2018

ISBN 978-3-943620-39-9 (Archive Books)

293446144